THE Church THROUGH History

Joseph Stoutzenberger

Harcourt
Religion Publishers

Harcourt Religion Publishers

Our Mission

The primary mission of Harcourt Religion Publishers is to
provide the Catholic and Christian educational markets with the
highest quality catechetical print and media resources.
The content of these resources reflects the best insights of current
theology, methodology, and pedagogical research. The resources are
practical and easy to use, designed to meet expressed market needs,
and written to reflect the teachings of the Catholic Church.

ISBN 0-15-901100-0

10   9   8   7   6   5   4   3   2

Contents

Chapter 1

BEGINNINGS 2
The Church of the Apostles

Chapter 2

SPREADING THE MESSAGE **32**
The Church Enters the Empire

Chapter 3

CHURCH VICTORIOUS. **54**
The Age of the Fathers

COVER AND CHAPTER OPENERS

Description and location of stained glass windows that appear on chapter opening pages.

Chapter One
Pentecost, Saint John's Church, Grand Marais, Minnesota

Chapter Two
Saints, Saint Joseph Cathedral, Sioux Falls, South Dakota

Chapter Three
Fathers of the Church, Saint Agatha Monastery, Cuijk, Netherlands

Chapter Four
Patrick, Saint Raymond's Cathedral, Joliet, Illinois

Chapter Five
Charlemagne, Saint Mark's, St. Paul, Minnesota

Chapter Six
Catherine of Siena, Saint Catherine's Church, Oak Park, Illinois

Chapter Seven
Theresa of Ávila, Sacred Heart, Winona, Minnesota

Chapter Eight
Jane Frances DeChantal, Saint Wilfrid Church, York, England

Chapter Nine
Isaac Jogues, Saint Helena's Church, Minneapolis, Minnesota

Chapter Ten
Francis Cabrini, Sacred Heart, Winona, Minnesota

Chapter Eleven
Vatican Council II, Resurrection Cathedral, Lincoln, Nebraska

Chapter Twelve
Fountain of Life, Saint Stephen's, Stephen's Point, Wisconsin

Epilogue
Calvary Episcopal Cathedral, Souix Falls, South Dakota

Cover

A varnished chi rho is imposed over layers of photos and the Julien calendar. Photos on the cover include Augustine of Hippo, Pentecost, Pope John Paul II, the procession of the bishops at Vatican II, the stoning of Stephen, the North American Martyrs, Dorothy Day, present-day high school students, and the earth from space.

ALLOWING THE PAST TO SPEAK

A Teacher's Prayer

Jesus, our model teacher, guide me as I lead my students into a journey through history. As they learn about the struggles faced by Christians of the past and the heroic steps they took to stay close to you, may they find reasons to believe in you and hope for a better world to come. Amen.

Overview

An introductory course on Church history attempts to help students come to an appreciation of two concepts: history and Church. The text describes history as story rather than as mere chronology. Church history describes how Christ has been and continues to be manifest through Christians in particular historical circumstances.

LESSON STRATEGIES

Introduction

Prayer

page vii

- **Music Suggestions**

  "Come, All You People" by Alexander Gondo from *Give Your Gifts, the Basics* (GIA, Harcourt Religion Publishers).

  "Song of the Body of Christ"/ "Canción del Cuerpo de Cristo" by David Haas, Spanish Trans. by Donna Peña, from *Gather (Comprehensive)* (GIA), *Walking by Faith* (Harcourt Religion Publishers, GIA), *Today's Missal* (OCP).

  "We Are Called" by David Haas from *Gather (Comprehensive)* (GIA), *Give Your Gifts, the Songs* (Harcourt Religion Publishers, GIA).

- **Scripture Suggestions**

  Sirach 32:14–16

  2 Thessalonians 2:13–17

  Luke 1:1–4

- **Prayer**

  Grant to me, O merciful God, that I might ardently love,
  prudently ponder, rightly acknowledge,
  and perfectly fulfill all that is pleasing to you,
  for the praise and glory of your name.

  Saint Thomas Aquinas, "Prayer Before Study or Reading."

page vii

Overview

Have the students read the **Introduction Overview** on page vii. Briefly discuss some of the points noted.

The Importance of Studying History

Understanding the past helps us appreciate ourselves and our world, why we are who we are, and possible ways to face upcoming challenges.

page viii

THE PRESENT BEGAN IN THE PAST

Storytellers: Bringing the Past to Life

1. Have the students read the material on page viii.

2. Then discuss with them the importance of knowing our personal and family history.

3. You might use the **Additional Activities, Storytelling,** and **Family Tree** to introduce this section to them.

Additional Activities

pages viii–x

Use the following activities to introduce storytelling and searching our history.

STORYTELLING

Ask the students to read over the sections on **Storytellers: Bringing the Past to Life** and **History versus Chronology** in the text, pages viii–x. Tell them that you would like to begin the course by giving them an opportunity to tell a story of their own.

Distribute **Handout–A, Telling My Story.** You may ask students to write a story for homework and bring it to class the next day, or you might simply give students a few minutes to think and jot down notes about a story related to one of the topics listed on the handout.

- Invite students to share their story in pairs.

- Then invite students to respond to the questions: Did the story you told reveal anything about yourself? If so, what?

FAMILY TREE

Ask students to draw their family tree as far back as they can. (You might offer a prize to the person who can list the greatest number of generations.)

- Invite students to make observations about the experience of drawing a family tree. For instance, take note whether some students have little sense of their own family history while others have a strong sense of it.

- Ask if they believe that people today are more or less attentive to their family history than people in the past. (If adopted students have some knowledge of their biological families, they may want to do a double family tree: adopted family and biological family. Students in blended families may get quite creative in their portrayal of their family tree.)

- Conclude the discussion with the question: What is the value of having a sense of one's family history? As part of that discussion, you might draw a tree on the board or overhead and include a cluster of roots for the tree. Point out to students that just as roots shape and nourish a tree, members of their family who came before them are the roots that nourish and shape their identity.

Concept Review

The text states that "History opens up new worlds to us. In so doing, it also sheds new light on our own world." Ask the students to do the following.

- Name an aspect of yourself or your life for which knowing some history could lead you to better understanding.
- Name three aspects of the Church today about which you would like to learn some history.
- How could historical information about the Church help you better understand the Church today?

pages ix–x

History Versus Chronology

To introduce the topic either have the students read and review the material on pages ix–x or complete the **Additional Activities, Who Likes to Study History?** or **Whom Would You Like to Interview?**

Additional Activities

Who Likes to Study History?

- Ask the students to rate themselves on how much they like the study of history, from 1 (I can't stand studying history) to 10 (I absolutely love studying history).
- Ask students, individually or in small groups, to identify reasons why they do or do not like to study history. List those reasons on the board or overhead.
- Then ask them if they can suggest ways that the study of history could become more interesting. List those ways on the board or overhead also, and ask a student to make a copy for you so that you can seek ways to incorporate their suggestions into the course.

Whom Would You Like to Interview?

1. Ask the students to think about one person, living or dead, whom they would like to interview.
2. Then ask them:
   - Why did you choose this person?
   - What questions do you want to ask?
   - What do you think you can learn from this person?
   - What story or stories do you think the person has to share?
   - Do you think this person does or could have an influence on your life? If so, how?
3. Invite the students to share their answers with the class or in small groups.
4. Then ask the students to consider: How is this exercise similar to the study of history?

Concept Review

Point out to the students that the text is attempting to communicate the fact that both history and chronology speak about the past. However, viewing the past as history gives it life, while viewing the past as chronology can make it seem lifeless. Explore with the students the difference between history and chronology to make sure that they understand the meaning of the difference.

page x **The Dynamics of History at Work**

Direct the students to complete the **In-Text Activity** as a way to make a transition to the concept of a dynamic perspective on history. You might use the **Additional Activity, A Dynamic Perspective on History,** to allow students to explore the concept further.

In-Text Activities

page x ACTIVITY

Using the Activity

Provide a forum for the students to share the results of this research, but make the sharing voluntary. Some students may have chosen an event that is private to the family and should not be shared. Respect this and refrain from implying that sharing is expected or that sharing will enhance a student's grade.

Additional Activities

The following activity allows students to examine changing perspectives on an issue similar to the example of attitudes toward nature described in the text. Have students complete the activity after they have read this section of the text.

A DYNAMIC PERSPECTIVE ON HISTORY

The text uses the example of changing perspectives on caring for nature to illustrate a dynamic, ongoing, interconnected understanding of history.

- Ask the students to think about other areas of concern that over time have undergone changes in perspective. List their suggestions on the board or overhead.
- Then place students in small groups and instruct each group to describe some of the ways that perspectives have changed and may continue to change on the topic. Some possible topics are: warfare, television viewing, computers and the Internet, music, medicine and medical care, nationalism, and violence in sports.

Concept Review

Write on the board or overhead the words *dynamic* and *history.* Point out that these two words are not separate concepts. History is dynamic, always changing, like a river that carries things downstream and continues on. Remind the students that they are recipients of history and also shapers of history.

Church History as the Story of Christ's Presence in the World

Church history describes how Jesus has been present to and through people over the past two thousand years.

pages xi–xii

HISTORY AND CHURCH HISTORY

1. At this point the introduction adds another essential element to a Christian understanding of history—namely, that Jesus has been and continues to be present in history. Therefore, in the words of the text, a Church history course "seeks to look at history with the 'eyes of faith.' "

2. After students have read and reviewed page xi, assign them the **In-Text Activity, Descriptions of Church,** to help them appreciate better the Church as Christ's presence in history.

3. The **Additional Activity, Who Embodies Church for You?** brings the concept of the Church as Christ's presence into the contemporary world. It also forms the basis for prayers with which to begin future classes.

In-Text Activities

page xi

DISCUSSION

Using the Discussion

Push the students to go beyond their younger explanations of what it means to follow Christ; address both concerns of teens and broader world problems. Point out that learning from the past has always been good advice for making decisions about the present and the future.

Additional Activities

DESCRIPTIONS OF CHURCH

Distribute **Handout–B, Descriptions of Church,** and read aloud the three statements found there. Then ask students to answer the questions on the handout. After a few minutes, review their answers with them.

WHO EMBODIES CHURCH FOR YOU?

Across a bulletin board or a section of the classroom wall place the words: The Church—The Communion of Saints.

- Ask the students to think about someone who embodies for them what it means to be Church. Hand out index cards. Instruct the students to write on the card their reasons for selecting this person.

- Have each student read his or her reasons and then post the index card on the bulletin board or wall under the "The Church—The Communion of Saints" heading.

- When all students have done so, point out to them that they have offered one another specific examples of what it means to be Church.

- Leave the cards on the board for a few days and select certain examples as the basis for a prayer to begin the next few class periods.

The Church—Ageless and Always Changing

The Catechism Describes the Church

Direct the students to read these two sections of the text on page xii and then use the
Additional Activity, Handing Down the Church to Our Children, to help them
understand the value of maintaining and carrying on traditions. The **In-Text Activity** might
be used as a homework assignment related to the topic or as a class discussion topic.

In-Text Activities

ACTIVITY

USING THE ACTIVITY

If time permits, use this **Activity** as a springboard for a class discussion.

Additional Activities

HANDING DOWN THE CHURCH TO OUR CHILDREN

1. One heading in the Introduction reads **The Church—Ageless and Always Changing;**
   see page xii.
   - Point out this heading to students. Ask the students, before reading the section if
     possible, to think about what the heading means.
   - Invite the students to explain the statement in their own words and to give
     examples of what the statement means.
   - Then ask a student to read aloud the paragraphs under the heading. Ask students
     if the meanings they provided coincide with what the text says about the ageless
     and always changing nature of the Church.
2. Then direct the students to project themselves twenty years into the future and to
   imagine that they are parents with children. Ask them to think about and to jot down
   their thoughts about the following questions. After a few minutes, invite students to
   comment on their responses to these questions.
   - What experience of Jesus and Church would you want for your children?
   - What aspects of your own experience of religion would you want for your
     children?
   - What aspects of Catholicism today do you hope will be available for your
     children?

CONCEPT REVIEW

Point out to the students that the text will make numerous references to the *Catechism of the Catholic Church* because it is a recent compilation of official Church teachings. The Catechism points out that the Church has both a visible manifestation and an invisible reality behind it. To help students appreciate this important concept, ask them to think about some dimension of themselves that few people, if any, know about. Although this aspect of themselves may not be directly known or visible, it probably has an impact on their visible manifestation to others. In similar fashion, the Church is a visible collection of flawed and imperfect people, but with "the eyes of faith" we recognize that Christ is present in and through us.

How to Study Church History

Valuable tools are available to students who wish to learn from a study of the Church's history.

page xiii

Tools that Help Us in Our Study of History

Use the **Additional Activity, Tools for Learning Church History,** as a lead-in for pointing out the checklist of tools that students will find on page xiii in the text.

Additional Activities

TOOLS FOR LEARNING CHURCH HISTORY

- Mention to the students that carpenters, medical doctors, and even teachers have certain tools available to them to help them achieve their goals.

- Invite the students to list what they might use to gain a better understanding of their own family history. How might these tools help them know about and appreciate developments in their family?

- Then have the students read about the six tools listed in the text for learning about Church history. Invite them to give examples that illustrate how each tool can provide insight into historical developments.

CONCEPT REVIEW

End the presentation of the introduction by reading aloud the section titled **Let's Get Started**.

TELLING MY STORY

Name_____ Date_____ Class period_____

Choose one of the following topics and write a story related to it. Look back into history to help you construct the story. Include as much detail as you can so that the account you give is a richly constructed story. Tell the story as a professional storyteller might.

1. Why I have my first, middle, Confirmation, and/or last name.

2. Why my family lives where it does.

3. Someone from my family, past or present, who has a story to be told.

4. An incident from my childhood that had a strong impact on me.

5. A family tradition associated with a holiday.

6. An unusual occurrence that happened during a vacation.

7. A funny or frightening event from my grade school days.

8. A classmate or friend who was a real character.

DESCRIPTIONS OF CHURCH

Name_____ Date_____ Class period_____

Read the following descriptions of the Christian Church. Then answer the accompanying questions.

Catholicism does not see the Church standing between the individual and God. When many people think of the Church they think only of the buildings, the rituals, the ministers, and bureaucracy of the Church. But the Church is truly the pilgrim people of God. The Church is the entire Christian community spread throughout the world today and reaching back to encompass all past generations.

> *How else can we come to know the good news except through the Church? If we read the Bible we are reading a book written by Church members and declared Scripture by the Church. If we hear the good news from another, chances are that person is a Christian and so a member of the Church.*

Richard Chilson, *Full Christianity* (New York: Paulist Press, 1985), 75–76.

> *Down through the ages, the church has struggled to follow in Christ's footsteps. The church has been concerned with the total needs of the whole person. The church is certainly dedicated to helping its members become whole people. This is accomplished in part by teaching them the basic Christian message and by sharing the sacraments with them. Teaching, though, is more than instruction in a few basic truths in which to believe; it also includes opening the eyes of the members to their role in establishing the kingdom of God by making their corners of the world more "Christian" places in which to live.*

Matthew F. Kohmescher, *Catholicism Today* (New York: Paulist Press, 1999), 40.

> *Believers united in a community preserve and illumine the total Christian mystery for one another. . . . We need the support of a community to continue believing. . . . We are sometimes shocked to find sinfulness present in the churches. But Christian community is not a gathering of those already completely saved. It is the place where we open ourselves to forgiveness and further conversion.*

Kathleen Fischer and Thomas Hart, *Christian Foundations* (New York: Paulist Press, 1995), 154–155.

1. What misrepresentations of Church are the authors concerned about?
2. What does each author emphasize about the nature of Church?
3. Based on these passages, what are some descriptions of the nature of Church that would help you explain it to others?
4. Write your own description of Church.

BEGINNINGS
The Church of the Apostles

A Teacher's Prayer

God of wisdom and compassion, kindle in my students a love for your Church. May your Spirit come upon them. Fill them with enthusiasm to do your will as active members of the Church. Inspire them with the realization that you are with them always. Amen.

Overview

While the chapter begins with the Pentecost experience of the early Christian community, it quickly steps back to review key themes within the Judaism that so shaped early Christianity's understanding of itself. Then the chapter examines the life and teaching of Jesus. It is important for students to realize that, even though the Church has constantly changed throughout history, it always looks to Jesus Christ for its purpose and meaning. Finally, it is important for students to understand that members of the Christian community, even at its earliest stages, discussed and debated issues, seeking the best ways to remain faithful to Christ.

An important but difficult concept for students to grasp is that the Church of the first century was not an ideal that later deteriorated into a less than perfect reflection of the ideal. Early Christians struggled to make the message of Jesus alive for themselves, as Christians do today. Early Christians debated issues about how to live the Christian life and about what language best captures what it means to follow Christ, as Christians do today as well. Many saintly people made up the Church then and they do now as well. The humanness of the Christian community is a great and wonderful mystery. That is, while the people who make up the Church have never been perfect, they are nonetheless Christ present among us.

Major Concepts Covered in This Chapter

1. **Introduction**
2. **Pentecost—The Birthday of the Church**
3. **The Jewish Roots of Christianity**
4. **The Early Church Lives out the Message of Jesus**
5. **Chapter Review and Conclusion**

Introduction

Prayer

pages
2–3

■ **Music Suggestions**

"Come and Fill Our Hearts" by Taizé from *Give Your Gifts, the Basics* (GIA, Harcourt Religion Publishers).

"Give Us Your Peace" by Michael Mahler from *Give Your Gifts, the New Songs* (GIA, Harcourt Religion Publishers).

"Psalm 104: Lord, Send Out Your Spirit" by Jeanne Cotter from *Give Your Gifts, the Basics* (GIA, Harcourt Religion Publishers).

"Send Down the Fire" by Marty Haugen from *Gather (Comprehensive)* (GIA), *Give Your Gifts, the Basics* (GIA, Harcourt Religion Publishers).

■ **Scripture Suggestions**

Isaiah 40:3–5

Acts 2:1–13

John 14:15–31

■ **Prayer**

See page 2 of the student text.

pages
2–3

Overview

Have the students read the **Chapter Overview** and timeline on pages 2–3. Briefly discuss some of the points and events noted.

page 4

Reflection on the Experience of the Early Church

1. Ask a student to read the paragraph with reflection questions that opens the chapter on page 4. Ask the students to reflect on the questions. Discuss the questions if appropriate with this group.

2. Near the beginning of each chapter, under **Before We Begin . . . ,** there are a few questions meant to lead students into reflecting on major themes to be addressed in that chapter.

   • Direct the students to read the questions under **Before We Begin . . . ,** on page 4. Ask them to spend a few minutes thinking and writing about one or more of the questions.

   • After a few minutes, invite the students to share responses to these questions.

   • Then ask them to discuss the question: In what ways do these particular questions address the period of the earliest days of the Church?

Pentecost—The Birthday of the Church

Inspired by the Holy Spirit, the followers of Jesus realize that he is present in and through them.

pages
5–6

PENTECOST

The Followers of Jesus before Pentecost

The Holy Spirit Stirs Jesus' Followers into Action

1. Have the students read and discuss page 5, including **FYI** and **Youth News.**

2. Following this, mention to the students that they are about to study an event that is so significant that it is often called the "birthday of the Church." For that reason, they will examine it closely. Have students read about Pentecost in the text.

3. Then assign some version of the activity **Additional Activity, The Pentecost Experience—A Role-Play.**

The **In-Text Activities** can be used as homework assignments accompanying this section.

In-Text Activities

page 5   FYI

YOUTH NEWS

page 6   ACTIVITY

Using the Activity

See number 2 in **Concept Review** on page 5.

Additional Activities

THE PENTECOST EXPERIENCE—A ROLE-PLAY

1. Place students in three groups. Tell students that they are to analyze how people who were there might have reacted to the Pentecost experience. Then assign each group to create a play depicting one of the following scenes:

   • The experience of the group gathered in the upper room before the coming of the Holy Spirit.

   • The experience of the group during and immediately after the coming of the Holy Spirit.

   • The experience and actions of the group following the coming of the Holy Spirit.

2. Allow about fifteen minutes for each group to prepare a brief play about its experience.

3. Direct each group to perform its play, and then discuss with the class the feelings and responses that the plays attempted to convey.

4. Conclude the discussion with these questions:

   • Has anyone in the class had an experience similar to any or all of the experiences that the followers of Jesus had at the first Pentecost? Would anyone be willing to tell the rest of the class about the experience?

- Can they imagine someone today having any or all of these experiences? If so, in what circumstances?

5. An alternative would be to assign one group of students to act out the entire Pentecost experience from the atmosphere in the room before the coming of the Holy Spirit, the event of the coming of the Spirit, and then the response of the people gathered. Students could either put on a live play or create a video presentation to be shown to the class. (Other groups of students can then be assigned to role-play or create a video on other important Church events.)

page 6 **Review Questions and Answers**

1. **What accounted for the attitude of uncertainty among the followers of Jesus who gathered at Pentecost?**

    The followers of Jesus had been filled with wonder at the deeds and teachings of Jesus, then their hopes were dashed during the crucifixion but restored with the resurrection, and finally Jesus' ascension left them feeling abandoned.

2. **Which book of the Bible tells about the actions of the early Church community?**

    The Acts of the Apostles is the book of the Bible that tells about the early Church.

3. **What two images indicated the presence of the Holy Spirit at Pentecost?**

    The Acts of the Apostles refers to experiences like those of wind and fire indicating the presence of the Holy Spirit at Pentecost.

4. **What new understanding came to the followers of Jesus as a result of the first Christian Pentecost?**

    At Pentecost, the followers of Jesus understood that Jesus was now present in and through them.

⌐ **CoNCepT ReVieW** ─────────

1. If you assigned the **In-Text Activity,** have students read their essays or poems or display their drawings.

2. After students have made their presentations, discuss with them the types of images and associations that they used to depict the Holy Spirit.

page 7 **Peter the Fisherman**

Chapter 1 provides a snapshot description of Peter, leader of the fledgling Christian community. Peter is particularly striking because in Scripture he is not presented in an idealized fashion but as a unique individual with clear human weaknesses and flaws.

- Direct the students to read the text material about Peter, page 7.

- Then have them in small groups complete the **Additional Activity, Peter, Model for Christians.**

- You might also assign students to find out more about all of the apostles by using the **Additional Activity, Symbols of the Apostles.**

PETER, MODEL FOR CHRISTIANS

Assign the students to look for references to Peter in a Concordance to the Bible.

1. Invite them to choose one story about Peter. They are to describe the story and to write about how the message of the story might be applied to their own life. Remind the students that they need to be able to analyze the symbolic meaning of elements in the stories if they are to apply them to themselves.

2. You might use the story of Peter walking on water as an example. Read Matthew 14:22–33. Ask the students how they would describe Peter and Peter's experience in this story. You could use the following statements to provoke discussion:

    - Peter immediately speaks up and questions Jesus.

    - Apparently unthinkingly and unquestioningly, Peter gets out of the boat in the middle of a stormy sea and heads toward Jesus.

    - Peter soon becomes afraid, which causes him to sink.

    - Jesus reaches out and saves him despite Peter's doubts and fears.

    - Peter joins Jesus in the boat, and the wind dies down.

3. Invite the students to think about how the various elements of this story can be applied to their own lives in symbolic ways. For instance:

    - What life experience is like being out in a stormy sea for you?

    - What might Jesus' being able to walk on water symbolize for you?

    - Do you tend to respond to situations in the ways Peter did? Explain.

    - Have you ever experienced a saving hand in your life? Do you think of Jesus as offering a saving hand to you?

    - When do you feel the safety of being in a boat? Does the Church serve that role for you? Explain.

SYMBOLS OF THE APOSTLES

Students often know little more than the names of the apostles. History has little to say about the apostles, and legends of uncertain origin about their exploits have been handed down to us. Yet by all accounts, the apostles were very active in effectively spreading the Christian message. They are recognized as patron saints of many groups of people and professions. They also have been adopted as patrons in many parts of the world. **Handout 1–A, The Shields of the Twelve Apostles,** gives students an opportunity to review the names of the apostles and the primary symbols associated with each one. The activity on the handout also invites students to learn more about a particular apostle. (Students might report to the class about the apostle they researched.) Finally, the handout invites students to think about their own lives and how they themselves might symbolize their own experience of the Christian life.

Concept Review

Ask the students:

- If you were an early Christian writer, would you have portrayed Saint Peter, the leader of the community to which you belonged, as having faults and shortcomings? Why or why not?

- Do you believe that the media should refrain from publicizing negative stories about important public figures, such as presidents and other leaders, and members of their families? Why or why not?

The Jewish Roots of Christianity

The first Christians recognize key themes in Judaism that reach their fulfillment in Jesus.

pages 8–10

JEWISH ROOTS OF THE CHURCH

Abraham: Father in Faith of the Christian Church

The Exodus Reveals a Loving God

1. Begin discussion of the Jewish roots of Christianity by reading aloud the Catechism quote and the first two sentences of the next paragraph on page 8: Historians today are emphasizing more and more the Jewishness of Jesus. That is, they are reminding us that we can't understand how people of his time viewed Jesus without understanding the Jewish culture in which he and they lived. Point out that we can't understand the Church apart from its Jewish roots either. Read the rest of text on the page.

2. To give students an opportunity to explore this concept, assign the **In-Text Activity** found on page 8.

3. Then have students read the sections on Abraham and the Exodus, pages 9–10.

4. The two **Additional Activities** accompanying this section allow students to explore further the major themes found in the Old Testament.

In-Text Activities

page 8   **ACTIVITY**

page 9   **DISCUSSION**

Using the Discussion

(1) Elements include: belief in one God, Old Testament of the Bible (including the psalms), some prayers, readings from Scripture during worship, Passover/Easter, holy places in Jerusalem.

(2) Probe the students to make connections between beliefs and moral decisions.

page 10   **WWW.**

Beginnings   7

JEWISH THEMES—CHRISTIAN THEMES

The chapter provides a synopsis of pre-Christian Jewish history in order to remind students that Christianity emerges from Jewish roots. As such, the Church not only grows out of Judaism historically, it also adopts and adapts major Jewish themes. **Handout 1–B, Jewish Themes—Christian Themes,** provides students an opportunity to consider ways that the Church incorporates Jewish themes into Church practices and beliefs.

- The assignment can be done individually or in small groups.

- The purpose of this activity is not for students to arrive at uniform answers but to help them realize how the Church used—and continues to use—the culture in which it found itself to express its identity and explain its role, especially the Jewish religion and culture in which God revealed himself in a special way.

JEWISH THEMES—HUMAN THEMES

Basic themes in Judaism and Christianity have parallels with universal human themes. **Handout 1–C, Jewish Themes—Human Themes,** gives students an opportunity both to examine these basic themes and also to think about how they might be applied to contemporary situations.

- The assignment can be done individually or in small groups.

- Invite students to read aloud their paragraphs to the rest of the class and discuss how each one applied the theme to a real-life situation.

CoNCept RevIEw

The questions under number 1 in the **In-Text Activity** on page 12 can serve as a review and application of the themes associated with Abraham and the Exodus.

pages 10–12

The Jews of Israel Versus the Hellenistic Jews

Point out to students that with this section they are learning about some of the social and historical background out of which Christianity emerged.

1. Have the students read the section beginning at the bottom of page 10 and ending on page 12.

2. Call on them to explain the impact of the following on the origins of Christianity:
   - The Babylonian Captivity
   - Jews of the Diaspora
   - Hellenization

   (The first two events placed many Jews in the middle of other cultures. Hellenization brought a broadening of Judaism firmly into the Greek culture and in turn brought many Greek elements into the Jewish faith. As a result, Christianity emerged not just from the Judaism of Palestine, but from a Hellenized Judaism; on Pentecost itself, many Hellenized Jews heard the good news and became followers of Jesus. Christianity spread quickly among the Hellenized Jews, thus paving the way for the conversion of many Gentiles. Thus Christianity soon became a religion to be reckoned with in the Roman Empire.)

3. Spend time with the map on page 11.

4. Questions 2 and 3 of the **In-Text Activity** on page 12 can be assigned in advance if you would like your students to explore these topics more deeply. The **Additional Activity, Greek Culture and Early Christianity,** and its accompanying handout provide a brief overview of Hellenization.

In-Text Activities

page 11 FYI

page 12 DISCUSSION

Using the Discussion

Both of these questions can generate heated responses. Emphasize and require tolerance and charity during the discussion.

ACTIVITY

Using the Activity

Answers will vary. The first question may lean toward responses such as sin, isolation, selfishness. The second question should eventually elicit the response "the kingdom of God." The third question may have responses along these lines: spreading the good news, worshiping with the community, making the world a better place, being signs of the kingdom of God, uniting with God.

Additional Activities

GREEK CULTURE AND EARLY CHRISTIANITY

The text points out that Christianity came into existence at a time when conflicts already existed—between Jews and non-Jews, between Jews living in Israel and those living outside of Israel, between Jews sympathetic to Greek culture and those who abhorred Greek culture. If they are to understand the development of Christian ideas, the students need to appreciate the influence of Greek culture on the early Christian era.

- **Handout 1–D, Greek Culture and Early Christianity,** gives a brief sketch of the influence of Greek culture, or Hellenization. You might assign the students to research some aspect of ancient Greek culture or the effect of Hellenization on Christianity. For instance, the students might already be familiar with Plato's allegory of the cave, one of the most well-known presentations of a Greek understanding of reality. If you or another faculty member is familiar with Plato's allegory of the cave, you might explain it and discuss with the students how Christian beliefs are similar to or different from those of Plato.

- A number of resources are available that explain Plato's allegory. **http://www.historyforkids.org** describes the allegory in these words:

    Plato also thought a lot about the natural world and how it works. He thought that everything had a sort of ideal form, like the idea of a chair, and then an actual chair was a sort of poor imitation of the ideal chair that exists only in your mind.

One of the ways Plato tried to explain his ideas was with the famous metaphor of the cave. He said, Suppose there is a cave, and inside the cave there are some men chained up to a wall, so that they can only see the back wall of the cave and nothing else. These men can't see anything outside of the cave, or even see each other clearly, but they can see shadows of what is going on outside the cave. Wouldn't these prisoners come to think that the shadows were real, and that was what things really looked like?

Suppose now that one of the men escaped, and got out of the cave, and saw what real people looked like, and real trees and grass. If he went back to the cave and told the other men what he had seen, would they believe him, or would they think he was crazy? Plato says that we are like those men sitting in the cave: we think we understand the real world, but because we are trapped in our bodies we can see only the shadows on the wall.

CoNCept RevIEw

Discuss these questions with the students:

- Why would some people outside of the United States today imitate aspects of U.S. culture?

- Why would some people outside of the United States resist imitating aspects of U.S. culture?

- Do you think that Jews accepted or rejected Greek culture around the time of Jesus for similar or different reasons? Explain.

page 12

Review Questions and Answers

1. **Why is it important that historians today are emphasizing more and more the Jewishness of Jesus?**

    Scholars point out that we cannot know Jesus and his followers unless we know about the culture in which they lived, especially the Jewish religion and culture in which God revealed himself in a special way.

2. **What three religions recognize Abraham as their father in faith?**

    Judaism, Christianity, and Islam recognize Abraham as their father in faith.

3. **What great test of faith did God lay before Abraham?**

    God commanded Abraham to sacrifice his son, Isaac.

4. **Name two Christian beliefs that reflect themes found in the story of Abraham.**

    Christian belief in one God and in Jesus' sacrifice on the cross are themes with connections to the story of Abraham.

5. **Describe the major events that encompass the Exodus story.**

    Israelite slaves in Egypt are set free when God sends Moses to lead them through the desert into the Promised Land, their ancestral home.

6. **How do modern Jews view the Exodus as it relates to their own lives?**

    Jews celebrate the Exodus each year at Passover. Pious Jews do not simply recall the historical event but also enter into it as participants. In other words, God didn't just free the ancient Israelites' ancestors from slavery; he also frees their descendents from spiritual and other slavery today.

7. **What Exodus theme runs through Church history?**

   As the Exodus is the story of liberation, so Church history is the story of God's liberating of people through the saving action of Jesus Christ.

8. **What was the Babylonian Captivity?**

   The Babylonian Captivity refers to the period when the nation of Judah was conquered by Babylonians and its leaders were forced to live in Babylon.

9. **What distinguished Jews in Israel from Jews of the diaspora?**

   Diaspora Jews were generally more comfortable with Greek culture and interactions with their non-Jewish neighbors than the Jews in Israel were.

10. **What is Hellenization?**

    Hellenization refers to the spread of Greek culture.

11. **What was the Septuagint? Why was it written?**

    The Septuagint is a translation of the Jewish Bible from Hebrew into Greek; it was produced around 200 B.C.

The Early Church Lives out the Message of Jesus

Both within and outside of the Jewish community, people join the Christian movement because it embodies the spirit and message of Jesus.

pages 13–14

BUILT ON THE GOOD NEWS

1. Remind the students that the Church cannot be separated from Jesus. Direct the students to read this section and to take note especially of the terms *conversion* and *reign of God*—two interrelated teachings of Jesus.

2. The **In-Text Activity** and the **Additional Activity, Experiencing Conversion,** offer students an opportunity to reflect personally on conversion. (The additional activity is more personal than the **In-Text Activity**.) You might mention that Catholics tend not to speak about "conversion experiences" and "being converted to Christ," but they do recognize the need for the experience. On the other hand, conversion is a cornerstone of the Protestant tradition, and speaking about it is common. Whichever activity you choose by which to elicit responses from the students regarding conversion, encourage them to take seriously this central teaching of Jesus.

In-Text Activities

page 14

ACTIVITY

Using the Activity

(1) Provide an opportunity for volunteers to share their poems and stories.

(2) Each of these statements can provide the basis for brainstorming. Write the students' responses on the board or overhead; then sort through the responses in a discussion and eliminate any that the majority of students disagree with.

(3) The first of these questions is private and should not be discussed, but the second is a good discussion question for small groups, as well as for the large group.

Experiencing Conversion

This section of the text speaks about the experience of conversion. Remind the students that a Church history course is the story of those who have been touched by Jesus. Experiencing Jesus and his message that God loves each of us personally is the experience of conversion. Experiencing conversion is unexplainable, as all love is. "Cradle Catholics," who were baptized into the faith in infancy through the decision of their parents, may claim not to have had any such "conversion experience." The following exercise provides students an opportunity to imagine what experiencing conversion might be like.

Invite the students to pause and reflect on the fact that Jesus calls everyone to experience conversion. Ask them to think for a few moments about what a conversion experience might be like. (You might suggest that they close their eyes to help them envision what conversion might be like.) After a few minutes ask them to think about words that would describe such an experience. Then instruct them to write down words or phrases that they would associate with conversion. (Perhaps different students will write the words: peace, forgiveness, freedom, love, joy.) If you think your students would be comfortable doing so, invite them to volunteer to say aloud a word or phrase that they wrote. Then end the session with a prayer such as the following:

> Jesus, our brother, you awaken us to the joy and peace of God's reign, where we
> can all get along because we know God's love for each of us. Turn our gaze to
> see ourselves, one another, and our world as you do—with the eyes of love. Set us
> free from worry, guilt, and fear. Sustain us with the experience of your love
> forever and ever. Amen.

Concept Review

Write on the following statement: Without Christ there would be no Church. Ask: Does anyone disagree? (Probably no one will.) Then write on the board or overhead: Without the Church there would be no Christ. Ask: Does anyone disagree? Whether or not anyone speaks up, point out that a case can be made that an implication of the Catholic teaching that Christ is present in the Church is that we need the Church to know Christ. This teaching points out the need for a Church history course, which could also be called a "Christ history course."

pages
15–17

The Beginning of the Church
Architects of the Early Church
Gamaliel's Words of Wisdom

1. Direct the students to read through these sections of the text.
2. Ask them to name characteristics of the Christian community at its earliest stage. Then ask them:
   - Do you think you would have joined this movement if you lived at that time?
   - Why do you think some people did not join this movement?
   - Why do you think many people did join this movement?

3. The **In-Text Discussions** offer students an opportunity to think about specific aspects of the early Church's experience in light of their own experience, and the **In-Text Activity** asks the students to look at the experience of three little-known early members of the Church.

In-Text Activities

page 15 **DISCUSSION**

Using the Discussion

Briefly connect this discussion with the difficulties faced by the members of the early Church.

page 17 **DISCUSSION**

Using the Discussion

Be sure those taking the agreement side of the debate make use of Gamaliel's words and back them up with examples.

ACTIVITY

Using the Activity

Definitely find class time for the students to share these stories.

page 17 **Review Questions and Answers**

1. **Name the two traditional sources of information we have about Jesus and two more recent sources.**

   The primary sources of information about Jesus are Scripture and Tradition. In the past century or so additional information has come from language, archaeological, and historical studies.

2. **Why was Jesus' reference to God as "Our Father" radical for his time?**

   Jesus' reference to God as "Our Father" expresses a tone of intimacy, familiarity, and informality in addressing God that was radical for his time.

3. **Give two indications that Jesus intended his community to continue his work.**

   Jesus' resurrection and his sending of the Holy Spirit are indications that he wanted his followers to continue his work.

4. **How did the early Christians view the coming of the reign of God?**

   Early Christians believed that the final reign of God was soon to come.

5. **What types of activities were required once the followers of Jesus realized that their earthly task would be a long-term one?**

   To carry on their movement long-term, Christians divided up work, chose leaders, clarified teachings, and resolved inevitable conflicts.

6. **What position did Gamaliel take on the treatment of Jewish Christians?**

   Gamaliel proposed leaving the Christians alone. If their movement succeeded, it indicated that God was with them.

Outlining the Acts of the Apostles

The Acts of the Apostles tells the story of the vitality present in the early Church and also describes successes and struggles of some early Christians. It is important for Church history students to become familiar with this text. One way to achieve this goal is to assign the students to outline the Acts of the Apostles. Students can then be assigned to report to the class on sections of the Acts.

Concept Review

Discuss with students the following question: From all that you know of the Christian movement during its earliest period, do you think that such a movement would succeed in attracting members today? Why or why not?

pages 18–23

Christians Inspire Hope

Early Christian Communities: Unity out of Diversity

Gentile Converts

1. Direct the students to read over these sections.

2. Then read to them the description of the Council of Jerusalem found in Acts 15. Discuss with them:
   - Why was the meeting called?
   - Who were the key figures at the meeting?
   - What positions on the issue were put forth, either explicitly or implicitly?
   - How was a decision made?
   - What was the decision made?

3. Use the **In-Text Discussion** and **Activities** to allow students to explore further the question of Gentile converts to the Church and the Council of Jerusalem.

4. The sections on Mary and Paul are dealt with in this lesson plan on pages 15 and 17.

page 18 **Discussion**

Using the Discussion

Spend some time with this discussion. It may take some probing to get below the surface of the discussion; make it real by giving comparisons from your locale or from the larger world—wealthy countries and developing countries, for example. Once the students can relate to the situation, zero in on the last question; challenge any "feel good" approach.

Mary, Model of the Church

1. The text includes a reflection on the Blessed Mother as model of the Church, using the mysteries of the Rosary to tell her story. Direct the students to read over this insert about Mary.

2. Then use the **In-Text Activity** on Mary and the Church according to Vatican Council II and the **Additional Activity** on **Personal Mysteries of the Rosary** to help the students appreciate the relationship between Mary and the Church and Mary and themselves.

3. Use the **In-Text Activity** to help students appreciate the humanness and saintliness of Mary through her Sorrowful, Joyful, and Glorious Mysteries.

In-Text Activities

ACTIVITY

Using the Activity

To prepare the students for this activity, share the mysteries of the Rosary with them, or brainstorm the mysteries with them.

Joyful Mysteries: 1. The Annunciation; 2. The Visitation; 3. The Nativity; 4. The Presentation; 5. Finding Jesus in the Temple.

Sorrowful Mysteries: 1. The Agony in the Garden; 2. The Scourging; 3. Crowning with Thorns; 4. Carrying the Cross; 5. The Crucifixion.

Glorious Mysteries: 1. The Resurrection; 2. The Ascension; 3. The Coming of the Holy Spirit; 4. The Assumption; 5. The Coronation of Mary as Queen of Heaven.

Additional Activities

MARY AND THE CHURCH ACCORDING TO VATICAN COUNCIL II

Vatican Council II placed its reflection on Mary in the "Dogmatic Constitution on the Church." **Handout 1–E—Mary and the Church** includes passages relating Mary to the Church from a paraphrase of the Vatican II document. Distribute the handout and instruct the students, individually or in small groups, to complete the assignment described there.

PERSONAL MYSTERIES OF THE ROSARY

The text describes the Rosary as a prayer that celebrates the life of Mary, dividing it into Sorrowful, Joyful, and Glorious Mysteries. Since all Christians are called upon to imitate Mary in living out the Christian life, ask the students to think about an experience of sorrow, of joy, and of glory that they have had in their life. After a few moments, ask them to write a prayer based on one of these sorrowful, joyful, or glorious mysteries.

Concept Review

To review the importance of Mary for the Church and its members, read aloud to students the passages about Mary from Handout 1–E.

In-Text Activities

page 20 ## ACTIVITY

Using the Activity

(1) Have the students first journal on this topic, and then break into small groups to share voluntary responses. Ask each group to present three insights to the large group. Discuss as needed.

(2) These experiences can be quite personal, so follow-up discussion in the large group with only voluntary sharing is best.

Concept Review

Mention to the students that people joined the Christian movement from traditional Jewish backgrounds, from Hellenized Jewish backgrounds, and from God-fearer and other Gentile backgrounds. All these people probably had differences in the way they experienced and practiced their common Christianity. Discuss with the students: Are there groups of people within Catholicism today who seem to experience and practice their faith differently from others? If so, who are these groups? What are some of the differences today?

page 20 ## Review Questions and Answers

1. **How can the relationship between Christians and Jews during the first decades after Jesus be misunderstood if the New Testament is read uncritically?**

   An uncritical reading of the New Testament suggests that from the beginning Christians were a clearly identifiable group separate from Jews, which was not the case.

2. **What were some of the characteristics of the lifestyle of the early Christians?**

   The early Christians worshiped together as Jews, shared meals and possessions, and lived closely together.

3. **Name two groups from which the Christian community formed.**

   People who joined the Christian community came from Palestinian Jews, Diaspora Jews, Gentiles known as "God-fearers," and other Gentiles.

Paul: The Apostle to the Gentiles

1. Direct students to read the insert about Paul and then ask: What made Paul particularly suited for his role as "Apostle to the Gentiles."

2. In conjunction with this section you might assign each student one of the following research assignments on which to report.

   - Read one of Paul's letters.
   - Describe one of Paul's missionary journeys.
   - Describe one of the places Paul visited during his missionary journeys.
   - Describe one experience Paul had during his highly productive life.

3. You might assign the activity **Demas—A Footnote to History** as an assignment to conclude discussion of the first Christian century.

Additional Activities

DEMAS—A FOOTNOTE TO HISTORY

Handout 1–F, Demas—A Footnote to History, describes the three references we have to a "fellow worker" with Paul named Demas. The exercise gives students an opportunity to use their imagination in re-creating what it might have been like to join Christianity during the time of Paul.

Concept Review

Point out to students that, like Peter, Paul was a unique personality. Read aloud to them Acts 16:16–40, or if they have Bibles, ask them to read the passage themselves. After they have heard the story of Paul and Silas in prison, discuss with them some of the characteristics Paul exhibited in the story. Conclude the discussion with the question:

- How could any of these characteristics have helped Paul to be the giant in the development of early Christianity that he was?

In-Text Activities

ACTIVITY

Using the Activity

As the students discuss this topic, write the arguments for both positions in two columns on the board or overhead. Then add a third column with the arguments found in Acts 15.

Review Questions and Answers

1. **What issue is illustrated in the story of Peter and Cornelius?**

   The story of Peter and Cornelius illustrates the issue of whether or not to accept Gentiles into the Christian community.

2. **What resolution resulted from the Council of Jerusalem?**

   The Council of Jerusalem proposed that Jewish Christians should continue to keep the Jewish law but that Gentiles could join the community without keeping most of these requirements.

Chapter Review and Conclusion

REVIEW

1. Ask the students to summarize the main points in the chapter using their own words. Write notes on the board from their contributions. To reinforce their summary, you might want to review the major concepts in this chapter in the teaching manual. Then read the **Conclusion** on page 23.

2. Review the vocabulary in this chapter:

ascension—the full entry of Jesus' humanity into divine glory in God's heavenly domain, forty days after his resurrection (page 5)

Acts of the Apostles—the book of the New Testament that depicts the actions of the early Church community (page 6)

Pentecost—for Christians, the day the Holy Spirit was manifested, given, and communicated as a divine Person to the Church, fulfilling the Paschal mystery of Christ according to his promise (page 6)

Exodus—God's saving intervention in history, as narrated in the Book of Exodus, by which liberated the Hebrew people from slavery in Egypt, made a covenant with them, and brought them into the Promised Land (page 10)

Passover—Jewish feast commemorating the deliverance of the Jewish people from death by the blood of the lamb sprinkled on the doorposts in Egypt, which the angel of death saw and "passed over" (page 10)

Babylonian Captivity—period from 587 to 539 B.C. when the Jewish nation did not exist and Jewish leaders were exiled to Babylon (page 10)

diaspora—scattering of the Israelites, Jewish people, from their homeland (page 11)

legend—a story regarded as historical although not verifiable (page 12)

conversion—a radical reorientation of the whole life away from sin and evil and toward God (page 13)

reign of God—also known as the kingdom of God; righteousness, peace, and joy in the Holy Spirit present in the person of Jesus and in our midst through the people of God and the Eucharist, and will be fully realized in heaven (page 13)

Messiah—In traditional Jewish belief, someone who will become king and restore Israel to peace and prosperity; Jesus radically challenged this definition with his divine mission of priest, prophet, and king (page 15)

Sanhedrin—in Jesus' time, a group of seventy-one men made up of the chief priest, scribes, and elders who made decisions regarding actions of the people of the Jewish community (page 17)

Gentile—a person of non-Jewish faith or origin (page 20)

God-fearers—Gentiles attracted to Judaism who maintained some association with local Jewish communities without becoming Jews (page 20)

Council of Jerusalem—the first Church council which was called to resolve the growing controversy over whether or not Gentile Christians would have to observe Jewish law (page 23)

TEST

Give the students the Chapter 1 Test or an alternative assessment. The tests have been placed on the Harcourt Religion Publishers' Web page. This has been done to enable the teacher to customize this material for local needs. First contact Harcourt Religion Publishers' high school consultant at 800-922-7696, ext. 3781 for a user ID and password. Then connect with the Harcourt Religion Publishers' Web site at **www.harcourtreligion.com** to download the information. Collect the tests for grading.

Chapter 1 Test Answers

MULTIPLE CHOICE (2 points each)

1. c	7. a	13. b	19. b	25. b
2. d	8. b	14. a	20. b	26. c
3. a	9. a	15. d	21. a	27. c
4. b	10. d	16. b	22. b	28. c
5. c	11. b	17. a	23. d	29. d
6. c	12. a	18. c	24. a	30. b

ESSAYS (5 points each)

1. The followers of Jesus went from being anxious, fearful, and uncertain to being confident that Christ was still with them, working in and through them.

2. Pentecost is called the "birthday of the Church" because it marked the first time that the followers of Jesus actively carried on his work, as the Church is called to do.

3. Students may answer the question in a number of ways. Part of their answer would need to include a description of Hellenization, which refers to incorporating Greek culture into the Jewish culture of the time.

4. Students may answer the question in a number of ways. The early Christians shared their resources together, took particular care of people in need, and spread the message with enthusiasm.

5. The early Christians "shared all things in common." They joined together for a common meal, which was radical for the time. They provided for the needs of widows, orphans, and others in need.

6. Students may answer the question in a number of ways. As part of their answer, they would need to explain the perspective of at least one of the groups listed in the question.

7. At the Council of Jerusalem, the Church leaders decided that non-Jews did not need to adhere to all of the traditional rules that Jewish members of the Christian community adhered to. Therefore, non-Christian Jews began to view Christianity as no longer a Jewish movement.

8. Students may answer the question in a number of ways. As part of their answer, students might point out that Paul provided a theology for the fledgling Christian movement, he wrote letters addressing many concerns faced by Christian communities, he was able to speak to a non-Jewish audience in ways that the other apostles could not, and he spread the message in many parts of the Roman Empire.

Prayer

MUSIC SUGGESTIONS

"**A Sign**" by Larry Schexnaydre and Yve Braud from *Give Your Gifts, the New Songs* (GIA, Harcourt Religion Publishers).

"**Come and Fill Our Hearts**" by Taizé from *Give Your Gifts, the Basics* (GIA, Harcourt Religion Publishers).

"**One in His Name**" by Larry Schexnaydre and Kenny Braud from *Give Your Gifts, the New Songs* (GIA, Harcourt Religion Publishers).

"**Send Us Your Spirit**" by David Haas from *Gather (Comprehensive)* (GIA), *Today's Missal* (OCP).

"**Send Us Your Spirit**" by Dan Schutte from *Glory & Praise (Comprehensive)* (OCP), *Today's Missal* (OCP).

SCRIPTURE SUGGESTIONS

Joel 3:26–29

Acts 10:34–48

John 14:15–21

PRAYER

Father in heaven,
[We celebrate] the fullness
of the mystery of your revealed love.
See your people gathered in prayer,
Open to receive the Spirit's flame.
May it come to rest in our hearts
And dispense the divisions of word and tongue.
With one voice and one song
May we praise your name in joy and thanksgiving.
Grant this through Christ our Lord.

Alternate Opening Prayer for the Vigil Mass of Pentecost, adapted.

Chapter 1 Test

Name_____ Date_____ Class period_____

Test is made up of questions with suggested values totaling 100 points.

Multiple Choice (2 points each)

_____ 1. The attitude of the followers of Jesus gathered at Pentecost before the coming of the Holy Spirit was
   a. filled with joy that Jesus was with them
   b. anxious to gain more followers for their group
   c. confused and uncertain about what to do
   d. dissention over the growing number of converts

_____ 2. The Holy Spirit was manifest at Pentecost in forms like
   a. Jesus walking through walls
   b. water and oil
   c. lightning and a dove
   d. wind and fire

_____ 3. Pentecost takes place
   a. fifty days after Easter
   b. the Sunday after Easter
   c. the first Thursday in spring
   d. late in August

_____ 4. The ascension refers to
   a. Mary's physical entrance into heaven
   b. Jesus' physical entrance into heaven
   c. the coming of the Holy Spirit
   d. Jesus rising from the dead

_____ 5. During the trial of Jesus, Peter
   a. stood up for Jesus
   b. planned a revolt
   c. denied knowing Jesus
   d. tried to negotiate Jesus' release

_____ 6. Jesus explained his mission by quoting from the
   a. Hebrew prophet Isaiah
   b. Greek philosopher Plato
   c. words of his Father
   d. Book of Exodus

_____ 7. Abraham came to believe in
   a. one god
   b. many gods
   c. Jesus
   d. Ten Commandments

_____ 8. God commanded Abraham to sacrifice his son
   a. Jacob
   b. Isaac
   c. Ishmael
   d. Lot

_____ 9. Three monotheistic religions are
   a. Judaism, Christianity, Islam
   b. Hinduism, Buddhism, Christianity
   c. Shinto, Zen, Sikhism
   d. Taoism, Confucianism, Islam

_____ 10. The person God sent to lead the Israelites during the Exodus was
   a. Abraham
   b. Isaac
   c. Jacob
   d. Moses

_____ 11. Jews celebrate the Exodus at
   a. Hanukkah
   b. Passover
   c. Rosh Hashanah
   d. Yom Kippur

_____ 12. A key theme of the Exodus is
   a. liberation
   b. renewal
   c. peace
   d. revenge

_____ 13. Passover specifically refers to
   a. the ten plagues in Egypt
   b. the lamb's blood sprinkled on doorposts
   c. passing through the Red Sea
   d. Pharaoh's daughter saving Moses

_____ 14. System developed by Jews who lived outside of their homeland to keep alive their faith
   a. synagogues
   b. temples
   c. animal sacrifice
   d. secret prayers

_____ 15. Jews who did not live in Israel were known as Jews of the
      a. empire
      b. Gentiles
      c. Samaritans
      d. Diaspora

_____ 16. Hellenization refers to
      a. women rulers of nations
      b. spread of Greek culture
      c. rebirth of Judaism
      d. the Roman Empire

_____ 17. The Septuagint is a
      a. Greek translation of the Old Testament
      b. candleholder used during Jewish worship
      c. synagogue in Egypt
      d. banner of the Roman army

_____ 18. Many Jews at the time of Jesus believed the messiah would be someone who would
      a. be sacrificed on a cross
      b. enter Jerusalem on a donkey
      c. restore peace and prosperity
      d. come from Rome

_____ 19. Scripture scholars suggest that many early Christians believed that the coming of the reign of God would happen
      a. when they died
      b. during their lifetime
      c. in the distant future
      d. when the empire ended

_____ 20. The Sanhedrin was
      a. Roman governors
      b. a group of Jewish leaders
      c. Jewish Christians
      d. a Greek translation of Bible

_____ 21. A person of non-Jewish origin was known as a
      a. Gentile
      b. Hebrew
      c. Christian
      d. Pharisee

_____ 22. Non-Jews who had some association with Jewish communities were known as
      a. Zealots
      b. God-fearers
      c. apprentices
      d. catechumens

_____ 23. Paul was originally a member of the
      a. Gentiles
      b. Zealots
      c. Sadducees
      d. Pharisees

_____ 24. Originally Paul
      a. persecuted Christians
      b. combined Judaism and Christianity
      c. was an early apostle
      d. was a soldier

_____ 25. Paul was sent to Rome for trial because he was
      a. a notorious criminal
      b. a Roman citizen
      c. an important Jewish leader
      d. a Christian

_____ 26. While in prison, Paul
      a. received the gifts of the Holy Spirit
      b. became a Christian
      c. wrote letters to Christian communities
      d. met with the Roman Emperor

_____ 27. Paul died by being
      a. crucified upside down
      b. stoned to death
      c. beheaded
      d. drowned at sea

_____ 28. The Council of Jerusalem decided that
      a. Christianity should become separate from Judaism
      b. Peter and Paul should travel to Rome
      c. non-Jewish Christians did not have to follow Jewish laws
      d. Christians should stop attending synagogue services

_____ 29. The Council of Jerusalem was called because
      a. Christians wanted to elect a permanent leader
      b. followers of Peter were fighting those of Paul
      c. Christians were being persecuted by Jewish leaders
      d. it wasn't clear whether converts needed circumcision

_____ 30. After the Council of Jerusalem
      a. Peter's power diminished and Paul's increased
      b. Gentile Christians were full members of the community
      c. Christian leaders decided to meet every ten years
      d. Judaism ceased to exist in the Roman Empire

Essays (5 points each)

1. If you underwent a transformation similar to the one the followers of Jesus did at Pentecost, what would it be like?

2. Why is Pentecost called the "birthday of the Church"?

3. If you were a Jew living during the century before Jesus, what would your attitude be toward Hellenization? Explain.

4. You have joined the Christian movement late in the first century. You and your fellow Christians realize that the movement needs greater structure and organization if it is to survive. What are some actions that you might take which would mirror the actions of the early Christians?

5. What are three characteristics of the lifestyle of the early Christian community?

6. Of the following groups, which one do you think would find Christianity most appealing: Gentiles (not the God-fearers), God-fearers, Diaspora Jews, or Palestinian Jews? Explain.

7. Why did the Council of Jerusalem play an important role in the separation of Christianity from Judaism?

8. Make a case that Paul was the most influential person in the early development of Christianity.

THE SHIELDS OF THE TWELVE APOSTLES

Name_____ Date_____ Class period_____

The chapel office at Northwestern University in Evanston, Illinois, is decorated with shields that symbolize the twelve apostles. Here is the description of each shield. Visit their web site at **www.stuaff.northwestern.edu/chaplain/office_staffdocs/shield.html.**
   After you have read the descriptions:

1. Write a report on one of the apostles. (We have little definite information about them, but accounts of their missionary activities and also legends about each apostle exist.)

2. Think about yourself in light of the Christian life. Design a shield that incorporates symbols appropriate for you.

Andrew—The Cross Saltire
Tradition has it that Andrew was put to death on a cross of this kind (X-shaped) while preaching in Greece.

James the Greater—The Three Shells
The escallop shell is the symbol of pilgrimage; legend says that James took the gospel all the way to Spain.

John—The Chalice and Serpent
Early Christian writers reported that an attempt was made to kill John by giving him a chalice of poison to drink.

Peter—The Crossed Keys
The key is the historic symbol of Peter, derived from Jesus' words to him: "I will give you the keys of the kingdom" (Matthew 16:18).

Philip—The Cross and Loaves
Philip was present when Jesus fed the multitude with the loaves and fishes.

Jude—The Ship
The ship symbolizes Jude's missionary journeys.

James the Lesser—The Saw
James died a martyr's death, and his body was "sawn asunder."

Matthew—The Purses of Money
The purses symbolize Matthew's work in the profession of tax collecting.

Simon—The Fish and Book
The Canaanite Simon is so symbolized because, as preacher of the gospel, he was a great fisher of men.

Matthias—The Book and Axe
Matthias was the apostle who replaced Judas Iscariot and who was ultimately stoned and beheaded after his missionary work in Judea.

Thomas—The Spear and Carpenter's Square
The square represents this patron saint of builders. Thomas was run through with a spear by a religious leader in India, where he was preaching.

Bartholomew—The Flaying Knives
According to tradition, Bartholomew was martyred by being flayed to death with such knives.

JEWISH THEMES—CHRISTIAN THEMES

Name_____ Date_____ Class period_____

Here are the major themes in Judaism. The earliest Christians would have been familiar with these themes and would naturally apply them to Jesus and to the life of the Church. For each theme, identify ways that the theme might apply to Jesus, the Church, or Christian beliefs and practices.

Creation: The world is God's good creation. Humans, created in God's image, play a special role in the world.

Fall and Redemption: Humans stray from God's plan. Nonetheless, God offers forgiveness and promises not to abandon the world and God's people. God promised and sent a redeemer.

The Covenant: God establishes a special relationship with the Jewish people. Jews, therefore, have privileges and responsibilities because they are "God's chosen people."

The Exodus: God frees the Israelites, ancestors of the Jewish people, from slavery. The "blood of the lamb" saves them from death, and God guides them through the desert to the Promised Land.

Kingship: The Jewish people receive a king. When the kingdom is destroyed, they long for a new king, a "son of David," a messiah.

The Prophets: Some members of the community, inspired by God, challenge people to return to God and to live and practice justice.

The Babylonian Captivity: Jewish leaders are sent off into captivity in a far land where practicing their beliefs is difficult and dangerous.

Restoration: The Jewish people are again set free and return to Israel where they practice their religion freely.

JEWISH THEMES—HUMAN THEMES

Name_____ Date_____ Class period_____

Themes found in the Jewish Scriptures are, in fact, universal human themes. To gain a sense of how traditional Jewish themes adopted by Christianity have a wider, basic human meaning to them, read over the following statements. Imagine that they are book titles. For one of the titles write a paragraph describing what the book might be about.

- A New Covenant with Creation

- Like Rain in the Desert

- We Are Redeemed, Not Perfect

- A Prophet Rejected in Her Own Land

- His Reign Will Last Forever

- Pilgrims Journeying to the Promised Land

Title chosen:_____

GREEK CULTURE AND EARLY CHRISTIANITY

Name_____ Date_____ Class period_____

WHAT IS HELLENIZATION?

Hellenization refers to the spread of Greek culture that took place beginning around the time of the conquests of Alexander the Great in the fourth century before Christ. Even though Jesus and his early followers lived in an empire that was politically Roman, the language and culture common to the empire was Greek. Similarly, if you were to travel around the world today, you would meet many people who know English and are familiar with U.S. movies, television, and so forth. At the time of Jesus, many people knew Greek language and culture.

WHAT IS THE CENTRAL BELIEF OF HELLENISTIC THOUGHT?

One aspect of ancient Greek culture that impressed so many thinkers around the known world was its emphasis on reason. Ancient Greeks emphasized learning and saw reason as an instrument by which people could gain insight into the workings of the world. Since Greek philosophy so dominated the empire, scholars from every culture had to explain themselves over against Greek philosophy and Greek philosophical ideas. That is, they used Greek categories and terminology to express their philosophical thought. For instance, one concept that was beginning to make sense to a majority of philosophers of the ancient world was that of monotheism, belief in one god. Greek and Roman popular culture had a system of polytheism, belief in many gods. Jewish, and later Christian, thinkers were able to appeal to reason to make a strong case for monotheism.

HOW DID HELLENIZATION AFFECT JUDAISM?

Many Jews, especially those living outside of Israel, embraced Greek culture and tried to combine Greek and Jewish thought and ideas. For instance, a group of Jewish scholars in Egypt translated the Bible into Greek and also added some books to the Bible originally written in Greek, not Hebrew. For other Jews, especially many Jews who lived in Israel, Hellenization was a form of infidelity that was eroding true Judaism. However, one way or another, everyone in the Roman Empire before and immediately after the time of Jesus had to address Greek culture and Greek concepts.

DID HELLENIZATION INFLUENCE JESUS AND HIS FIRST FOLLOWERS?

Jesus and his earliest disciples lived mostly in the part of Israel that was least influenced by Greek culture. However, even in Galilee, Greek culture was present. Jesus himself referred to the Old Testament to speak about himself and his role. But some of his followers did use Greek concepts to explain Jesus. For instance, the beginning of the Gospel according to John refers to Jesus as the *Logos,* a Greek term meaning "word," or "idea," or "reason." Greek thought normally viewed God and the ideal world (the world of ideas) as separate from the physical world. When Christianity proclaimed Jesus to be the "word made flesh," it was a challenge to the typical Greek under-standing of reality. In the end, this belief, which baffled so many Greek thinkers, won out and became the dominant belief in Greek and Roman civilization.

MARY AND THE CHURCH

Name_____ Date_____ Class period_____

Mary, the Blessed Mother, has always held a place of great reverence in the Church. Here are some statements about the relationship between Mary and the Church from a paraphrase of the document on the Church first issued by the bishops of Vatican Council II. For each statement, describe a message that it contains for members of the Church.

Bill Huebsch, *Vatican II in Plain English: The Constitutions*
(Allen, TX: Thomas More, 1997).

Mary was free to say yes or no to God.
Her role was not forced upon her. (#55)

[S]ince she played such a pivotal role
in the life and work of Christ,
we now realize that she is
the first to receive the grace we also seek. (#61)

The Church takes Mary as its example
and always tries to imitate her life
and always seeks to give birth
to the presence of Christ in the world. (#64)

Mary's place is with God in heaven.
This gives us great hope
of what we ourselves can look forward to. (#68)

DEMAS—A FOOTNOTE TO HISTORY

Name_____ Date_____ Class period_____

The early Church wasn't very interested in the personalities or life stories of the apostles and disciples. It was more interested in proclaiming the message that the reign of God was at hand. Therefore, it left us with some interesting questions about the people who made up the Christian community at its beginning stages. For instance, we know about someone named Demas who joined the movement and worked diligently to spread the Christian message.

Demas is mentioned three times in Scripture, all in letters written by Paul. In his letter to the Colossians (4:14), Paul writes: "Luke, the beloved physician, and Demas greet you." In verses 23 and 24 of his letter to Philemon, Paul writes: "Epaphras, my fellow prisoner in Christ Jesus, sends greetings to you, as do Mark, Aristarchus, Demas, and Luke, my fellow workers." Since both of these letters were probably written between A.D. 61–63, during Paul's first Roman imprisonment, it appears that Demas had become a true "fellow worker" with Paul in his ministry. Demas had joined the movement and gave his time and energy spreading the Christian message.

The third mention of Demas seems sad. Somewhere between 63 and 67, Paul was once again in a Roman prison from which he wrote letters to Timothy, whom he left in charge of the Church at Ephesus. In his Second Letter to Timothy (4:9), Paul writes: "Do your best to come to me soon, for Demas, in love with this present world, has deserted me and gone to Thessalonica."

Who was this Demas? What led him to join Paul in actively participating in the Christian movement and then to fall "in love with the present world," apparently leaving Paul and the Christian community? Even this little that we know of him makes him a fascinating figure.

Writers of historical fiction take bare-bones accounts, such as the one we have of Demas, and create stories of possible scenarios to flesh out what might have happened. Use your imagination to write the story of Demas: What led him to join the Christian movement, to give himself to spreading its message, and then to leave it? What would it have been like to work beside the great Paul during these exciting and dangerous days?

CHAPTER TWO

SPREADING THE MESSAGE
The Church Enters the Empire

A Teacher's Prayer

Jesus, you laid down your life so that people would know the extent of God's love. Grant my students and me the joy of living life as passionately as your early followers did. As the spark of your message was kept burning through the sacrifice of holy martyrs, may I impart to my students a heartfelt appreciation for those who have come before us and for what they believed in so strongly. Amen.

Overview

The deep enthusiasm for their faith, characteristic of Christians of this era, is particularly evident in two ways: (1) the number of people who refused to renounce their faith in the face of extreme torture, and (2) the intensity of the debates about what to believe and how to practice those beliefs. These two experiences of the pre-Constantinian Church make up the two major concepts of this chapter. It is important for the students, who may take for granted the opportunity to practice their religion or who experience the sacraments nonchalantly, to realize that for hundreds of years being baptized and participating in the Eucharist could be a self-imposed death sentence. Therefore, one objective of this lesson is that the students will be helped to come to a greater appreciation of their own faith by spending time reflecting on the question: Why did the martyrs die for their faith?

Major Concepts Covered in This Chapter

1. Introduction

2. The Church of the Martyrs

3. The Church Takes Shape

4. Chapter Review and Conclusion

LESSON STRATEGIES

Introduction
Prayer

pages
24–25

■ **Music Suggestions**

"All That We Have" by Gary Ault from *Glory & Praise (Comprehensive)* (OCP), *Gather (Comprehensive)* (GIA).

"Come and Follow Me" by Francis Patrick O'Brien from *Give Your Gifts, the Songs* (GIA, Harcourt Religion Publishers).

"I Say 'Yes,' Lord" / "Digo 'Sí,' Señor," by Marty Haugen and Donna Peña from *Gather (Comprehensive)* (GIA), *Give Your Gifts, the Songs* (Harcourt Religion Publishers, GIA).

"Seed Scattered and Sown" by Dan Feiten from *Today's Missal* (OCP).

"We Walk by Faith" by Marty Haugen from *Gather (Comprehensive)* (GIA), *Today's Missal* (OCP), *Glory & Praise Comprehensive*.

■ **Scripture Suggestions**

Psalm 61:1–4

Acts 2:43–47

Matthew 24:9–14

■ **Prayer**

See page 24 of the student text.

pages
24–25

Overview

Have the students read the **Chapter Overview** and timeline on pages 24–25. Briefly discuss some of the points and events noted.

The Church of the Martyrs

The first three hundred years of Christianity are marked by intermittent but often extremely torturous persecutions. Christian martyrs keep alive and strengthen the faith until, in the end, the persecuted triumph over the persecutors.

pages
26–27

MARTYRS
Inter-Jewish Conflicts Lead to Christian Persecutions

1. Begin discussion of the early Christian martyrs by having the students privately write their thoughts on the **Before We Begin . . .** questions at the beginning of the chapter. You might point out that our contemporary world is known for skepticism, which undermines believing in anything or anyone intensely. Discuss with the students what the experience of witnessing on behalf of someone or some belief, such as the early Christians did, might have been like.

2. If few or no students report having such an experience, or are reluctant to share, place them in small groups and ask them to name movies in which characters felt strongly enough about something that they risked suffering, ridicule, or even death because of it. (Many blockbuster films—for example, *Pearl Harbor*—feature such a premise. Many teen-oriented movies also place characters in a situation in which they must decide whether or not to stand up for what they feel is right.)

3. The text will discuss some modern-day martyrs in the last chapters. You might want to delay this assignment until then, or use it to alert the students that the willingness of some Christians to give their lives for the faith did not end with the early Church. Since the students will encounter during the course numerous stories of martyrs, you might set aside a bulletin board or a file folder listing the names and stories of Christian martyrs through the ages.

In-Text Activities

page 27   ## DISCUSSION

Using the Discussion

The Church recognizes that without the early martyrs—those who died for the faith—the message of Christ may not have continued and certainly would not have had the life and intensity that it did. Therefore, it is appropriate that the day after the birth of Christ the Church celebrates the life given to Christianity through the sacrifice of the martyrs, symbolized by the first martyr, Stephen.

Additional Activities

MODERN-DAY DEACONS

The role of deacon existed very early in Church history. Following Vatican Council II in the 1960s, the Catholic Church decided that there should be permanent deacons to perform the same work done by deacons early in Church history. (Prior to Vatican Council II, being a deacon was, except in rare cases, the last step toward becoming a priest.) You might direct the students to interview a permanent deacon in an area parish to find out what his duties are. You might also invite a permanent deacon to speak to your class about his experience as a deacon.

CONCEPT REVIEW

Remind the students that the Acts of the Apostles and other writings from the early Church focus a great deal on the persecutions endured by the apostles and other members of the early Church. Discuss with the students: How do you think the fact that early Christianity was marked by martyrdom and persecution affected its worldview—the way Christians saw themselves?

page 28   ## The Roman Persecutions

Direct the students to read the section **The Roman Persecutions** on page 28. Discuss the **Factors That Made Christianity Susceptible to Persecution** to be sure the students understand the relevance of each point.

In-Text Activities

ACTIVITY

Using the Activity

1. Assign the students to work in small groups and make sure each group is researching a different modern-day martyr. Provide in-class time for the students to share their research with the whole class. Encourage students to draw connections between their lives and the lives of the martyrs.

34   *Chapter Two*

2. Resources: *The Catholic Martyrs of the Twentieth Century: A Comprehensive World History* by Robert Royal (Crossroad, 2000), *By Their Blood: Christian Martyrs of the Twentieth Century* by James C. Hefley and Marti Hefley (Baker Books, 1995), *American Martyrs from 1542* by Albert J. Nevins (Our Sunday Visitor, 1987), *No Strangers to Violence, No Strangers to Love: Twentieth Century Christian Heroes* by Boniface Hanley (Ave Maria Press, 1983), *Six Modern Martyrs* by Mary Craig (Crossroad, 1985).

page 29   **An Age of Persecutions**

Instruct the students to read the section **An Age of Persecutions** on page 29, paying special attention to the information about Pliny. In preparation for the mock trial **In-Text Activity,** direct students to reread the **Factors that Made Christianity Susceptible to Persecution** box found on page 28.

In-Text Activities

page 29   **Activity**

Using the Activity

Assign a small group of students to serve as lawyers defending Christianity and another small group to serve as lawyers for the empire. Give them a few minutes to prepare arguments for their position. You might have another small group play the role of Christians and a group serve as a jury that would comment on the arguments when the trial is completed and make a decision about what to do with the Christians based on the arguments presented.

Additional Activities

THE STORY OF SAINT TARCISIUS

After the students have read about the Roman persecutions of the early Christians, you might distribute **Handout 2–A, The Story of a Youthful Martyr,** to provide them another account of a martyr. The activity accompanying the handout is intended to give the students an opportunity to discuss the role that the stories of martyrs should play in Catholic education.

CoNCept RevïEw

Read aloud the last line from the paragraph under **The Roman Persecutions** on page 28: "Christianity's beliefs and practices came into direct conflict with the purposes of the emperor and the persecutions began." Discuss with the students: Are Christian beliefs and practices a threat in any way to the political, social, or economic agenda of our society? If so, how? If not, should they be?

The Legend of Deacon Laurence

Ask for a volunteer to read aloud the legend of Deacon Laurence. After the students have heard the story, ask them to respond to the following questions:

1. What values are presented in the story that could be considered counter-cultural during Laurence's time?

   Laurence equated "wealth" with the poor, sick, and needy of Rome.

2. What are some adjectives you might use to describe Laurence?

   Laurence was bold, fearless, faith-filled, and confident in his Christian beliefs.

3. Whether or not the legend is true, does this story reflect perspectives characteristic of early Christianity? If so, what are those perspectives?

   The story illustrates some of the appeal of early Christianity in that the movement included both "haves" and "have nots" on an equal level. People in need were particularly prized and respected in the Early Church. People such as Laurence were willing to stand up to power and to sacrifice their lives for their beliefs.

Perpetua and Felicity

When the students have read the story of these two martyrs, point out to them that Perpetua wrote about her life and a later writer described the circumstances surrounding her death. In her diary Perpetua describes a number of dreams she has as she awaits her martyrdom, which she knows is coming. Her dreams are highly symbolic, as dreams tend to be. Perpetua sees beyond the suffering and death that awaits her to the full entrance into life with Christ that comes with her martyrdom.

From Outsiders to Insiders
Martyrs—Heroes of the Church

Direct the students to review pages 31–32.

- Ask: Why does the text say that the year 313 marks the end of an era for the Christian Church? (In that year it becomes legal to practice Christianity in the Roman Empire. Shortly after that, Christianity becomes not only legal and acceptable but also the preferred religion of the empire. In time Christianity becomes the official religion of the empire.)

- Discuss with the students how this change might have affected the experience of being Christian. For instance, before Constantine, being Christian might have led to persecution and was viewed as subversive to the state. Eventually, some time after Constantine, not being Christian was an affront to the state and set oneself outside of the mainstream. Ask the students to keep this important difference in mind when we come to the next chapter and the next historical period.

page 31   YOUTH NEWS

Using the Activity

Invite the students to write or draw a symbolic description of a Christian perspective on martyrdom and the life that follows it. Ask some students to read or present and describe their accounts or simply suggest images that they used in their descriptions.

Additional Activities

THE LEGACY OF THE MARTYRS

Handout 2–A, The Story of a Youthful Martyr, provides the students with an opportunity to examine the phenomenon of martyrdom in Christianity. Many Christian martyrs are portrayed as if they were seeking death. In fact, in the circumstances in which they lived, martyrdom represented the strongest and clearest affirmation of their faith that they could make. Allow the students, either individually or in small groups, to complete the assignment on the handout and then review their responses with them.

CoNCept ReviEw

Point out to the students that Saint Justin Martyr, who died for his faith by being beheaded around the year 165, suggested that never before had common people gone to death for their beliefs with such joy as had the early Christians. Discuss with the students:

- How should members of the Church today look upon the martyrs?
- In what ways does the Church commemorate the martyrs?

In-Text Activities

page 32   WWW.

page 32   **Review Questions and Answers**

1. **Who is the first known Christian martyr?**

   Saint Stephen is the first known Christian martyr.

2. **Which group of Christians was the primary target of Jewish persecutions?**

   Christians of Hellenistic Jewish background were the primary target of Jewish persecution of Christians.

3. **In what city were the followers of Jesus first called *Christians?***

   The followers of Jesus were first called Christians in Antioch, the capital of Syria.

4. **List three reasons why Christians were particularly susceptible to Roman persecution.**

   Answers could include:

   - Christianity spread quickly throughout the empire.
   - Christianity rejected emperor worship.
   - Christianity accepted Gentiles as members.
   - Christianity became distinct from Judaism, and its members met in secret assemblies.

5. **Who was the Roman emperor who first persecuted Christians? Why did he do so?**

Nero was the first Roman emperor to persecute Christians, blaming them for a fire that destroyed much of Rome in the year 64 A.D.

6. **What did Diocletian do to try to restore order to the empire?**

Diocletian divided the empire into sections and reinstated mandatory emperor worship.

7. **What did the Edict of Milan grant?**

The Edict of Milan granted Christians freedom to practice their religion.

8. **Who was the first emperor to become Christian?**

Constantine was the first emperor to become Christian.

The Church Takes Shape

From the second to the fourth century, members of the Church address the issues of how to express their beliefs, how to celebrate those beliefs, and how the Church should be structured.

page 33

THE CHURCH TAKES SHAPE

1. Before the students read these sections, ask them to name the various elements characteristic of any religion. Possible answers are:
   - a set of beliefs
   - prayer
   - Scriptures
   - sacraments
   - a community of people
   - statements about right and wrong behavior

   Alert the students that elements such as these developed in early Christianity and are the subject of this section of the text.

2. Direct the students to read the section, **The Church Takes Shape** on page 33. As they are doing so, write the words CREED, CULT, and COMMUNITY on the board or overhead. Point out that Christianity began with a group of people who shared an experience of Jesus as Christ. To keep the experience alive, to share it with others, to give it shape for the future, and to prevent it from becoming distorted, the Christian community naturally had to address the issues discussed in the remainder of this chapter.

pages
34–36

Apologists Explain and Defend the Faith

ORTHODOXY AND HERESY

THE DEBATE ABOUT CHURCH PRACTICES

1. Write on the board or overhead the terms: HERESY, ORTHODOXY, HERETICS, and APOLOGISTS. Direct the students to read **Apologists Explain and Defend the Faith** on page 34 and the chart on **Prominent Criticisms Addressed by Apologists** and the text on **Orthodoxy and Heresy** on page 35. Ask for definitions of the terms to be written on the board or overhead.

2. Direct the students to read the section on **The Debate about Church Practices** on pages 35 and 36. Point out that the early Church needed to decide on what was acceptable regarding many of its practices. Mention to them that the essentials of the sacraments remain intact from the earliest days of the Church but that discussion about other, less essential aspects of Church practices still takes place today.

In-Text Activities

page 35
DISCUSSION

Using the Discussion

Use the **In-Text Discussion** to examine controversies in which the Church is involved today. The activity may be done individually, in small groups, or as a class unit. If the activity is done individually or in small groups, allow time for class discussion.

Additional Activities

DEBATING CHURCH PRACTICES

Handout 2–C, Debating Church Practices, gives the students an opportunity to think about and discuss some questions of Church practice related to the sacraments that parishes at times must address. In addition to determining whether they agree or disagree with each of the statements, the activity on the handout asks the students to examine how their local Church addresses some of the practices related to the sacraments.

Concept Review

Discuss with the students the following statement: The Church would be better off today if early Christian thinkers had simply agreed to disagree and had not attempted to come up with one orthodox understanding of Christian teachings.

In-Text Activities

page 36
FYI

Using the FYI

Churches in the East and West calculate the date of Easter by the same principle, established by the Council of Nicea in 325 A.D. Easter is to be celebrated on the Sunday following the first full moon after the March Equinox. However, differences in dating occur because Churches follow different calculations of the equinox and the full moon. Recently, there has been a move to use modern scientific calculations to determine when Easter is to be celebrated, using the meridian of Jerusalem as the point from which to make the calculation. However, local Churches fear that making the change will weaken their unique identity.

DISCUSSION

Using the Discussion

Introduce the **Discussion** by mentioning to the students that members of certain religions stand out because of the dress that they wear or the positions they take on issues. Then ask them:

- Do Catholics stand out because of their beliefs or behavior?
- Should Catholics stand out from the rest of society because of their behavior? If so, how? If not, why not?

SETTING THE CANON—THE CHURCH IDENTIFIES ITS SCRIPTURES

Direct the students to read the section on **Setting the Canon—The Church Identifies Its Scriptures** on pages 37 and 38.

1. Ask them to describe the three stages of Gospel development described in the text (see box, page 37).
2. Explain to them the close relationship between Scripture and Church held by Catholics, especially as manifest in the Church's understanding of Tradition. Discuss with the students:

   - Does the fact that the Church decided which books should be included in the New Testament diminish or increase your appreciation of the Scriptures as the word of God?

   (Point out that many Catholic beliefs, such as the mystery of the incarnation, the Holy Spirit as human intimate experience of God, and the Church as Christ's presence in the world, affirm that God is manifest through the human. The Scriptures, while they are the word of God chosen by divine guidance, are also human works both in their writing and in how they are chosen.)

⌐ CoNCept ReViEw ⎯⎯⎯⎯⎯⎯

Read aloud the statement on page 37 from the Catechism about Scripture and Tradition. Point out to the students that, according to the Catechism, Scripture and Tradition have the same source and the same goal—making present and fruitful the mystery of Christ. Discuss with the students: How have Scripture and Tradition made present and fruitful the mystery of Christ for you? How might they do this more clearly for you?

Beginnings of a Sacramental Life

INITIATION INTO THE CHURCH

1. Instruct the students to read pages 39–41 on the sacramental life.
2. Ask the students to explain the difference between the Greek and Latin understandings of sacramental life. (The Greek perspective emphasized the entire life of the Christian as the mystery of life with Christ. The Latin Church emphasized specific rites or sacraments that celebrated and made present the mystery of life with Christ.)
3. Follow this explanation by assigning the **In-Text Activity** on page 40 to be done in small groups.

page 40   ACTIVITY

Using the Activity

Use the **Activity** items as an invitation for the students to describe sacramental experiences that have helped them experience Christ's presence in their lives.

page 41   **FYI**

Additional Activities

GUEST SPEAKER

Invite a new Catholic who participated in the RCIA to speak with the class. (Alternative: a member of an RCIA team.) Have the class brainstorm and prioritize questions prior to the presentation, and be sure to allow enough time for questions.

pages
42–43

An Institutional Structure Emerges: One Body, Different Functions

1. Direct the students to read the section **An Institutional Structure Emerges: One Body, Different Functions,** pages 42–43, and then mention to the students that many people question whether or not Jesus intended to found the Church.

2. Discuss: Based on information in the text, did Jesus intend to found the Church?

   (The short answer is "yes," although the text points out that Jesus did not provide an exact blueprint for how the Church should be structured. The early Church adopted some variety in the way it was structured. The current structure of the Catholic Church came to be standard for the Church.)

In-Text Activities

page 42   DISCUSSION

Using the Discussion

1. The answers could include:
   - Deacon
   - Eucharistic minister
   - Music minister
   - Parish council member
   - Youth minister
   - Hospice volunteer
   - Someone who visits the sick or elderly

2. Use the **In-Text Activity** as a springboard for discussion regarding opportunities available for youths to minister within their parish, community, or family. Some ideas include:
   - Tutoring
   - Visiting the sick or elderly
   - Babysitting
   - Youth group participation
   - Music minister

HIPPOLYTUS, THE FIRST ANTI-POPE

Handout 2–D, Hippolytus—The First Anti-pope, tells the story of a brief, early schism that took place in the Church when a good but overly zealous Christian arranged for some of his friends to elect him "pope," thus setting himself up as an anti-pope. The handout mentions more modern Church leaders who also set themselves apart from officially recognized Church leadership. You might read the story on the handout and assign a few students to research the two more modern figures mentioned in the handout.

CONCEPT REVIEW

Discuss with your students the following statement: The Church is not a democracy. You might use the following questions to further the discussion.

- What would people who make this statement be implying about the Church?

- Do you agree with this statement?

- If the Church is not a democracy, what is it?

- What models of involvement and governance or what improvements would you propose for the Church?

pages
43–44

WOMEN IN THE EARLY CHURCH

1. After the students have read this section, ask them:

   - What is meant by the sentence: "Determining what roles women had in the early Church requires a kind of detective work." (The Bible does not focus on women or on the work they performed.)

   - Is this statement true for all historical records from earlier times? (Typically historical records focus on the male leadership that existed in the patriarchal societies of the time.)

   - What evidence exists that women were active and equal members of the early Christian community?

2. Then read aloud the quote by Pope John Paul II on women in history.

   Unfortunately, a certain way of writing history has paid greater attention to extraordinary and sensational events than to the daily rhythm of life, and the resulting history is almost only concerned with the achievements of men. This tendency should be reversed. "How much still needs to be said and written about man's enormous debt to women in every other realm of social and cultural progress!" (*L'Osservatore Romano,* English edition, 31 May 1995, #6.)

page 44

DISCUSSION

Using the Discussion

Note for the students the fact that Paul was writing in a time when the patriarchal structure was strong in families. Statements in these readings that seem to put down women and children and thus bother modern readers should be read and discussed in the context of the times in which they were written. This is an area in which adaptation to the culture of the present day is necessary.

Using the Activity

Discuss with the students: Do you think that joining the Christian community in the early centuries was empowering to women? (Evidence suggests that the Christian community was more equal than the dominant culture. Despite restrictions in the dominant culture, women seem to have been actively involved in leadership and ministry from the time of Jesus on.)

page 45   ## Review Questions and Answers

1. **As applied to the Church, what do the words *creed, rite,* and *community* mean?**
   - Creed refers to the way the Church expresses its beliefs.
   - Rite refers to the way the Church celebrates and ritualizes its beliefs.
   - Community refers to the way the Church structures itself.

2. **Describe a major difference between Jewish and Greek thought.**

   Jewish thought focused more on right behavior while Greek thought focused more on right thinking.

3. **What is theology?**

   Theology refers to the rational, intellectual study of religious matters.

4. **What function did apologists serve in the early Church?**

   Christian apologists defended and explained Christian beliefs.

5. **What is the difference between orthodoxy and heresy?**

   Orthodoxy refers to right, accurate statements about religious beliefs. Heresy refers to wrong, inaccurate statements about religious beliefs.

6. **What was the debate about people who were called *lapsi?***

   The *lapsi* controversy addressed the issue of what to do about people who leave the Christian community and wish to return to it.

7. **What does "setting the canon" mean in regard to Scripture?"**

   "Setting the canon" means determining which writings are accepted as official Scriptures.

8. **What principles did Church leaders use in setting the canon?**

   Church leaders based their decision about the canon on the following questions:
   - Was a particular work written by an eyewitness to events, by someone who actually knew Jesus, or by an apostle?
   - Did the writing accurately reflect the teachings of Jesus as the apostles remembered them?
   - Had the piece of writing been consistently used in liturgical settings by Christian communities for some time?
   - Was there a general consensus that a particular writing was sacred and special?

9. **What two sources does the Church use to determine Christian teachings? What is their common source?**

   Scripture and Tradition are the two sources the Church uses to determine Christian teachings. The source of both is God who communicates through Christ and his Church.

10. **What is the pre-Christian meaning of the term *sacramentum?***

   Sacramentum referred to the secret initiation rite that members of the Roman army underwent.

11. **How did Greek-speaking churches refer to what Latin churches called sacraments?**

   Greek-speaking churches used the term *mysterion* to describe what the Latin churches called sacraments.

12. **What does it mean to say that sacraments became more formalized and spiritualized?**

   Over time, the sacraments became more formalized because they were performed in uniform fashion. The physical actions of the sacraments, such as bathing and eating, were eventually reduced so that, for instance, eating became more of a spiritual meal than a physical one.

13. **Outline the basic transformation that took place in the early Church's institutional structure.**

   As the Church grew, clearly defined structures of authority grew with it. Fairly early the model that exists in the Catholic Church today became standard, with bishops and presbyters having leadership in local communities.

14. **Who were Junia and Phoebe?**

   Junia and Phoebe were two women leaders in the early Church. Saint Paul refers to Junia as "prominent among the apostles" and to Phoebe as a "deacon of the church."

Chapter Review and Conclusion

REVIEW

1. Ask the students to summarize the main points in the chapter using their own words. Write notes on the board from their contributions. To reinforce their summary, you might want to review the major concepts in this chapter in the teaching manual. Then read the **Conclusion** on page 45.

2. Review the vocabulary in this chapter:

   deacon—third degree of the Sacrament of Holy Orders; an assistant to a bishop or a priest; in the early Church, someone appointed to serve those who were poor or otherwise needy in the community (page 27)

   martyr—a witness to the truth of the faith, in which the martyr endures even death to be faithful to Christ (page 27)

   Edict of Milan—declaration allowing religious freedom in the Roman Empire (page 31)

   heretic—one who holds a position on an article of faith that conflicts with officially defined teachings (page 34)

   apologist—a Christian thinker who defended and explained Christian beliefs (page 34)

   atheism—the denial that God exists (page 35)

incarnation—the fact that the Son of God assumed human nature and became man in order to accomplish our salvation (page 35)

orthodoxy—correct teachings about basic Christian beliefs (page 35)

heresy—a position on an article of faith that conflicts with officially defined teachings (page 35)

canon—the authentic list of books which makes up the Old and New Testament; chosen through apostolic Tradition (page 38)

Tradition—the deposit of faith as found in the preaching of the apostles, handed on through the apostolic succession in the Church (page 38)

sacrament—an efficacious sign of grace, instituted by Christ and entrusted to the Church, by which divine life is dispensed to us through the work of the Holy Spirit (page 39)

catechumen—an unbaptized person preparing for membership in the Church (page 41)

assimilation—members of minority groups adopting the values and characteristics of the dominant culture in which they live (page 41)

bishop—means "overseer"; in the Catholic faith the word refers to one who has received the fullness of the Sacrament of Holy Orders; the shepherd of a particular church entrusted to him (page 43)

presbyter—another name for elder or priest; in the early Church presbyters served in leadership positions in some faith communities; one who has received the second order in Holy Orders (page 43)

Test

Give the students the Chapter 2 Test or an alternative assessment. The tests have been placed on the Harcourt Religion Publishers' Web page. This has been done to enable the teacher to customize this material for local needs. First contact Harcourt Religion Publishers' high school consultant at 800-922-7696, ext. 3781 for a user ID and password. Then connect with the Harcourt Religion Publishers' Web site at **www.harcourtreligion.com** to download the information. Collect the tests for grading.

Chapter 2 Test Answers

Matching (2 points each)

1. n	4. h	7. l	10. a	13. d
2. e	5. j	8. g	11. o	14. i
3. f	6. b	9. m	12. k	15. c

Short Answer (5 points each)

1. Emperor Nero blamed Christians for starting a fire that burned much of Rome in 64 A.D.

2. Laurence presented people who were poor, disabled, and needy as the "treasure of the Church."

3. Perpetua's servant and companion was Felicity.

4. The feast of Stephen is celebrated on December 26.

5. Some altars contain relics of martyrs as a reminder of the legacy of the early Church.

6. The Edict of Milan proclaimed religious freedom in the Roman Empire.

7. *Orthodoxy* means "right teaching" or "right thinking."

8. Criticisms of Christianity addressed by apologists were the belief that it was a form of atheism, the mystery of the Incarnation, certain Christian practices, and the disruptive nature of Christian social structure.

9. The "Easter controversy" refers to the fact that the Eastern and Western Churches calculated when Easter was to be celebrated differently.

10. "Canon" means rule or measure. In regards to Scripture, it refers to the officially recognized books of the bible.

11. The actual words and actions of Jesus were the first stage of Gospel development. Secondly, his followers circulated stories about these words and actions. Finally, certain writers gathered sayings and stories into the form we know today as a gospel.

12. Sacraments are "efficacious" in the sense that through them Christ accomplishes what they symbolize.

13. The Greek Church referred to the sacraments as "mysteries."

14. Answers may vary.

Prayer

MUSIC SUGGESTIONS

"Be Not Afraid" by Bob Dufford from *Glory & Praise (Comprehensive)* (OCP), *Today's Missal* (OCP), *Gather (Comprehensive)* (GIA), *Lead Me, Guide Me* (GIA).

"For Living, For Dying" by Donna Peña from *Give Your Gifts, the Songs* (GIA, Harcourt Religion Publishers).

"Raise Me Up" by Eric Becker from *Give Your Gifts, the New Songs* (GIA, Harcourt Religion Publishers).

"Send Down the Fire" by Marty Haugen from *Give Your Gifts, the Basics* (GIA, Harcourt Religion Publishers).

"With You by My Side" by David Haas from *Give Your Gifts, the New Songs* (GIA, Harcourt Religion Publishers).

SCRIPTURE SUGGESTIONS

Revelation 21:1–5a

James 5:7–11

Mark 16:14–20

PRAYER

Give us, O God, the vision which can see your love in the world in spite of human failure.

Give us the faith, the trust, the goodness, in spite of our ignorance and weakness.

Give us the knowledge that we may continue to pray with understanding hearts, and show us what each one of us can do to set forth the coming of the day of universal peace.

The crew of Apollo 8, while orbiting the moon.

CHAPTER 2 TEST

Name_____ Date_____ Class period_____

Test is made up of questions with suggested values totaling 100 points.

Matching (2 points each)

_____   1. Deacon

_____   2. Martyr

_____   3. Stephen

_____   4. Herod Agrippa I

_____   5. Nero

_____   6. Constantine

_____   7. Laurence

_____   8. Perpetua

_____   9. Diocletian

_____   10. Pliny

_____   11. Heretic

_____   12. Apologist

_____   13. *Lapsi*

_____   14. Bishop

_____   15. Presbyter

A. Roman governor who wrote the emperor seeking guidance about what to do with Christians

B. First Christian Roman emperor

C. Early name for priest or elder

D. Christians who left the faith but wanted to return

E. Means "witness"

F. First Christian martyr

G. Early Christian who kept a diary in prison and died for the faith

H. Ruler of Palestine who persecuted Christians in Jerusalem

I. Means "overseer"

J. First emperor to persecute Christians

K. Someone who defends and explains the faith

L. Roman deacon who died while being burned over hot coals

M. Emperor who began dioceses and the "great persecution" of Christians

N. Office in the Church intended to serve those who are poor

O. Someone espousing a position contrary to officially defined teachings

Short Answer (5 points each)

1. What event led to the persecution of Christians in Rome?

2. What did Laurence present as the "treasure of the church"?

3. Who was Perpetua's servant and companion?

4. When is the feast of Saint Stephen?

5. What do some altars in Catholics churches contain as a reminder of the legacy of the early Church?

6. What did the Edict of Milan proclaim?

7. What is meant by the term *orthodoxy?*

8. Name two criticisms of Christianity that apologists addressed.

9. What was the "Easter controversy"?

10. What is the canon?

11. Name the three stages of Gospel development.

12. What does it mean to say that sacraments are "efficacious"?

13. What term did the Greek Church use for sacraments?

14. Name a woman who played a leadership role in the early Church.

THE STORY OF A YOUTHFUL MARTYR

Name_____ Date_____ Class period_____

In 1854 an English cardinal wrote a novel about a young woman who worked for the Church in Rome during the third and fourth centuries. In his novel he repeated a story of an earlier Christian martyr that had been told for a long time. Many people thereafter thought that the story was fictitious since it was written in a novel; but actually Pope Damasus, who served as pope from 366 to 384, had written a poem commemorating the young martyr as well.

The story is about a young boy named Tarcisius who lived in Rome during the time of Emperor Valerian's persecutions (around the year 257). Many Christians were in the Roman prisons, and priests could not freely bring them the Eucharist. Tarcisius, perhaps under twelve at the time, received permission to take Communion to the prisoners. He would go almost daily to visit the Christians awaiting death and bring them Communion. Since he was so young, guards didn't challenge him or search him carefully. One day, however, some non-Christian children called him over to play with them. Tarcisius told them that he was too busy to play. The other children asked him what he was hiding and tried to take the Communion bread from him. Tarcisius would not give up the Eucharist, so the children beat him until he was dead. Some Christians rescued his body and took it to the cemetery of Saint Callistus for burial.

In the poem that Pope Damasus wrote about Tarcisius, he compared him to the first martyr, Saint Stephen. Since Stephen was a deacon, some people adopted the belief that Tarcisius was also a deacon. It appears more likely that he was merely a youthful member of the Church who volunteered for a dangerous job that brought joy and sustenance to fellow members of the community. In doing so he gave his life.

Tarcisius is the patron saint of altar servers, Eucharistic ministers, and first communicants. His feast day is August 15.

Up until the 1960s, young children preparing for First Communion typically heard the story of the brave young Tarcisius who guarded the Eucharist with his life. Do you think that young Catholics today should hear this story? Why or why not?

THE LEGACY OF THE MARTYRS

Name_____ Date_____ Class period_____

The experience of the martyrs colored early Christianity's understanding of itself. During certain times in Christianity's first three hundred years, the possibility of martyrdom was for Christians a fact of life, not something of their choosing. Many writers spoke of martyrdom as the Christian ideal. However, it is important to keep martyrdom in perspective. For instance, to say that being a martyr was the Christian ideal did not mean that Christians sought out or welcomed martyrdom. Instead, the glowing reports about martyrs that are a major part of the Christian story must be understood in light of the following five perspectives:

- Martyrs placed faith in God above life itself.
- Martyrs are a reminder that earthly life pales in comparison to the joys of heavenly life.
- Enduring suffering for the right reason is a painful but positive experience.
- Love demands sacrifice.
- Martyrdom demonstrates the presence of God's life among us.

Here are some writers' reflections on martyrdom:

I pray, my brothers, that we may be found worthy to be cursed, censured, and ground down, and even to be executed in the name of Jesus Christ, as long as Christ Himself is not killed in us.

Paulinus of Nola (353–431)

The martyrs are perfected in righteousness, and they earned perfection through their martyrdom. For them the church does not pray: for the other departed faithful she prays, but not for martyrs. They have gone out of this world so perfected that instead of being our clients they are our advocates.

Augustine of Hippo (354–430)

Now, at last I begin to be a disciple! Let nothing visible or invisible hinder me, through jealousy, from attaining to Jesus Christ. Come fire, come cross, come whole herds of wild beasts, come drawing and quartering, scattering of bones, cutting off of limbs, crushing of the whole body, all the horrible blows of the devil—let all these things come upon me, if only I may be with Christ.

Ignatius of Antioch (killed c. 107 by wild beasts)

God does not require of us the martyrdom of the body; he requires only the martyrdom of the heart and the will.

John Vianney (1786–1859)

Quotes from Jill Haak Adels, *The Wisdom of the Saints* [New York: Oxford University Press, 1987].

Name_____ Date_____ Class period_____

FOR DISCUSSION

1. What would you say to someone who asked you the following questions:

   • Do Christians welcome suffering?

   • Do Christians welcome death?

   • Did the early Christian martyrs want to suffer and die?

2. Give examples to illustrate the meaning of the four perspectives on Christian martyrdom in the quotes of Paulinus of Nola, Augustine of Hippo, Ignatius of Antioch, and John Vianney.

3. Explain in your own words what each of the above authors is saying about martyrdom.

DEBATING CHURCH PRACTICES

Name_____ Date_____ Class period_____

Answer **Agree, Disagree,** or **Uncertain** to the following statements. Explain why you take the stand that you do. If a parish in your neighborhood or your diocese has a policy on any of these issues, describe what it is.

_____ 1. People should not kneel while receiving Communion if the stated practice of a parish is to stand during reception of Communion.

_____ 2. Individual parishes should vote on whether or not to have both altar boys and altar girls serving at Mass.

_____ 3. A priest should not offer the option of face-to-face Sacrament of Reconciliation if he is uncomfortable without a confessional screen.

_____ 4. People should not say the rosary or practice other forms of personal devotion during the Mass so that they can participate fully in the Eucharist.

_____ 5. Parishes that have no priest available should have a layperson preside over a prayer service, deliver a homily, and distribute Communion on Sundays.

_____ 6. Every diocese should decide for itself when young people are eligible to receive the Sacrament of Confirmation.

_____ 7. Catholic couples should plan their own wedding ceremonies under the guidance of a priest, including the readings to be used at the wedding Mass.

_____ 8. Parish councils should determine the amount of preparation that a couple should receive prior to having their child baptized.

HIPPOLYTUS—THE FIRST ANTI-POPE

Name_____ Date_____ Class period_____

During its two thousand years, the Church has had almost forty men claiming to be pope who were not. These men are known as anti-popes, people who claim to be or exercise the office of pope without valid authority to do so. Some anti-popes were deliberately elected by factions of Church leaders. Others were chosen during a time of confusion when rules for election were unclear or when the legitimate pope had been deposed or sent into exile. As you can imagine, having someone who claims to be bishop of Rome who is not a validly chosen pope can cause deep divisions in the Church. The first such anti-pope was named Hippolytus, who claimed to be pope in the year 217. An interesting and unusual character, Hippolytus—even though an anti-pope—ended up being canonized a saint of the Church.

Hippolytus was a scholar and a respected priest of the Church of Rome. He wrote much, and was often quoted because of his strong stand against heresies having to do with the nature of Christ. He was an excellent speaker, and people came from great distances to hear him preach. A bit of an actor, Hippolytus presided at Eucharist with great flair. He even wrote the Eucharistic Prayer that is now Eucharistic Prayer II and often is used at Mass.

With a background in speaking out forcefully against heresies, Hippolytus was impatient with Pope Zephyrinus, whom he felt was too permissive in allowing heresy to go unchecked. After Pope Zephyrinus's death, his close advisor Callistus was chosen to succeed him. Hippolytus believed that Callistus was a poor choice. He therefore had a small band of his followers elect him as "pope." He called his group the "Catholic Church" and referred to the rest of the Roman Church as "The Roman Christian School of Callistus." He continued to claim to be pope through the reign of two successors to Callistus.

In the year 235, Emperor Maximus Thrax began a concentrated attack on Church leadership in Rome. Both Pontian, the pope, and Hippolytus, the anti-pope, were sent to the salt mines of Sardinia. Because he did not want the Church in Rome to be without a leader, Pontian resigned the papacy—the first pope to do so. While exiled together, Pontian and Hippolytus were reconciled; Hippolytus and his group were reconciled with the Church. Both Pontian and Hippolytus are recognized as saints today.

Within the Church, Catholics continue to debate and disagree on certain matters. Sometimes Catholics take stands that lead them out of the Church itself. Find out what you can about Archbishop Marcel LeFebvre and Father Leonard Feeney and tell their stories.

CHAPTER THREE

CHURCH VICTORIOUS
The Age of the Fathers

A Teacher's Prayer

O Lord, you inspired the Fathers and Mothers of your Church. During our study of their age, grant that your Spirit come upon us so that my students and I may find a place within ourselves where we too can know your love and find joy and peace. Amen.

Overview

This chapter tells the story of the radical transformation that took place when Christianity became the religion of the empire. On the one hand, emperor and Church leaders together began to set standards for both society and the Church. This marriage of secular and religious characterizes Christianity until after the Reformation. On the other hand, many Christians chose to flee this liaison between the secular and the religious and live a life of strict self-denial, which became a distinguishing mark of the Church of the day. During this period also, great thinkers, known collectively as the Fathers of the Church, hammered out a formulation of orthodox Christian teachings that continues to be standard Catholic theology today. The rapid spread of Christianity brought with it controversy over the meaning of core Christian beliefs, leading to a series of councils to define what those core beliefs were.

These three major concepts, examined in this chapter (relations between Church and state, monasticism, and the creed), continue to be themes important to Catholicism today.

Major Concepts Covered in This Chapter

1. Introduction

2. The Religion of the Empire

3. Church Fathers and Mothers Guide the Christian Community

4. The Beginnings of Monasticism

5. Chapter Review and Conclusion

Introduction

Prayer

■ **Music Suggestions**

"A Sign" by Larry Schexnaydre and Yve Braud from *Give Your Gifts, the New Songs* (GIA, Harcourt Religion Publishers).

"Change Our Hearts" by Rory Cooney from *Glory & Praise (Comprehensive)* (OCP), *Gather (Comprehensive)* (GIA), *Today's Missal* (OCP).

"For Everything There Is a Time" by Donald Reagan from *Glory & Praise (Comprehensive)* (OCP).

"If God Is for Us" by Grayson Warren Brown from *Today's Missal, Glory & Praise Comprehensive* (OCP).

"Prayer of Saint Francis" by Sebastian Temple from *Today's Missal* (OCP), *We Celebrate* (J.S. Paluch Co., Inc.), *Glory & Praise Comprehensive* (OCP).

"Psalm 23: Shepherd Me, O God," by Marty Haugen from *Give Your Gifts, the Basics* (GIA, Harcourt Religion Publishers).

"Sing to the Glory of God" by James E. Moore Jr. from *Give Your Gifts, the New Songs* (GIA, Harcourt Religion Publishers).

■ **Scripture Suggestions**

Psalm 108:1–5

Romans 8:24–30

Matthew 14:22–33

■ **Prayer**

See page 46 of the student text.

Overview

Have the students read the **Chapter Overview** and timeline on pages 46–47. Briefly discuss some of the points and events noted.

The Religion of the Empire

With Constantine, Christianity becomes intertwined with the Roman Empire. Church leaders call a number of councils to define orthodox Christian beliefs. In the West, Church leaders play a major role in meeting the threat from nomadic tribes known collectively to history as barbarians.

THE RELIGION OF THE EMPIRE

The Edict of Milan Changes Christianity

Constantine—From Roman General to Christian Ruler

1. The **Before We Begin** . . . activity gives the students an opportunity to reflect on Christianity's great appeal leading up to the major event of this time period, the favorable decision of Emperor Constantine and the eventual merging of Christianity and the empire.

2. After you and your students have completed discussion of the **Before We Begin . . .** activity and before they have read these sections of the chapter, ask them to write a definition of the term *empire*. After they define the term, ask them to write words or images that they associate with the term. Finally, discuss with them the following question:

   • Should there be a Christian Empire? Why or why not?

   (The students often have negative impressions of empire, associating it with totalitarianism. Point out to them that during its history the Roman Empire was at times more totalitarian and at other times more democratic.)

3. Then direct the students to read the sections about the Edict of Milan and Constantine on page 49. Ask the students:

   • What impact did Christianity's becoming the religion of the empire have on the Christian community?

   (If need be, point out to the students that being Christian is less challenging and more comfortable when those in power are also Christian. However, it is also important for the students to realize that Christian leaders took on new, important, and challenging roles once Christianity became the empire's religion.)

In-Text Activities

page 50   **WWW.**

ACTIVITY

Using the Activity

The students will discover that, even though Constantine did not receive Baptism until on his deathbed, nonetheless he instituted laws for the empire based on Christian teachings.

Additional Activities

THE CHURCH-STATE ISSUE

1. The issue of the relationship between the Church and the state will arise a number of times during this course since the problem faces Church leaders in a number of different periods. At this point in the course, you might mention this fact and discuss with the students:

   • What would you like the relationship between the Church and the state to be?

   • Should the president of the United States consult with the pope on moral matters? Should the president consult with other religious leaders such as the Dalai Lama or Muslim clerics? Explain your response.

   • Should Christians do whatever they can to make their beliefs the law of the land? Why or why not?

   • Should Church leaders ever address political matters? If so, in what context?

2. As part of your discussion about this issue, mention that Vatican Council II in the 1960s marked a turning point in the Catholic position regarding the relationship between Church and state. The council's document on religious freedom advocates separation of Church and state and freedom to practice the religion of one's choice in all nations. At the same time, the council's document on the Church in the modern world does see a place for Church leaders and individual Christians being involved in political, social, economic, and moral concerns. You might read over these two documents and refer to significant quotes as part of your discussion.

CoNCept RevieW

Discuss the following statement with the students. Defend and explain your response. Jesus would have wanted Constantine and the empire to embrace Christianity.

(A case could be made for either a "yes" or a "no" answer. The students may observe that Jesus said that his kingdom was not of this world, bringing up the issue of the relationship between "this world" and heaven. The students may note that Jesus lived his life as an outcast himself, not as someone who possessed earthly power. The students may also refer to Jesus on the cross, a manifestation of powerlessness, not power. On the other hand, Jesus lived and preached a message calling for healing and well-being for people who were hurting. That is, he did concern himself with matters of this world. Isn't a "Christian empire" one way to achieve the agenda he sought? What better way to carry out Jesus' earthly agenda than to wed his mission with that of the empire? Don't Church leaders today attempt to influence governments on all levels?)

page 50

Review Questions and Answers

1. **Name three changes in the Church's role and practice that came about after Christianity gained power in the Roman Empire.**

   After Christianity gained power in the Roman Empire:
   - Church leaders provided guidance in secular affairs and vice versa.
   - Divisions within the empire led to divisions in the Church and vice versa.
   - Christian worship became a public ceremony.
   - Christian missionaries spread not only the faith but also Roman civilization.

2. **How did Constantine's decision to move his capital from Rome to Constantinople affect the Eastern and Western sections of the empire?**

   Because Constantine moved the empire's capital to Asia Minor, the center of civilization also moved from West to East.

3. **Give an example illustrating how Constantine continued to hold onto non-Christian ways.**

   Constantine continued to refer to himself as *Pontifex Maximus,* seeing himself in the priestly role held by pre-Christian emperors.

pages
51–52

THE COUNCIL OF NICAEA

Instruct the students to read the section entitled **The Council of Nicaea,** including pages 51–52, and assign the **In-Text Activity.**

Church Victorious

57

page 52   ## ACTIVITY

Using the Activity

At the age of 32, Athanasius (295–373) became bishop of Alexandria in Egypt. As secretary to the previous bishop, Athanasius had actively participated in the Council of Nicaea. He fiercely defended the decisions of the council against Arius, who was also a priest of Alexandria. Bitter conflict between the two groups (those of Athanasius and those of Arius) sometimes led to violence and often to political turmoil and personal accusations. Three times Athanasius was exiled, and at one time there was a price on his head. From the time of his death, however, he was venerated as a saint.

Additional Activities

EXAMINING THE NICENE CREED

Place the students in small groups and give them copies of **Handout 3–A, The Nicene Creed.** Ask them to make a list of specific beliefs stated in the creed, such as belief in God the Father who created everything. Instruct them to think about possible beliefs or understandings that the creed may have been trying to address. (For instance, many people of the time believed in the Roman pantheon of gods or saw the physical world as evil and only the spiritual realm to be that of God—two understandings rejected in the creed.) Invite representatives from various small groups to report on the statements from the creed and beliefs or understandings that may have contradicted the belief statements in the creed. The purpose of the activity is to give the students an opportunity to review the creed and also to realize that the creed addressed specific false beliefs and understandings held at the time.

CONCEPT REVIEW

1. Saint Athanasius, a leading voice against Arianism, wrote eloquently about the significance of the human and divine natures united in Christ. His ideas guided the formation of the Nicene Creed. Here is one image he used to describe the importance of Christ's full divinity and full humanity. Write on the board or overhead the following quote and discuss with your students what Saint Athanasius means as it applies to Jesus.

   You know how it is when some great king enters a large city and dwells in one of its houses; because of his dwelling in that single house, the whole city is honored, and enemies and robbers cease to molest it.

   On the Incarnation, Chapter II.

2. After your discussion, read the way Athanasius explained the image:

   Even so is it with the King of all; He has come into our country and dwelt in one body amidst the many, and in consequence the designs of the enemy against mankind have been foiled and the corruption of death, which formerly held them in its power, has simply ceased to be. For the human race would have perished utterly had not the Lord and Savior of all, the Son of God, come among us to put an end to death.

Councils Further Clarify Christian Beliefs

pages 53–54

1. Have the students read the section on **Councils Further Clarify Christian Beliefs** on pages 53–54.

2. Review the chart on page 54, making sure the students understand the issues of each council.

In-Text Activities

page 54   ### ACTIVITY

Using the Activity

1. Apollinarianism is somewhat based on the teachings of Apollinarius (c. 310–390), a bishop of Laodicea. While he opposed Arianism, Apollinarius believed that Christ did not have a human intellect or a human soul. Thus he taught that Jesus had only one nature—divine.

2. Nestorianism is named for Nestorius, who was bishop of Constantinople from 428 to 431, when he was deposed following the Council of Ephesus. Nestorius denied that the human and divine natures of Christ were united in one divine Person. One conclusion of his thinking was that, if Christ's human nature was totally unique and different from ours, then he could not save us.

3. Pelagianism originated with Pelagius (c. 350–425), a teacher in Rome. Pelagius over-emphasized human freedom, believing that humans were capable of doing good completely on their own. He did not believe that humans were born with a tendency toward sin, nor did he believe that grace was necessary for humans to choose the good.

page 54   ## Review Questions and Answers

1. Who was Arius, and what is the principal teaching of Arianism?

Arius was an Egyptian priest who began a popular and long-lasting heresy. The principal teaching of Arianism was that Jesus was not of the same substance as God the Father.

2. Who called for the Council of Nicaea? What does it mean to say that it was the first ecumenical council?

Emperor Constantine called for the Council of Nicaea in order to restore order to the empire. This gathering was the first ecumenical council because it was the first time that all bishops of the world were invited to meet and address Church matters together.

3. What is the Nicene Creed, and how does it describe the relationship between God the Father and Jesus?

The Nicene Creed is the summary of essential Christian beliefs decided upon at the Councils of Nicaea and Constantinople. Jesus is described as "one in Being with the Father."

4. What is Monophysitism, and what response did the Council of Chalcedon make to it?

Monophysitism is the belief that Jesus possessed only one divine nature rather than both a divine and a human nature. The Council of Chalcedon condemned this teaching and affirmed that Jesus is one divine Person who possesses two natures, human and divine.

WESTERN ROMAN EMPIRE FALLS
The Bishop of Rome as Emperor of the West

1. Direct the students to read these sections and ask them:
   - What does it mean to say that the pope became, in effect, the "emperor of the West"?
   - What was the *Pax Romana* and how was it threatened by invading tribes from the North and East?

2. Then place the students in small groups and assign them to create a list of what North American ways of thinking and living have become common to the world during the past fifty years, as directed in the **In-Text Activity.**

In-Text Activities

FYI

FYI

DISCUSSION

Using the Discussion

Be sure the groups list both negative and positive influences; in fact, you may want them to create two lists: *Negative North American ways of thinking and living* and *Positive North American ways of thinking and living*. Quite likely, when the lists are shared in the large group, there will be some heated discussion as to whether certain items are negative or positive. Use the teachings of the Church to decide each issue.

Saint Leo the Great

1. Before they read about this important pope, ask the students to discuss the following:
   - Name as many roles as you can think of that the pope performs today.

     They may answer:

     —being head of the Catholic Church

     —speaking out on moral issues

     —calling for peace among nations
   - What other roles would you like to see the pope perform?

2. Then direct the students to read about Saint Leo the Great. Ask the students:
   - Why is Saint Leo given the title "the Great"?
   - Was Leo a secular as well as religious leader in the same way the pope is today? Explain how his role was similar to and different from the pope's role today.

Chapter Three

Concept Review

Present the following scenario to the students, and discuss with them their responses.

- You are the leader of a nomadic group living along the frontier of the Roman Empire. Part of your means of survival for some time has been raiding Roman settlements in order to take crops and livestock; you have lost a number of men in the process. You have also learned about the ways of the Romans and about their religion, Christianity. Do you actively seek to become part of the empire? Do you decide that you and your people will become Christians? Explain your decisions.

page 58

Review Questions and Answers

1. **Who were considered barbarians by citizens of the Roman Empire?**

   Nomadic tribes who lived outside of the Roman Empire were considered to be barbarians.

2. **Which invading group first took control of Rome?**

   The first group to take control of Rome was the Visigoths.

3. **What type of Christianity did the tribes from the North and East usually adopt when they became citizens of the Roman Empire?**

   The Northern and Eastern tribes usually adopted Arianism when they became Roman citizens.

4. **Who was Attila, and what did Pope Leo the Great convince him not to do?**

   Attila was leader of the Huns who made their way to the outskirts of Rome. Pope Leo the Great convinced Attila not to sack Rome.

5. **What does it mean to say that *Rome* meant more than a city or an empire?**

   Rome meant not only a city or an empire but also order, stability, universal law, and civilization.

6. **What did Leo the Great do to shape the papacy?**

   Pope Leo the Great stated that each pope succeeds Saint Peter rather than the previous pope. This strengthened the position of the papacy, identifying it with the powers given by Jesus to Peter.

Church Fathers and Mothers Guide the Christian Community

Through their writings, teaching, and exemplary lives, men and women of the time known as the Age of the Fathers interpret the meaning of Christian beliefs and applications of those beliefs to living the Christian life.

pages 59–63

The Fathers of the Church

The Patristic Period

SAINT AMBROSE (339–397)

SAINT AUGUSTINE OF HIPPO (354–430)

SAINT JEROME (331–420)

Church Victorious   61

Literal and Spiritual Worldviews

1. Ask the students to name some of the "founding fathers" of the United States or Canada and to describe a contribution that each person made to the country. Point out to the students that men and women during the centuries when Christianity first dominated the Roman Empire served similar roles, shaping the Church's beliefs and practices.

2. Direct the students to read the sections on pages 59 to 63. You might assign a specific section to each of six small groups and direct them to report to the class about the main ideas presented in that section.

In-Text Activities

page 59
FYI

Using the FYI

1. As part of your discussion, ask the students:
   - Is it important for you to know how the founders of your nation, state, or province envisioned it to be? If so, how can that information be helpful for us today?
   - How well do you know the vision of the founders of your nation, state, or province?
2. Then ask the students these same questions regarding the Church.

page 62
ACTIVITY

Using the Activity

If this activity is given, it should be assigned before covering the material in class. In addition to library resources, the students can find information on and writings of the Church Fathers on the Internet.

page 63
ACTIVITY

Using the Activity

You might suggest that the students take a biblical story and use their imagination to represent a possible deeper meaning to the story.

Additional Activities

SAINT AUGUSTINE'S CONVERSION

1. The students often note that Augustine underwent a classic conversion experience, spending much of his youth pursuing pleasures of the flesh and then renouncing them when he was older. According to his account in his *Confessions*, Augustine was in a garden with a copy of the Letters of Saint Paul when a young boy's voice said to him, "Pick up and read." Augustine read the last section of Romans 13, and his life changed forever.

2. Distribute copies of the New Testament (or the Bible) to the students. Ask them to page through the Gospels and Letters searching for a passage that they feel might lead someone to a conversion experience. After five minutes or so, ask the students to read the passages they found and to comment about why and how they believe the message could change a person's life.

CoNCept ReViEw

1. Write on the board the following statement:
   - The Church Fathers were right: To be Christian one must be able to see below the surface of things.

2. Invite the students to think about and to illustrate with examples what the statement means. You might point out that many stories about Jesus require seeing below the surface:
   - his birth in a stable instead of in a palace
   - his humble early life as a village carpenter
   - his riding into Jerusalem on a donkey
   - his death by crucifixion

3. You might also use as examples core Christian beliefs:
   - Jesus is both human and divine.
   - There is one God, but three Persons in one God.
   - The Holy Spirit dwells within people.

page 63

Review Questions and Answers

1. What role did the Fathers of the Church perform?

Church Fathers were the great thinkers of the early Church. Their writings and exemplary lives helped Church members then and now in deciding matters of Christian beliefs and practices.

2. What view of reality did Manicheans have?

Manicheans viewed reality as a struggle between forces of the spiritual (good) and the physical (evil).

3. What is the *Vulgate?*

The *Vulgate* is Saint Jerome's translation of the Bible into Latin.

4. What role did Saint Jerome play in helping Christians understand the Bible?

Jerome translated the Bible into the language of the common people and also engaged students, many of them women, in the study of the Bible.

5. What was a central theme found in the teachings of the Fathers of the Church?

Church Fathers tried to help people see the deeper, spiritual meaning of all things and the events of history.

6. What crisis did Saint Augustine address in his *City of God?*

In *City of God*, Saint Augustine addressed the impending fall of Rome to invading tribes.

7. What was the dominant worldview of the medieval period?

The dominant worldview of the medieval period was that the spiritual is more important than the physical and that everything should be looked at in the light of eternity.

The Beginnings of Monasticism

During this period many men and women practice asceticism and live apart from society, establishing monasticism as the ideal form of the Christian life throughout the Middle Ages.

pages
64–66

MONASTICISM

Eastern Monasticism

1. Begin the lesson on monasticism by having the students complete the **In-Text Activity** on page 67. Invite some students to read their responses to Saint Basil.

2. Then direct the students to read the material on monasticism on pages 64–66 and discuss its contents.

3. Point out to the students that in most religious traditions there has existed some form of monasticism. Ask them why they think this simple and austere lifestyle has held such universal appeal.

page 65

Saint Anthony of Egypt

Saint Anthony of Egypt was inspired by two scripture passages which changed his life. Ask students to spend some time reading Scripture and to share with the class passages which inspire them in everyday life.

Teaching and Living the Faith

The text gives several examples of both men and women teaching and living the faith. Use this information to begin a class discussion of ways to teach and live the faith in the world today.

In-Text Activities

page 66

FYI

YOUTH NEWS

Using the Youth News

Check with your diocesan youth ministry office for the latest information regarding spiritual-growth opportunities for teens.

page 67

ACTIVITY

Using the Activity

Provide an opportunity for volunteers to share their responses with the class.

WISDOM OF THE DESERT

The men and women who lived their lives in the austerity of isolated monasteries have wisdom to share with people struggling to live the Christian life today. **Handout 3-B, Wisdom of the Desert,** contains quotes from such men and women. The activity invites the students to think about these teachings and to write about the value of the instruction for today. The activity can be used as a homework assignment accompanying this section of the chapter or it might be completed in small groups.

LIVING THE MONASTIC LIFE

The students typically have questions about the value of living the monastic life. Shouldn't a Christian be helping people instead of living apart from people? Today especially, people are judged by what they do rather than simply on their being. Monks provide a reminder to everyone of some important Christian concepts:

- God loves us as we are and for who we are, not for what we do.
- We don't earn God's love. God's love is there for us to delight in if only we take the time to experience it.
- A monastery is a reminder that, beyond the hustle and bustle in which most of us are absorbed, lies our true home, our true happiness, which Christians call *heaven.*

The students can better appreciate monasticism if they understand specific aspects of living the monastic life. **Handout 3–C, Living the Monastic Life,** describes aspects of the monastic life and gives the students an opportunity to think about how they might apply monastic practices to their own lives. Distribute the handout and have the students follow the directions as stated, perhaps as a homework assignment. After the students have written their responses, discuss with them the value of monasticism.

MONASTICISM—THE TRADITION CONTINUES

Handout 3–D, Monasticism Today, includes an activity meant to remind the students that there are still Christians today who live the monastic life. Either distribute the handout or simply read the information found there. Explain the assignment and have the students report to the class on the results of their findings.

CoNCept RevieW

Discuss these questions with the students:

- What led to the monastic movement in the early Church?

  In the early Church, those who were drawn to the monastic life felt that living within society was too comfortable and distracted them from living the Christian life fully. They wanted to give their all to experiencing life with Christ, which they found in the desert and monasteries.

- Is this still the reason why some people are drawn to the monastic life today?

  For the most part, monastic life today seems to hold the same allurement for those who are drawn to it.

- Can you see the appeal of monasticism?

  Answers may vary. This question is meant to raise questions in the students about what would truly bring them joy.

Review Questions and Answers

1. **Who was the first known Christian monk?**

   Saint Anthony of Egypt is the first known Christian monk. His story was told by Saint Athanasius.

2. **What contribution to Christianity was made by Saints Basil and Macrina in the East and Saints Benedict and Scholastica in the West?**

   Saints Basil and Macrina and Saints Benedict and Scholastica began monasteries for men and for women where monks and nuns could live solitary lives together in community.

3. **How were the monasteries in Ireland different from those in the East and the West?**

   Irish monks did not remain in monasteries but traveled about spreading the good news of the Christian message.

Chapter Review and Conclusion

REVIEW

1. Ask the students to summarize the main points in the chapter using their own words. Write notes on the board from their contributions. To reinforce their summary, you might want to review the major concepts in this chapter in the teaching manual. Then read the **Conclusion** on page 67.

2. Review the vocabulary in this chapter:

   Pontifex Maximus—the term means "the greatest bridge-builder"; title for emperors and, eventually, the pope (page 50)

   Arianism—a heresy denying that Jesus is truly God (page 51)

   ecumenical council—a meeting to which all bishops of the world are invited in the exercise of their collegial authority for the purpose of addressing common concerns facing the worldwide Church (page 52)

   Council of Nicaea—meeting of bishops in 325 that condemned Arianism and formulated the Nicene Creed (page 52)

   catholic—a word that means "universal" or "everywhere" (page 52)

   Nicene Creed—summary of essential Christian beliefs written and approved at the Councils of Nicaea (325) and Constantinople (381) (page 52)

   Monophysitism—belief that Jesus has only a divine nature, instead of the traditional Christian teaching that Jesus has two natures—human and divine (page 53)

   Visigoths—a Germanic tribe who settled primarily in Spain; the first such group to lay siege to Rome (page 55)

   Vandals—one of the most destructive nomadic tribes; adopted Arianism when they converted to Christianity (page 55)

Huns—a tribe originating in China; one of the last barbarian groups to invade Western Europe (page 56)

Pax Romana—literally "Roman Peace"; the time of stability and order afforded people who lived in the Roman Empire during the height of its power (page 56)

Apostolic See—a term used for the papacy, identifying papal power with that of the apostles; also called the "Holy See" (page 57)

Fathers of the Church—a designation for Church leaders during the early centuries of Christianity whose teachings collectively formulated Christian doctrine and practices (page 59)

Manicheism—a religious movement that viewed reality as a constant struggle between the forces of spiritual good and physical evil; the physical world is entirely evil (page 61)

Vulgate—Saint Jerome's Latin translation of the Bible; the word *vulgate* is derived from the same Latin root as *vulgar*, which originally simply meant "of the common people" (page 62)

monastic movement—living alone or in community apart from the rest of society in order to experience God's presence, especially through regular prayer and self-denial, marked by the profession of religious vows (page 64)

monk—a person who lives the monastic life (page 64)

desert fathers—Christian men who lived alone in the desert territories of northern Africa and the Middle East in order to sacrifice their lives to Christ (page 64)

convent—the residence of religious women who are bound together by vows to a religious life (page 66)

TEST

Give the students the Chapter 3 Test or an alternative assessment. The tests have been placed on the Harcourt Religion Publishers' Web page. This has been done to enable the teacher to customize this material for local needs. First contact Harcourt Religion Publishers' high school consultant at 800-922-7696, ext. 3781 for a user ID and password. Then connect with the Harcourt Religion Publishers' Web site at **www.harcourtreligion.com** to download the information. Collect the tests for grading.

Chapter 3 Test Answers

MULTIPLE CHOICE (1 point each)

1. b	3. a	5. a	7. a	9. c	11. a
2. d	4. d	6. b	8. a	10. d	12. c

MATCHING (1 point each)

1. F	3. D	5. E	7. I	9. C
2. J	4. G	6. A	8. H	10. B

TRUE OR FALSE (1 point each)

1. F	3. T	5. F	7. T	9. T
2. T	4. F	6. T	8. F	10. F

IDENTIFICATION (2 points each)

1. *Pax Romana*—literally "Roman peace"; the time of stability and order afforded people who lived in the Roman Empire during the height of its power

2. *Pontifex Maximus*—the term means "the greatest bridge-builder"; title for emperors and, eventually, the pope

3. *The City of God*—monumental work of Saint Augustine in which he reassured his readers that, while earthly kingdoms rise and fall, the City of God lasts forever.

4. **ecumenical council**—a meeting to which all bishops of the world are invited in the exercise of their collegial authority for the purpose of addressing common concerns facing the worldwide Church

5. **Apostolic See**—a term used for the papacy, identifying papal power with that of the apostles; also called the "Holy See"

6. **Fathers of the Church**—a designation for Church leaders during the early centuries of Christianity whose teachings collectively formulated Christian doctrine and practices

7. **desert fathers**—Christian men who lived alone in the desert territories of northern Africa and the Middle East in order to sacrifice their lives to Christ

8. **Manicheism**—a religious movement that viewed reality as a constant struggle between the forces of spiritual good and physical evil; the physical world is entirely evil

9. **Vulgate**—Saint Jerome's Latin translation of the Bible; the word *vulgate* is derived from the same Latin root as *vulgar* which originally simply meant "of the common people"

ESSAY (5 points each)

1. After Christianity became the religion of the Roman Empire, members of the Church were insiders and powerbrokers—people who expected to participate in leadership and civilization needed to be Christian, Christians were no longer subject to possible persecution, and some people joined the Church without a great sense of understanding or commitment.

2. Lessons to learn from the Arian controversy and the Council of Nicaea are: that controversies over Christian teaching have been part of Church history for a long time, that councils provide a procedure for the Church to settle matters of conflict, that wise leaders emerge during conflicts to clarify and keep alive the Christian message, and that the Christian message is not just about eternal life but is also concerned about temporal affairs in light of eternity.

3. Arianism flourished in the fourth century because it taught that Jesus was not of the same substance as God the Father. This teaching resonated with some pre-Christian concepts of Greek superheroes. Secondly, Arius himself was a popular and persuasive teacher.

4. Pope Damasus (366–384) first used the term *Apostolic See* to refer to the papacy, strengthening the connection between his office and the apostles. Pope Leo the Great (440–461) convinced Attila the Hun to spare destruction of Rome. Thus he acted both as the city's spiritual and as the city's temporal ruler.

5. The Fathers of the Church helped clarify Christian teaching during the formative period of Christian history. They sustained the Church during times of controversy and challenge.

6. The Fathers of the Church viewed all aspects of the world in light of the life and message of Christ.

7. Saint Augustine wrote the first true biography called *Confessions*. He also wrote *The City of God*, which explained that Christianity would outlast and overcome the tribulations accompanying the fall of the Roman Empire.

8. As being Christian became comfortable and aligned with temporal power and concerns, men and women left society to live a life with Christ in isolation, which became the foundation for monasticism.

9. Saint Anthony took to heart two gospel passages: "Go, sell all that you have and give it to the poor" and "Be not concerned about tomorrow."

10. Three women who had an impact on the Church during the fourth and fifth centuries were Saints Macrina and Scholastica, who helped establish monasticism, and Saint Clotilde, who helped convert her husband, King Clovis of the Franks, to Christianity.

Prayer

MUSIC SUGGESTIONS

"Bring Forth the Kingdom" by Marty Haugen from *Gather (Comprehensive)* (GIA).

"Earthen Vessels" by John Foley from *Glory & Praise (Comprehensive)* (OCP), *Today's Missal* (OCP).

"Givin' Back the Gifts" by Larry Schexnaydre and Rhett Glindmeyer from *Give Your Gifts, the New Songs* (GIA, Harcourt Religion Publishers).

"Make Me a Channel of Your Peace" by Franciscan Communications from *Gather (Comprehensive)* (GIA).

"On Holy Ground" by Donna Peña from *Give Your Gifts, the Songs* (GIA, Harcourt Religion Publishers).

"On That Day" by Kate Cuddy from *Give Your Gifts, the New Songs* (GIA, Harcourt Religion Publishers).

"We Believe" by Christopher Walker from *Today's Missal* (OCP).

SCRIPTURE SUGGESTIONS

1 Samuel 1–10

Ephesians 4:17–5:2

Luke 5:1–11

PRAYER

O Lord,
I place myself in your hands and dedicate myself to you.
I pledge myself to do your will in all things—
To love the Lord God with all my heart, all my soul, all my strength . . .
To honor all persons . . .
To clothe the naked. To visit the sick. To bury the dead.
To help in trouble. To console the sorrowing.

To hold myself aloof from worldly ways.
To prefer nothing to the love of Christ.
Not to give way to anger.
Not to foster a desire for revenge . . .
Not to make a false peace. Not to forsake charity . . .
To speak the truth with heart and tongue . . .
Never to despair of your mercy, O God of Mercy.

Saint Benedict

CHAPTER 3 TEST

Name_____ Date_____ Class period_____

Test is made up of questions with suggested point values totaling 100 points.

Multiple Choice (1 point each)

_____ 1. Emperor Constantine moved the capital of the empire to
   a. Antioch
   b. Byzantium
   c. Rome
   d. Capernaum

_____ 2. Demonstrating that he retained non-Christian ways, Constantine kept for himself the title
   a. *Maximus Gladiatrix*
   b. *Princeps*
   c. *Rex Romanorum*
   d. *Pontifex Maximus*

_____ 3. Arius taught that
   a. Jesus is not truly God
   b. the Holy Spirit does not exist
   c. the pope is not Peter's successor
   d. Jesus is not human

_____ 4. Church leaders composed most of the official Christian creed used all over the world today at the
   a. Council of Constantinople
   b. Council of Jerusalem
   c. Vatican Council
   d. Council of Nicaea

_____ 5. The word *catholic* literally means
   a. universal
   b. Christ-like
   c. truthful
   d. holy

_____ 6. The person who called the first ecumenical council was the
   a. pope
   b. emperor (Constantine)
   c. patriarch of Constantinople
   d. bishop of Alexandria

_____ 7. Monophysitism was a heresy that taught that Jesus
   a. had only a divine nature
   b. was human but not divine
   c. was both human and divine
   d. did not die on the cross

_____ 8. The invading group that first overtook Rome were the
   a. Visigoths
   b. Huns
   c. Francs
   d. Vikings

_____ 9. Attila the Hun is famous for
   a. speaking Latin and Greek
   b. killing the pope in battle
   c. sparing Rome from destruction
   d. accepting Baptism as a Christian

_____ 10. Manicheans believed in
   a. living a life of pleasure
   b. returning to pre-Christian religion
   c. worship of the sun-god Ra
   d. struggle between matter and spirit

_____ 11. *Confessions* was written by
   a. Augustine
   b. Ambrose
   c. Jerome
   d. Monica

_____ 12. *City of God* addressed the issue of
   a. the Arian heresy in Egypt
   b. building Constantinople
   c. the fall of the Roman Empire
   d. sinfulness in the Church

© Harcourt Religion Publishers

Matching (1 point each)

_____ 1. Anthony of Egypt

_____ 2. Benedict

_____ 3. Leo the Great

_____ 4. Nonna

_____ 5. Arius

_____ 6. Jerome

_____ 7. Monica

_____ 8. Helena

_____ 9. Augustine

_____ 10. Ambrose

A. Translated the Bible into Latin

B. Politician induced to become bishop of Milan

C. Wrote the first true autobiography

D. Prevented the sacking of Rome

E. Began a heretical movement

F. First known Christian monk

G. Converted her husband; mother of three saints

H. Emperor Constantine's mother

I. Augustine's mother

J. With his sister, began monasteries in the West

True or False (1 point each)

_____ 1. Emperor Constantine became Christian when he signed the Edict of Milan.

_____ 2. Constantine named his new capital city Constantinople.

_____ 3. The Council of Nicaea condemned Arianism.

_____ 4. Arianism died out when its founder was exiled.

_____ 5. The Nicene Creed was written by the apostles in the first century.

_____ 6. Descendants of Monophysites traveled to India and China.

_____ 7. When the capital of the empire moved to the East, the pope became the leading authority in the West.

_____ 8. Saint Augustine was a Christian during his entire life.

_____ 9. Saint Jerome taught Scripture to a group of women.

_____ 10. The Church Fathers taught that everything should be understood strictly on a literal level.

Identification (2 points each)

1. *Pax Romana*—

2. *Pontifex Maximus*—

3. *The City of God*—

4. ecumenical council—

5. Apostolic See—

6. Fathers of the Church—

7. desert fathers—

8. Manicheism—

9. Vulgate—

Essays (5 points each)

1. Describe three differences that occurred after Christianity became the religion of the Roman Empire.

2. The text lists four lessons to be learned from the Arian Controversy and the Council of Nicaea. Name three of these lessons.

3. Give two reasons why Arianism flourished in the fourth century.

4. Explain how the papacy was strengthened under Pope Damasus and Pope Leo the Great.

5. Describe contributions made by two Fathers of the Church.

6. Give an example of the worldview advocated by the Fathers of the Church.

7. Name Saint Augustine's two most famous written works. Describe a contribution made by one of them.

8. What developments in Roman society led initially to the monastic movement?

9. What messages from Scripture led Anthony of Egypt to become a hermit in the desert?

10. Name three women who had an impact on the Church during the fourth and fifth centuries.

THE NICENE CREED

Name_____ Date_____ Class period_____

At a later council Church leaders added a minor addition to the wording of the Creed formulated at the Council of Nicaea. For each statement, state what viewpoints the council fathers might have wanted to counteract and clarify. (For instance, Christians believe in one God rather than many gods. Christians believe that all creation is God's handiwork rather than the physical world being evil and only the spiritual being good.)

We believe in one God,
    the Father, the Almighty,
    maker of heaven and earth,
    of all that is seen and unseen.

We believe in one Lord, Jesus Christ,
    the only Son of God,
    eternally begotten of the Father,
    God from God, Light from Light,
    true God from true God,
    begotten, not made, one in Being with the Father.
    Through him all things were made.
    For us men and for our salvation
      he came down from heaven:
    by the power of the Holy Spirit
      he was born of the Virgin Mary, and became man.
For our sake he was crucified under Pontius Pilate;
    he suffered, died, and was buried.
    On the third day he rose again
    in fulfillment of the Scriptures;
    he ascended into heaven
      and is seated at the right hand of the Father.
    He will come again in glory to judge the living and the dead,
      and his kingdom will have no end.

We believe in the Holy Spirit, the Lord, the giver of life,
    who proceeds from the Father and the Son.
    With the Father and the Son he is worshiped and glorified.
    He has spoken through the Prophets.
    We believe in one holy catholic and apostolic Church.
    We acknowledge one baptism for the forgiveness of sins.

We look for the resurrection of the dead,
    and the life of the world to come.

WISDOM OF THE DESERT

Name_____ Date_____ Class period_____

A few hundred years into the Christian era, many Christians—women and men—left the comforts of society to live in deserted areas where they could devote all of their energies to living the Christian life and experiencing God. A twentieth-century monk, Thomas Merton, collected some of their sayings in a book called *The Wisdom of the Desert* (New York: New Directions Books, 1960). Based on the following passages, write an essay about what you think these early Christians have to say to us today.

A brother asked one of the elders: What good thing shall I do, and have life thereby? The old man replied: God alone knows what is good. However, I have heard it said that someone inquired of Father Abbot Nisteros the great, the friend of Abbot Anthony, asking: What good work shall I do? and that he replied: Not all works are alike. For Scripture says that Abraham was hospitable and God was with him. Elias loved solitary prayer, and God was with him. And David was humble, and God was with him. Therefore, whatever you see your soul to desire according to God, do that thing, and you shall keep your heart safe. (pages 25–26)

An elder said: Here is the monk's life-work, obedience, meditation, not judging others, not reviling, not complaining. For it is written: You who love the Lord, hate evil. So this is the monk's life—not to walk in agreement with an unjust man, nor to look with his eyes upon evil, not to go about being curious, and neither to examine nor to listen to the business of others. Not to take anything with his hands, but rather to give to others. Not to be proud in his heart, nor to malign others in his thoughts. Not to fill his stomach, but in all things to behave with discretion. Behold, in all this you have the monk. (pages 28–29)

Abbess Syncletia of holy memory said: There is labor and great struggle for the impious who are converted to God, but after that comes inexpressible joy. A man who wants to light a fire first is plagued by smoke, and the smoke drives him to tears, yet finally he gets the fire that he wants. So also it is written: Our God is a consuming fire. Hence we ought to light the divine fire in ourselves with labor and with tears. (page 55)

Once some robbers came into the monastery and said to one of the elders: We have come to take away everything that is in your cell [monk's room]. And he said: My sons, take all you want. So they took everything they could find in the cell and started off. But they left behind a little bag that was hidden in the cell. The elder picked it up and followed after them, crying out: My sons, take this, you forgot it in the cell! Amazed at the patience of the elder, they brought everything back into his cell and did penance, saying: This one really is a man of God! (page 59)

A brother asked one of the elders, saying: There are two brothers, of whom one remains praying in his cell, fasting six days at a time and doing a great deal of penance. The other one takes care of the sick. Which one's work is more pleasing to God? The elder replied: If that brother who fasts six days at a time were to hang himself up by the nose, he could not equal the one who takes care of the sick. (pages 59–60)

LIVING THE MONASTIC LIFE

Name_____ Date_____ Class period_____

Monasticism has taken many forms during its history. However, certain characteristics are common to living the monastic life. Choose three or more of the practices listed below. Write a paragraph explaining how it could be helpful for developing your own spiritual life.

Silence—Monks spend most of their time in silence. In doing so, they are not attempting to shut out the world and other people but to be more attentive. Silence can be used to cut oneself off from others or to create a space within ourselves to listen more intently. By being silent, monks are not "talking to themselves" but are listening to God.

Prayer—Jesus asks Christians to "pray always." Prayer can take many forms. In a monastery, monks pray formally on a regular basis throughout the day and night. By taking time out to pray formally, they experience all their activities—working, eating, reading, conversing, or sleeping—as prayer as well.

Solitude—Monks typically spend a great deal of time alone. The earliest monks went to great extremes to live alone. In a monastery, monks have cells, small private rooms, where they spend quiet time. The goal is not to be alone but to commune with God.

Simple living—Monks own few possessions. Meals are simple affairs, albeit healthier than what most of us eat. Simple living does not devalue material things but actually accentuates the personal appreciation of things.

Living close to nature—Although some monasteries can be in cities, monks usually live close to nature and follow the natural rhythms of the day and the seasons.

Communal living—Early Christian communities reportedly "shared all things in common." Monks continue this tradition. Besides a few robes and a pair of sandals, monks have nothing that they can call their own.

Self-discipline—Monks live a disciplined life. We might tell ourselves that eating snacks between meals is not healthy. Monks actually live this discipline. We might say that we would like to pray more. Monks follow a regimen of regular prayer.

Communion with God—The goal of a monk's lifestyle is not different from the goal of the Christian life—to experience God.

MONASTICISM TODAY

Name_____ Date_____ Class period_____

During the time of persecutions, martyrs shedding their blood for Christ were not an unusual occurrence. When people in Ireland, the British Isles, and Western Europe became Christian, they learned about the courage of the early martyrs from missionaries who introduced them to the faith. Many people in these newly Christianized lands wanted to give their own lives as the martyrs had done. To do so they set off into the wilderness to sacrifice their lives for Christ apart from the comforts of family or social life. Desolate forests and mountains served as the setting for this new type of martyrdom. They are known as "green martyrs," to distinguish them from the "red martyrs" who shed their blood during the persecutions. An astounding number of Christians, women and men, chose to live in solo or group isolation until the end of the Middle Ages.

Today monasteries still dot the Christian landscape. Although fewer in number compared to the Middle Ages, Christian men and women still seek the joy and peace of communion with Christ by living in monasteries. They go about their chores behind monastery walls or out in the country where visitors are rare. Every few hours they gather in their chapel to pray, even waking in the middle of the night to pray so that the cycle of prayer is unbroken. Some men and women monks have spent decades never venturing beyond their monastery walls.

If possible, visit a monastery or a cloistered convent where men or women live the life of constant prayer and work rather than the active life of direct service to their surrounding community. See if there is someone associated with the monastery whom you might interview. Otherwise, read about the monastic life as it is lived today, and report your findings to your class.

CHAPTER FOUR

EXPANSION AND GROWTH
Creating a Christian European World

A Teacher's Prayer

Good and gentle Jesus, may your divine light shine upon me as I search for ways to lead my students to you—the one who waits for us with open arms. May the saints, your missionaries who spread your message with courage and conviction, inspire me to enliven your message for my students. Amen.

Overview

Three important developments occurred in the Church during this period: the increasing division between Eastern and Western Christianity, the expansion of European Christianity, and the pope's initiation into being the ruler of an autonomous state. The chapter also briefly addresses relations among Christians, Muslims, and Jews. The issue of the pope as a secular ruler and the involvement of the Church in political affairs will resurface regularly throughout the course. A number of activities are available as part of the lesson plan for this chapter to help your students explore missionary activity, which has been part of Christianity from the beginning and continues today.

Major Concepts Covered in This Chapter

1. **Introduction**
2. **Christianity—East and West**
3. **Christianizing Life Experiences**
4. **The Conversion of Europe**
5. **Chapter Review and Conclusion**

Introduction

Prayer

- **Music Suggestions**

  "Anthem" by Tom Conry from *Glory & Praise (Comprehensive)* (OCP), *Today's Missal* (OCP), *Gather (Comprehensive)* (GIA).

  "City of God" by Dan Schutte from *Glory & Praise (Comprehensive)* (OCP), *Gather (Comprehensive)* (GIA), *Today's Missal* (OCP).

  "Come and Follow Me" by Francis Patrick O'Brien from *Give Your Gifts, the Songs* (GIA, Harcourt Religion Publishers).

  "Seed Scattered and Sown" by Dan Feiten from *Today's Missal* (OCP).

  "Service" by The Dameans from *Glory & Praise (Comprehensive)* (OCP).

  "The Summons" by John L. Bell and Iona Community from *Give Your Gifts, the Basics* (GIA, Harcourt Religion Publishers).

  "Yes, Lord," by Darryl Ducote from *Give Your Gifts, the Songs* (GIA, Harcourt Religion Publishers).

- **Scripture Suggestions**

  Isaiah 26:1–4

  Acts 13:1–3

  Mark 6:7–13

- **Prayer**

  See page 68 of the student text.

Overview

Have the students read the **Chapter Overview** and timeline on pages 68–69. Briefly discuss some of the points and events noted.

Christianity—East and West

Divisions with the Roman Empire lead to establishing two major centers of Christianity, Eastern (Greek) and Western (Latin).

CHRISTIANITY EAST AND WEST

1. Depending on how you approached the lesson on monasticism in Chapter Three, your students might find the **Before we begin . . .** activity on page 70 redundant. If the students identify practices that may help young people develop their spiritual lives, you might ask them to choose one such practice and to do it faithfully for a few days, write about the experience, and then report to the class about what the experience was like.

2. After the students have read pages 71–72, divide the class into small groups and ask the groups to list five important statements about the Church and its beliefs. Then have the small groups share the lists with the class. Discuss as needed.

page 71 **DISCUSSION**

Using the Discussion

Quite likely there will be a difference of opinion on the value of ornate church buildings. While many of the students would prefer to spend money on good works, it is important to recognize that those who built ornate churches in the past did so with the best of reasons. They sincerely believed that this was a worthwhile way to praise God. For many people, the church building was the only place of real beauty in their lives, and the church did therefore help them to raise their minds and hearts to God. If it were not for the many wonderful old church buildings in Europe, and to a lesser degree in the Americas, we would not have such a marvelous storehouse of art and architecture available to all to enjoy—and to help us even today to raise our minds and hearts to God and the work of Jesus on earth.

page 72 **DISCUSSION**

Using the Discussion

Be sure the students understand that today Catholic missionaries would never baptize an entire tribe just because the tribe's leader converted to Christianity. On the other hand, acknowledge that many societies are much more communal than our own is, and it is possible that an entire group would be of one mind in this regard. It is the responsibility of the missionaries to catechize as much as possible all those who desire Baptism.

Additional Activities

PRAYER SPACE

1. Instruct a group of the students to arrange the classroom, the chapel, or some other indoor or outdoor space into a setting that would be conducive to prayer.

2. Assign another group to design a prayer service that would appeal to young people using the prayer space.

THE MARKS OF THE CHURCH

1. After the students have read pages 71–72, ask them to explain the meaning of each of the four marks of the Church (one, holy, catholic, and apostolic).

   • One: The Church is one because of its source (the Trinity), its founder (Christ), and its soul (the Holy Spirit). The Church's unity is assured by visible bonds of communion—its profession of faith, its common worship (especially the sacraments), and apostolic succession through Holy Orders. (See Catechism #s 813, 815.)

   • Holy: The Church is the holy people of God, united with Christ and sanctified by him. (See Catechism #s 823–824.)

   • Catholic: The Church is catholic or universal because Christ is present in it and because it has been sent out by Christ to bring the gospel to all people. (See Catechism #s 830–831.)

- Apostolic: The Church is apostolic because it is founded on the apostles in three ways—(1) It is build on the foundation of the apostles and sent out on mission by Christ. (2) With the help of the Holy Spirit, the Church keeps and hands on the teachings of the apostles. (3) The Church is taught, sanctified, and guided by the apostles through their successors, the college of bishops, who are assisted by priests, all in union with the pope, who is the successor of Peter. (See Catechism #857.)

2. Discuss with them: Would you add other "identifying marks" that would indicate that a Church is an authentic Christian Church?

Concept Review

Use the photograph of Hagia Sophia on page 71 to point out to the students the great transformation that occurred in Christianity from its humble beginnings to its glory days entering the Middle Ages.

page 72 **Review Questions and Answers**

1. What is Hagia Sophia?

Hagia Sophia, which means "Holy Wisdom," is the great church built in Constantinople (Istanbul, Turkey) by Emperor Justinian in 537. It was later used as an ideal model for other mosques, and today it is a museum.

2. Why did Christians build magnificent church buildings?

Christians built magnificent churches both as gathering places and as monuments representing their faith in God.

3. What are the four marks of the Church?

The four marks of the Church refer to characteristics associated with the Church of Christ—one, holy, catholic, and apostolic.

MAJOR CHRISTIAN CENTERS

pages 73–74

1. Assign the students to read the section of the text on pages 73–74, and then discuss with them the **In-Text Activity.**

2. Use one of the additional activities to allow the students an opportunity to explore Eastern Christianity.

In-Text Activities

page 73 **FYI**

Using the FYI

Explain to the students that this designation is more accurate before the schism that split East and West. Today there are Orthodox churches that are not in union with Rome and other Eastern Rite churches that are in union with Rome; both are sometimes referred to as Eastern Churches. Likewise, there are Orthodox churches and Eastern Rite churches in the West.

Using the Discussion

You might have the students work in small groups for a brief time to discuss this item. Responses may vary from quiet, centering prayer to greeting other members of the community gathered to worship.

Additional Activities

EASTERN CHRISTIANITY

1. If your students are not familiar with Eastern Christianity, invite them to research the topic and to bring in some representation of Orthodox or Eastern Rite Catholic Christianity—for example, a photo of an icon or a crucifix with an Eastern design, a photo of an Eastern Rite or Orthodox church, or a photo of an Eastern Rite or Orthodox service or cleric.

2. Discuss with the students:

   • What atmosphere or spirituality is evoked by the objects you have seen?

   • How is the atmosphere or spirituality different from that of the Church in the West?

   (Churches in the East tend to be ornate and decorated with many icons. The liturgies are elaborate and lengthy, with emphasis on mystery and the mystical.)

ANCIENT CHRISTIAN PATRIARCHATES

Divide the class into five groups. Assign to each group one of the five patriarchates listed in the text: Rome, Alexandria, Constantinople, Antioch, and Jerusalem. Ask the groups to research the Church as it developed in its area and to prepare a presentation on its patriarchate, including, if possible, a video component.

Concept Review

The text points out that Eastern Christianity flourished under the protection of the Eastern emperor in Constantinople during a period when the Church in the West was struggling to maintain itself. Discuss with the students how Eastern Christian leaders might have viewed the Western Church at this time. (For instance, while the bishop of Rome as pope had long been viewed as successor to Peter and thus as holding a special position in the Church, the crises facing the Western Church diminished his ability to exercise authority over the Eastern patriarchs.)

page 74   ## Review Questions and Answers

1. **What role did patriarchs play in the early Church?**

   Patriarchs were leaders of the Christian community in major cities of the Roman Empire.

2. **How did other patriarchs view the pope of Rome?**

   Sometimes other patriarchs recognized the pope as having a primacy of authority; sometimes other recognized a "primacy of honor" but did not believe that he had the power to make decisions without consulting them.

3. Name two ways that Eastern and Western Churches' understanding of liturgy differed.

Eastern spirituality underlying the liturgy tended to be more mystical. For Eastern Christians, therefore, the liturgy was the time when the union of humans and God was most evident and when humans especially shared in the divine life. Liturgy in the West was above all a celebration of the Paschal mystery by which Christ accomplished the work of our salvation.

pages 75–76

CHRISTIANITY MEETS ISLAM

1. Direct the students to read this section that briefly outlines the beginnings of Islam on pages 75–76. While the course is not a world religions course, it is important for the students to realize that over a period of one hundred years Islam overtook Christianity as the dominant religion in much of what had been the Roman Empire. And, to this day, Islam is an important consideration in world events.

2. The **In-Text Activity** on page 76 identifies research topics that can help the students understand the impact made by Islam on Christianity during this period. Ask the students who do these research projects to report to the class on their findings.

In-Text Activities

page 76

FYI

ACTIVITY

Using the Activity

1. Follow the presentations with a discussion on Islam and Christianity then and now.

2. See the Web site www.usccb.org/seia/islam.htm for resources on Islamic-Catholic Relations.

CONCEPT REVIEW

Discuss with the students the following question: When Islam spread to formerly Christian-dominated lands, do you think Christians who converted to the new religion saw it as a rejection of Christianity or as an out-growth of Christianity?

(Muslims tend to view their religion as a further development, based on new revelations to Muhammad, of Jewish and Christian beliefs.)

page 76

Review Questions and Answers

1. Who was the founder of the Muslim faith?

Muhammad founded Islam following what he considered to be revelations from God.

2. What significance does the *hijrah* have for Muslims?

The *hijrah*, or flight from Mecca to Medina in 622, marks the beginning of the Muslim calendar because it was the first time that the people of an entire community dedicated themselves to living as Muslims.

3. How did Muslims view Jews and Christians in territories they conquered?

Muslims considered Jews and Christians to be fellow believers in the one true God and "people of the book" who, along with Muslims, believed that God spoke through the prophets of the Old Testament and through Jesus.

4. Name two reasons why many Christians converted to Islam.

For one thing, non-Muslims in Muslim-controlled territories had to pay additional taxes. However, the majority of Christian converts probably found Islam appealing because of its message, the enthusiasm of its followers, and its spreading power.

5. Why is the Battle of Tours important?

At the Battle of Tours in 722 Charles Martel defeated the Muslim army, preventing Muslims from gaining control of Europe.

Christianizing Life Experiences

Members of the Church develop numerous practices to sustain and foster the Christian life.

pages 77–80

THE CHRISTIAN EXPERIENCE

A World of Grace

THE CHRISTIAN CALENDAR

Developments in Church Practice

1. Have the students read the sections of the text from pages 77–80. As they are doing so, write on the board the vocabulary words found in the margins.

- grace
- liturgical calendar
- Rogation Days
- baptistry
- basilica
- Gregorian chant
- celibacy
- Sacrament of Reconciliation

2. When they have finished reading the material, ask the students to explain what significance each of the terms listed on the board had for the Christian life of people in the Western Church of the time.

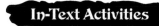
In-Text Activities

page 78

FYI

ACTIVITY

Using the Activity

Encourage the students to emphasize the positive experiences in their lives and in their actions. On the other hand, difficult times can also be experiences of grace and are best understood in that way.

Using the Activity

1. Some students are interested in historical fiction. This medium is a fairly painless way to acquire a wealth of information about this period of history. Encourage students who have delved into this time period through fiction to share their knowledge with the class.

2. This activity is an excellent classroom project.

Additional Activities

LISTENING TO GREGORIAN CHANT

Bring in a CD of Gregorian chant. Turn out the lights in the room and direct the students to relax, close their eyes, and listen to the music. Play four or five minutes of the music, and then ask the students to jot down in their notebooks the atmosphere or images that the music evoked. After a few minutes, invite the students to share their reflections with one other person. Then call on the students for their observations. This activity is a good prelude to the above Activity #2.

THREE STAGES IN THE DEVELOPMENT OF RECONCILIATION

The Sacrament of Reconciliation demonstrates the type of change that occurred in sacramental practices throughout history since it underwent essentially three stages of development. **Handout 4–A, The History of Reconciliation,** briefly describes those stages. Distribute the handout to provide the students an overview of the major changes that took place in the practice of the sacrament.

CONCEPT REVIEW

Discuss the following statements with the students:

• Christians should be more attentive to the liturgical calendar today.

(You might draw your students' attention to a liturgical calendar and ask them how they might benefit from being alert to the changes of the liturgical year. Be sure they know and understand the significance of the season currently being celebrated.)

• Churches should be designed so that a baptistry clearly indicates entrance into a church building and into the Church.

(Discuss possible creative designs and placements for a baptistry.)

• The Church should make greater use of Gregorian chant during services.

(Invite suggestions about how music is best incorporated into the liturgy.)

Review Questions and Answers

1. **What purpose did the liturgical calendar play during the expansion of Christianity?**

   The liturgical calendar Christianized the seasons of the year, relating them to the life of Christ.

2. **When did the Church officially recognize the existence of seven sacraments?**

   The Church officially defined the seven sacraments at the Second Council of Lyons in 1274.

3. **What was a baptistry? What led to the standard practice of performing Baptisms in a church?**

   A baptistry was a building used for celebrating Baptisms. As the practice of infant Baptism became the norm, Baptisms were performed in churches themselves.

4. **What was the standard design of a basilica?**

   Basilicas were typically rectangular in shape with one rounded end.

5. **What effect did the use of altar rails and screens have on the way the Eucharist was experienced?**

   The use of altar rails and screens led to a sense that the priest was offering the Eucharist *for* the people rather than *with* them.

6. **When did celibacy become officially required of priests in the Western Church?**

   Celibacy became an official requirement for priests in the Western Church in 1123 at the First Lateran Council.

7. **How did Reconciliation change after the 700s?**

   Up until the 700s Reconciliation was a reinitiation process that was public and overseen by a bishop, and that often lasted for a period of years. After 700 the practice of private penance became the popular and eventually the officially recognized form of the sacrament.

8. **What development resulted in Church leaders becoming involved in performing weddings and in regulating marriages?**

   As Church leadership became more stable than civil government, bishops and priests became more actively involved in performing wedding ceremonies and regulating marriages.

The Conversion of Europe

Missionaries spread the Christian message, transforming Europe into a Christian world.

pages
81–83

THE WORK OF MISSIONARIES

The Conversion of Ireland

The Conversion of England

Direct the students to read the sections on pages 81–83.

page 81   YOUTH NEWS

Using the Youth News

Some missionary groups provide material for use in the classroom. Check into the Web sites before the students do for assistance in processing the material.

page 83   FYI

Expansion and Growth

MISSION IS FOR EVERYONE

Handout 4–B, Mission Is for Everyone, gives the students an opportunity to think about Catholic mission work in the contemporary world as well as their own involvement in mission work. Have the students complete the assignment individually. Go over their responses to the questions, and then ask volunteers to describe their drawings and what meaning they find in them.

POPE JOHN PAUL II ON MISSIONARY WORK

1. Pope John Paul II is the most traveled pope in history. He has met with Catholics as well as people of all faiths during his many journeys. **Handout 4–C, Pope John Paul II on Missionary Work,** includes quotes from his encyclical in which he most directly addressed mission activity. You might direct the students to complete the activity listed on the handout.

2. Then discuss with them: Is Pope John Paul II's vision of mission similar to or different from the approaches to missionary activity described in the text? Describe possible similarities and differences.

   (Augustine of Canterbury and Patrick demonstrated respect for local culture during their evangelizing. Boniface may have taken a more headstrong approach in his missionary activity.)

AUGUSTINE OF CANTERBURY'S APPROACH TO EVANGELIZATION

1. Read aloud the following passage from Venerable Bede's *Ecclesiastical History of the English People.* (Quotes are from the Medieval Sourcebook Web site.)

   As soon as (Augustine and his companions) entered the dwelling place assigned to them (in Canterbury), they began to imitate the course of life practiced in the primitive church: applying themselves to frequent prayer, watching, and fasting; preaching the word of life to as many as they could; despising all worldly things, as not belonging to them; receiving only their necessary food from those they taught; living in all respects conformably to what they prescribed to others, and being always disposed to suffer any adversity, and even to die for that truth which they preached. In short, several believed and were baptized, admiring the simplicity of their innocent life and the sweetness of their heavenly doctrine.

2. Then ask the students:
   - Describe Augustine's approach to evangelization.
   - Is his approach the way you understood mission work to have taken place? Explain.
   - In what other ways might mission work be carried out?
   - Would you approve of Augustine's approach today?
   - Of what methods of missionary activity would you not approve? Do you think these methods are employed by any religions today? Explain.

3. Following this discussion, read the following passage from Pope Gregory the Great's instructions to the missionaries in England. Then use the last question above to discuss Gregory's instructions.

When Almighty God shall bring you to the most reverend Bishop Augustine, our brother, tell him what I have, after mature deliberation on the affairs of the English, determined upon, namely, that the temples of the idols in that nation ought not to be destroyed, but let the idols that are in them be destroyed; let holy water be made and sprinkled in the said temples—let altars be erected, and relics placed. For if those temples are well built, it is requisite that they be converted from the worship of devils to the service of the true God; that the nation, seeing that their temples are not destroyed, may remove error from their hearts and, knowing and adoring the true God, may the more familiarly resort to the places to which they have been accustomed.

CoNCepʈ RevɪEw

Ask the students:

- What cultures do you think of as being "Catholic cultures"?
- What are the origins of Catholicism in those cultures?
- Is there anything unique about the expression of Catholicism in these different cultures?
- If so, what are those differences?

(The students might point out, for instance, that Irish Catholicism is distinctly different in many ways from Italian Catholicism or Polish Catholicism. Such differences sometimes caused conflicts during the immigrant phase of American Catholicism, as we will see later in the course.)

page 84

Saint Hilda, Abbess of Whitby

After the students have read the insert about Saint Hilda on page 84, point out that they are reading about a woman who ran a thriving double monastery, hosted a very important meeting for the English Church, and actively participated in the decision-making. Saint Hilda is one of many women who exerted leadership during the Church's history.

pages 84–87

The Conversion of Europe

ENTANGLEMENTS OF CHURCH AND STATE

After the students have read this section on pages 84–87, ask them:

- What was the Donation of Pepin?

    (The Donation of Pepin was his designation of the central part of Italy to be governed by the pope. With his donation, Pepin made the pope a secular ruler. While the pope had previously been involved in secular matters, now he became a head of state like other European secular leaders.)

- How did this change the role of the pope?

    (Popes after this often acted more like secular leaders than spiritual leaders.)

- How long did this state of Church affairs continue?

    (The pope was a secular ruler into the nineteenth century. After 1870 popes lost control of the Papal States and became primarily spiritual leaders.)

page 85 **WWW.**

FYI

Using the FYI

The Christmas tree is a good example of the Christianizing of a custom of a converted people. In pre-Christian times tree worship was practiced in some places, and the practice of decorating with trees and greenery was common. Recall, for example, the legend of Saint Boniface cutting down a tree dedicated to the god Thor. By medieval times some towns were celebrating Christmastime with a "Paradise Play," in which a tree was a standard prop for settings from the garden of Eden to the crucifixion. Martin Luther is said to have decorated a tree at Christmas, using candles on the tree to represent the stars in the sky at that time of year. As a result Germany quickly developed a tradition of the Christmas tree.

page 87 **DISCUSSION**

Using the Discussion

Be sure the students recognize that it is possible to be religious in a pluralistic culture without assuming that everyone is Christian. The U.S. prayerful response to the terrorist attack on the World Trade Center and the Pentagon shows a sensitivity to non-Christians and their beliefs and practices.

Concept Review

Discuss with the students the following statement: Creation of the Papal States represents a downturn in the history of the Church.

(The point of this discussion is to recognize that through his generous gift, Pepin created a situation that required later popes to serve a function not previously performed by popes—being secular rulers.)

page 87 ## Review Questions and Answers

1. What did missionaries do for Christianity?

Missionaries spread the Christian message to other groups of people, specifically in non-Christian areas.

2. Briefly sketch the outline of Saint Patrick's life.

As a teenager, Patrick was captured and taken to Ireland where he lived as a slave. He escaped to France and became a priest and then a bishop. He returned to Ireland and for the rest of his life traveled the island converting the Irish to Christianity.

3. What Roman monk headed the missionary activities in England?

Pope Gregory the Great sent Augustine of Canterbury to spread Christianity in England.

4. What controversy did the Synod of Whitby solve?

In England at the time, Roman and Irish Christian practices differed somewhat. The Synod of Whitby determined that Roman customs would be followed in all matters.

5. **What is Saint Boniface reported to have done to convince the Germans of the power of the Christian God?**

   According to legend, Saint Boniface cut down a tree dedicated to the god Thor. When he wasn't struck dead for doing so, those who observed this deed accepted Christianity.

6. **Who were Clovis and Clotilde?**

   King Clovis was the first leader of the Franks to become Christian following his marriage to the Christian woman Clotilde.

7. **What did Saint Boniface do for Pepin the Short, and what gift did Pepin give the pope in return?**

   Acting as the pope's representative, Saint Boniface crowned Pepin King of the Franks. In return, Pepin rewarded the pope by declaring him ruler of the middle section of Italy known from then until 1870 as the Papal States.

8. **What took place on Christmas day in the year 800?**

   On Christmas day in 800, Pope Leo III crowned Charlemagne Holy Roman Emperor.

9. **Give reasons why popes during the later years of the eighth century felt compelled to side with the Frankish kings rather than with the emperor in Constantinople?**

   The Frankish kings, not the emperors in Constantinople, really held power in Europe. The pope could communicate and work with the Frankish kings much more readily than he could with the emperor.

page 88   ## THE JEWISH PEOPLE

After the students have read the section, ask them:

- Why was Saint Augustine's position on Jews both good news and bad news for them?

  (Augustine advocated that Jews should be left alone but should not prosper.)

- What have studies concluded about the way Jews generally were treated by popes and by other Christians during the early Middle Ages?

  (Generally, Jews and Christians lived together without bitterness and persecution during this period.)

CoNCepl RevieW

Discuss with the students what aspects of Catholicism would lead to special appreciation for Judaism and what within Catholicism might lead to animosity toward Judaism.

(Christianity has its roots in Judaism; Jews are our elders in faith. The covenant God made with the Jewish people stands forever; Jesus extended the covenant to all people through his death and resurrection. Much of Catholic liturgy has roots in Jewish prayer. Sadly, a literal reading of some of the New Testament, written when some Christians were in conflict with some Jews, led later Christians to view Jews and Judaism in an unfortunate and negative manner. Today the Church has a better understanding of the historical background at the time of the early Church and, therefore, a greater appreciation for Judaism.)

Review Questions and Answers

1. **What two reasons did Saint Augustine give for not harming Jews?**

   Saint Augustine said Jews should not be harmed because (1) the Old Testament, to which Jews continue to witness, demonstrates that Christianity has deep and ancient roots, and (2) the demise of Judaism illustrates what happens when a people denies Jesus Christ as the Messiah. His reasons illustrate good and bad responses to Judaism and the Jewish people.

2. **What was the overall atmosphere in Jewish-Christian relations in the early Middle Ages?**

   In general, during the early Middle Ages, Jews and Christians lived next to each other without noticeable antipathy.

Chapter Review and Conclusion

REVIEW

1. Ask the students to summarize the main points in the chapter in their own words. Write notes on the board from their contributions. To reinforce their summary, you might want to review the major concepts in this chapter in the teaching manual. Then read the **Conclusion** on page 89.

2. Review the vocabulary in this chapter:

   Hagia Sophia—Church of the Holy Wisdom built in Constantinople and currently serving as a museum in Istanbul, Turkey (page 71)

   marks of the Church—four characteristics mentioned in the Nicene-Constantinopolitan creed that are associated with the true Church of Christ: one, holy, catholic, and apostolic (page 72)

   patriarch—leader of the Christian community in major cities of the Roman Empire (page 73)

   Paschal mystery—Christ's work of redemption accomplished principally by his passion, death, resurrection, and glorious ascension (page 74)

   Muhammad (560–632)—founder of the Islamic religion (page 75)

   Muslim—a member of the religion of Islam (page 75)

   hijrah—the flight of Muslims from Mecca to Medina in 622; event marks the beginning of the Muslim calendar (page 75)

   Islam—a religion based on submission to God's will as it was revealed to Muhammad (page 75)

   grace—participation in the life of God and the free and undeserved gift that God gives us to respond to our vocation to become his adopted children (page 77)

   liturgical calendar—division of the year to mark events in the life of Christ (page 77)

   Rogation Days—three days of prayer and penance before the Solemnity of the Ascension to ask God's blessing on the harvest (page 78)

Chapter Four

baptistry—the place where Baptisms are celebrated; originally a separate building and now typically a section of a church (page 79)

basilica—a Greek word meaning "king's hall"; currently the term is used to designate a certain church of historical significance that continues to play an important part in the religious life of a particular region (page 79)

Gregorian chant—of song in which one vocal part predominates and no instruments are used; mainly uses chords D, E, F, and G (page 79)

celibacy—the state or condition of those who have chosen to remain unmarried and refrain from sexual intercourse for the sake of the kingdom of heaven in order to give themselves entirely to God and to the service of his people (page 80)

Sacrament of Reconciliation—one of the Sacraments of Healing in which one is forgiven and healed of sin and reunited with God in the Christian community (page 80)

missionaries—people who spread the Christian message to other people, usually in other lands (page 81)

Synod of Whitby—A meeting of Roman and Celtic Christians to determine which style of Christianity would be followed in England (page 83)

Donation of Pepin—King Pepin's designation of the central part of Italy to be governed by the pope (page 86)

Papal States—section of Italy ruled by the pope until 1870 (page 86)

Charlemagne—King of the Franks who was crowned Roman Emperor by the pope (page 86)

TEST

Give the students the Chapter 4 Test or an alternative assessment. The tests have been placed on the Harcourt Religion Publishers' Web page. This has been done to enable the teacher to customize this material for local needs. First contact Harcourt Religion Publishers' high school consultant at 800-922-7696, ext. 3781 for a user ID and password. Then connect with the Harcourt Religion Publishers' Web site at **www.harcourtreligion.com** to download the information. Collect the tests for grading.

Chapter 4 Test Answers

MATCHING (3 points each)

1. O	4. B	7. L	10. I	13. K
2. F	5. M	8. C	11. N	14. H
3. A	6. J	9. E	12. G	15. D

SHORT ANSWER (3 points each)

1. Three ancient patriarchates were Alexandria, Antioch, and Jerusalem (along with Rome and Constantinople).
2. The common language of the Church in the East was Greek, while the Western Church used Latin.
3. The Eastern Church viewed the liturgy as an event when the union of humans and God was most evident. Liturgy in the West tended to be viewed as a celebration of the Paschal Mystery by which Christ accomplished the work of salvation.

4. According to Islam, Muhammad received messages from God telling him to call people back to strict monotheism.

5. The Battle of Tours prevented the armies of Islam from establishing control of Europe beyond the Spanish peninsula.

6. Dionysius Exiguus believed that a calendar should be based on Christian origins rather than on the legendary founding of Rome as the calendar of the time was.

7. The word "basilica" refers to a large royal building in the Roman Empire. Under Christianity, it came to refer to a large church building.

8. Saint Columban and other Irish monks introduced the practice of private confession.

9. Pope Gregory I witnessed a young boy from England being sold as a slave, moving him to seek the conversion of the people of Angle-land.

10. According to legend, Saint Boniface cut down a tree sacred to the gods of the Germanic people. When he didn't die for his deed, many people converted.

11. Venerable Bede wrote a history of Christianity in England.

12. Unlike in Roman society, in Celtic society free women held near-equality with men.

13. The Christmas tree had its origins in pre-Christian Germany.

14. The Franks were *foederati* with the Romans, meaning that Roman leaders viewed them as partners and not as enemies.

15. The emperor in Constantinople considered himself the only emperor of the Roman Empire, even though he had no control over matters in Western Europe.

ESSAYS (5 points each)

1. Some missionaries, such as Saint Patrick in Ireland and Saint Augustine of Canterbury in England, made use of pre-Christian elements in their missionary activity. Other missionaries, such as Saint Boniface in Germany, did battle with pre-Christian elements and attempted to overcome them and replace them entirely with Christian beliefs and practices.

2. The Papal States, territory that cuts across the middle of the Italian peninsula, were a gift from the Frankish ruler Pepin to the pope. With this gift, the pope became both a spiritual leader as well as the ruler of that separate body of land up until 1870. (Student critiques of the creation of the Papal States may vary.)

Prayer

MUSIC SUGGESTIONS

"All the Ends of the Earth" by Bob Dufford from *Gather (Comprehensive)* (GIA), *Lead Me, Guide Me* (GIA), *Today's Missal* (OCP), *Glory & Praise Comprehensive* (OCP).

"Canticle of the Sun" by Marty Haugen from *Gather (Comprehensive)* (GIA), *Glory & Praise (Comprehensive)* (OCP), *We Celebrate* (J.S. Paluch Co., Inc.), *Today's Missal* (OCP).

"Come, All You People" by Alexander Gondo from *Give Your Gifts, the Basics* (GIA, Harcourt Religion Publishers).

"Lead Me, Lord" by John Becker from *Today's Missal* (OCP).

"Seed Scattered and Sown" by Dan Feiten from *Today's Missal* (OCP).

"Sign Me Up" by Kevin Yancy and Jerome Metcalfe from *Lead Me, Guide Me* (GIA).

"The Harvest of Justice" by David Haas from *Gather (Comprehensive)* (GIA).

"Unless a Grain of Wheat" by Bernadette Farrell from *Today's Missal* (OCP), *Gather (Comprehensive)* (GIA).

"With You by My Side" by David Haas from *Give Your Gifts, the New Songs* (GIA, Harcourt Religion Publishers).

SCRIPTURE SUGGESTIONS

Genesis 1:1, 11–12, 29–31

1 Peter 4:7–11

Mark 4:26–29

PRAYER

Let us bless God, whose might has created the earth and whose providence has enriched it. God has given us the earth to cultivate, so that we may gather its fruits to sustain life. As we thank God for this bounty, let us learn also, as the Gospel teaches, to seek first God's way of holiness: then all we need will be given us besides.

Rogation Days prayer, *Catholic Household Blessings & Prayers*
(Washington, DC: USCC, 1988).

CHAPTER 4 TEST

Name_____ Date_____ Class period_____

Test is made up of questions with suggested point values totaling 100 points.

Matching (3 points each)

_____ 1. Donation of Pepin

_____ 2. Synod of Whitby

_____ 3. Hagia Sophia

_____ 4. Marks of the Church

_____ 5. Patriarch

_____ 6. Charles Martel

_____ 7. Rogation Days

_____ 8. *Hijrah*

_____ 9. Patrick

_____ 10. Gregory the Great

_____ 11. Hilda

_____ 12. Boniface

_____ 13. Charlemagne

_____ 14. Augustine of Hippo

_____ 15. Augustine of Canterbury

A. Emperor Justinian's creation

B. One, holy, catholic, and apostolic

C. Muslim flight

D. Led conversion of the English

E. Returned to the land where he was enslaved

F. Settled controversy for the English Church

G. Led conversion of Germans

H. Taught that Jews should be left alone

I. Sent missionaries to England

J. Won the Battle of Tours

K. First Holy Roman Emperor

L. Prayers for a successful harvest

M. Leader in a major Christian center

N. Hosted the Synod of Whitby

O. Made the pope a secular ruler

Short Answer (3 points each)

1. Name three ancient patriarchates.

2. What was the common language of the Church in the East? Of the Church in the West?

3. Describe a difference in how the Eastern and Western Churches viewed the liturgy.

© Harcourt Religion Publishers

4. What led Muhammad to preach the religion of Islam?

5. What was the result of the Battle of Tours?

6. Why did Dionysius Exiguus decide to create the Christian calendar?

7. What is a basilica?

8. What practice did Saint Columban and other Irish monks introduce to the Church?

9. According to legend, what led Pope Gregory I to seek the conversion of the Angles?

10. According to legend, what did Saint Boniface do to convince non-Christians to convert?

11. What did Venerable Bede write about?

12. How did the position of women differ in Celtic society compared to Roman society?

13. Name a practice popular among Christians today that had its origin in pre-Christian Germany.

14. What does it mean to say that the Franks were *foederati?*

15. Why was the crowning of Charlemagne an insult to the emperor in Constantinople?

Essays (5 points each)

1. Describe two approaches to missionary activity as demonstrated by leading missionaries of the sixth through eighth centuries.

2. Explain and critique the creation of the Papal States.

THE HISTORY OF RECONCILIATION

Name_____ Date_____ Class period_____

THE NEW TESTAMENT ERA

Jesus proclaimed, "Your sins are forgiven." The Church of the apostles represented a movement that brought diverse people together.

FROM THE SECOND TO THE SIXTH CENTURIES

"Reconciliation" meant returning to the Christian community after separating oneself from it by committing serious offenses. Reconciliation took years and involved public penance until, along with other penitents, one was received back into the Church community by the local bishop. This form of Reconciliation was available only once in a person's lifetime.

FROM THE SIXTH CENTURY TO THE MID-TWENTIETH CENTURY

Irish monks introduced private confession of faults, a monastic practice which then became popular with laypeople. This form of Reconciliation was private, between a penitent and a priest, and was available whenever needed. To avoid possible scandal when a woman confessed to a priest, the practice of confessing behind a screen eventually became commonplace.

FOLLOWING VATICAN COUNCIL II

By the 1970s, the Sacrament of Reconciliation underwent changes mandated by a commission to carry out the teachings of Vatican Council II. The goal of the changes was to restore a communal and Scripture-based approach to the sacrament. Since that time, communal penance services centered on Gospel readings followed by private confession of sins and absolution have become popular.

MISSION IS FOR EVERYONE

Name_____ Date_____ Class period_____

Mission work, which means spreading the good news of Jesus to others, is not just in the hands of specific people known as missionaries. It is not just something done overseas, in strange lands. Whether Christians like it or not, mission work takes place wherever and whenever they encounter others.

Here are some questions and a drawing exercise to help you examine being a missionary today.

1. Over the past century, the percentage of the United States population that is Catholic has risen steadily. Do you believe that this increase has made a difference in the country? If so, how?

2. Some estimates suggest that in a few decades Catholics will make up over half of the United States population. If that were to occur, do you believe that it would make a noticeable difference in the country? If so, how?

3. Do you see yourself in any sense as a missionary, spreading the good news of Jesus to others? If so, how?

4. On the back of this sheet, draw an image of what you see as the biggest obstacle preventing you from doing all that you can to spread the message of Jesus.

POPE JOHN PAUL II ON MISSIONARY WORK

Name_____ Date_____ Class period_____

In 1990 Pope John Paul II wrote an encyclical about missionary work in which he called upon all Catholics to participate in that work. Read over the following statements from his "On the Permanent Validity of the Church's Missionary Mandate" *(Redemptoris Missio)*. Describe in your own words what the pope means in each statement and also why he wants us to hear its message. That is, what does this statement say about Pope John Paul II's vision of mission?

Proclaiming Christ and bearing witness to him, when done in a way that respects consciences, does not violate freedom. Faith demands a free adherence on the part of man, but at the same time faith must also be offered to him, because the "multitudes have the right to know the riches of the mystery of Christ—riches in which we believe that the whole of humanity can find, in unsuspected fullness, everything that it is gropingly searching for concerning God, man and his destiny, life and death, and truth. . . . This is why the Church keeps her missionary spirit alive, and even wishes to intensify it in the moment of history in which we are living." (#8)

The kingdom [of God] aims at transforming human relationships; it grows gradually as people slowly learn to love, forgive and serve one another. (#15)

St. John tells us that "God is love" (1 Jn 4:8,16). Every person therefore is invited to "repent" and "believe" in God's merciful love. (#13)

On her part, the Church addresses people with full respect for their freedom. Her mission does not restrict freedom but rather promotes it. *The Church promotes; she imposes nothing.* She respects individuals and cultures, and she honors the sanctuary of conscience. (#39)

THE CHURCH AND WORLD UNITED

Toward the High Middle Ages

A Teacher's Prayer

Jesus, our brother, as my students and I journey in search of you, may we pause to discover your presence in the story of humanity's journey and also in our own story. Help us find inspiration in the dedication of reformers and philosophers, artists and architects, knights and pilgrims. Amen.

Overview

This chapter covers a number of concepts significant to the development of Catholicism. For many people, characteristics of the Middle Ages continue to be associated with Catholicism (for instance, ornate cathedrals, wandering friars, Church leaders leading princely lives along with secular rulers, and crusaders). Beginning with Charlemagne, it is not clear who rules the Church—emperor or pope. It takes centuries to sort the matter out. During this period, the remaining non-Christian (as well as non-Jewish and non-Muslim) tribes of Europe convert to Christianity. However, Christian unity is torn apart by the East–West Schism. In Europe, every activity has a religious significance to it. The chapter looks at a number of activities strongly associated with the Middle Ages that held religious meaning. The last section of the chapter looks at the crusades, which started out with religious fervor and ended in disaster. During the same period a new form of religious life—the mendicant orders—swept across Europe, enlivening the Church with renewed vigor.

Major Concepts Covered in This Chapter

① **Introduction**

② **The Medieval World**

③ **Institutional Problems and Church Reforms**

④ **The East—West Schism**

⑤ **The Christian Life during Christendom**

⑥ **Crusaders and Reformers**

⑦ **Chapter Review and Conclusion**

LESSON STRATEGIES

Introduction
Prayer

pages
90–92

■ **Music Suggestions**

"All the Ends of the Earth" by Bob Dufford from *Gather (Comprehensive)* (GIA), *Lead Me, Guide Me* (GIA), *Today's Missal* (OCP), *Glory & Praise Comprehensive* (OCP).

"Come, All You People" by Alexander Gondo from *Give Your Gifts, the Basics* (GIA, Harcourt Religion Publishers).

"Give Us Your Peace" by Michael Mahler from *Give Your Gifts, the New Songs* (GIA, Harcourt Religion Publishers).

"On That Day" by Kate Cuddy from *Give Your Gifts, the New Songs* (GIA, Harcourt Religion Publishers).

"Standin' in the Need of Prayer," spiritual from *Gather (Comprehensive)* (GIA), *Lead Me, Guide Me* (GIA).

"We Will Serve the Lord" by David Haas or Rory Cooney from *Gather (Comprehensive)* (GIA).

■ **Scripture Suggestions**

Sirach 9:17–10:5

1 Corinthians 1:10–17

John 13:12–17

■ **Prayer**

See student text, page 90.

Overview

1. Have the students read the **Chapter Overview** and timeline on pages 90–91. Briefly discuss some of the points and events noted.

2. Have the students complete the "**Before We Begin . . .**" activity on page 92. (You might instead assign this activity as homework before beginning the chapter and ask the students to report on their findings.)

The Medieval World

During the Middle Ages, Christianity becomes the dominant worldview for Europe, while developments within European society help to shape Christianity.

pages
92–94

THE MEDIEVAL WORLD
Saints and Sinners
When Were the "Middle Ages"?

1. The chapter begins with the presumption that the students have some preconceptions about the Middle Ages. Brainstorm with the students and explore impressions that they already have about the Middle Ages and then have them complete the **Before We Begin . . .** activity. (You might instead assign this activity as homework before beginning the chapter and ask the students to report on their findings.)

2. Have the students read these sections of the text and draw their attention to the word *Christendom*. Ask them what images this term brings to mind. (They might mention bishops elaborately dressed presiding at liturgy in a grand cathedral where lords and knights wear crosses on their shields. They might mention a medieval town dominated by a cathedral, which serves as the center of its activity.) Emphasize that during the Middle Ages in Europe Christianity and all aspects of life were intimately intertwined. Thus this period in particular deserves to be called *Christendom*. The term suggests a unified blending of one religion and secular power such as Europe had not know before and has not known since.

In-Text Activities

page 93   **FYI**

page 94   **DISCUSSION**

Using the Discussion

You might direct the students to the areas of school (treatment of others, conscientious study), work (honest effort, fair wages), home (respect, charity, common values and goals), politics (tolerance, respect for life at all stages, just treatment in domestic and foreign affairs), and so on.

CoNCept RevieW

Discuss the implications for medieval Christendom in the topic of the **In-Text Discussion**.

pages 95–97

Charlemagne and the Holy Roman Empire

CHARLEMAGNE, THE CHRISTIAN EMPEROR

CHAOS OVERTAKES CHARLEMAGNE'S EMPIRE

1. Direct the students to read these three sections. After the students have read these sections of the text, ask them:
   - How did Charlemagne see his role in the Church?
   - Why did he see himself in that role?
   - Was Charlemagne good or bad for the Church? Give your reasons.
   - Should the Church be subject to a secular ruler? Explain.
2. Following your discussion, point out to the students that Charlemagne brought to his palace the most renowned theologian and educator of his time, Alcuin. Alcuin served as an advisor to Charlemagne and as head of the palace school. Here is a prayer attributed to Alcuin, which demonstrates the depth and sincerity of the spiritual vision found at Charlemagne's court:

Eternal Light, shine into our hearts;
Eternal Goodness, deliver us from evil;
Eternal Power, be our support;
Eternal Wisdom, scatter the darkness of our ignorance;
Eternal Pity, have mercy upon us—
so that with all our heart and mind
and soul and strength
we may seek your face
and be brought by your infinite mercy
into your holy presence,
through Jesus Christ our Lord.

Breakfast with the Saints, selected by LaVonne Neff (Ann Arbor, MI: Servant Publications, 1996), 11.

page 96 ## ACTIVITY

Using the Activity

(Until fairly recently, some laws of the United States were enacted simply because they reflected Christian beliefs rather than a natural-law premise. For instance, for most of U.S. history, states had laws restricting stores from being open on Sundays or religious holidays. These laws were called blue laws.)

Additional Activities

THE DARK AGES

1. For centuries historians designated a variety of time frames as the *Dark Ages*. Charlemagne's time and immediately after it were typically included under this title. Direct groups of students to research living conditions in Europe during the ninth and tenth centuries. Ask them to prepare a presentation for the class making a case for or against the following statement: The so-called Dark Ages were not as dark as we might think.

2. Direct the students to include in their presentation discussion of the role of the Church during this period. (You might point out the observation made in the text that Charlemagne emphasized learning and brought many scholars to his imperial city. Even the Vikings, although feared by Christian Europe, had one of their number—Leif Erikson—travel as far as North America during this supposedly "dark" period [AD 1000]).

CoNCept RevIEw

Direct the students' attention to the picture of Charlemagne on page 95. Discuss with them:

- Based on the information about him found in the text, does Charlemagne deserve the title "the great"? Why or why not?

- Given what you know of the age of Charlemagne, what are the strengths and weaknesses of each of the following models for Europe of the time?

    — The emperor has ultimate authority over all of Christendom, including the pope.

    — The pope has ultimate authority over all of Christendom, including the emperor.

    — The emperor has ultimate authority over political matters; the pope has ultimate authority over spiritual matters.

pages 98–99 ## Feudalism: The Medieval Way of Life

FEUDALISM AND THE CHURCH

The students may be familiar with feudalism from a history course. This section looks at three ways feudalism affected the Church: Church leaders as part of the feudal system, Church structure mirroring the feudal structure, and theologians viewing relationships among levels of beings in feudal terms. To address the first implication, read aloud the quote from Anthony E. Gilles on page 99. Remind the students that the spiritual role we associate with bishops today was only part of a bishop's responsibility during the Middle Ages. As part of the feudal system, bishops (and abbots) were lords and vassals as well.

page 99   ACTIVITY

          Using the Activity

          1. Before assigning this activity, have the students read the sections of the text on feudalism and then assign the **In-Text Activity.**

          2. Draw on the board or overhead a vertical line or a pyramid-shaped triangle with smaller horizontal lines across it. Ask a student to come to the board to fill in words that should be placed on the horizontal lines based on the Great Chain of Being (God at the top, followed by angels, and so on).

          3. Instruct the students to make a drawing illustrating an alternative view of reality.

          4. After the students have made their drawings, you might allow them to walk around the room to observe one another's drawings. Then discuss with them their alternative views. End the discussion with the question: Is there a dominant view of reality in the world today? If so, what is it?

Additional Activities

FEUDALISM AND THE CHURCH

          Handout 5–A, Feudalism and the Church, contains passages from the 1909 edition of *The Catholic Encyclopedia,* which is available on the Internet. The passages point out how Church leaders came to be unwittingly involved in the feudal system and faced accompanying dangers from this involvement. Although reforms addressed abuses stemming from the great secular power held by Church leaders, not until the Reformation was the system itself challenged. You might simply read the passages on the handout and ask the students the accompanying questions, or distribute the handout in order that the students can write their responses in the space provided. Discuss with them each passage to make sure that they understand its meaning.

CoNCept ReviEw

Ask the students to write an explanation of feudalism for someone unfamiliar with the term. Then discuss with them: What effect did feudalism have on the Church of the Middle Ages?

page 99   **Review Questions and Answers**

          1. **Which centuries encompass the Middle Ages?**

                The broadest time span for the Middle Ages is from 476 to 1600. However, the central period of the Middle Ages lasted from around 800 to 1300.

2. **Why can the term the *Middle Ages* carry a negative meaning?**

   Some people consider the period between the classical age and the age of the Enlightenment as a time of medieval superstitions.

3. **Why are the Middle Ages in Europe also known as the time of Christendom?**

   Except for relatively small communities of Jews, European rulers and common people alike followed Christianity as the guiding principle for their lives.

4. **What does it mean to say that Charlemagne was a "holy emperor" and the "second Constantine"?**

   Like Constantine, Charlemagne attempted to form Western Europe into one family of faith.

5. **Name two ways that Charlemagne attempted to serve the Church as Holy Roman Emperor.**

   - Charlemagne promoted Christian learning by supporting monasteries and the copying of ancient writings.
   - He took an active role in establishing Church practices for his empire.
   - He made the form of worship uniform throughout the empire.
   - He instituted rules for monasteries and clergy.
   - He enacted laws against heresy.

6. **Who were the Vikings, Saracens, and Magyars?**

   These three were non-Christian groups who attacked areas of Christian Europe for around one hundred and fifty years after Charlemagne.

7. **What kind of work did serfs do?**

   Serfs worked the land in exchange for the leadership and protection of a lord who owned the land.

8. **How did the feudal system function?**

   The feudal system was a division of society based on interlocking duties and responsibilities meant to make productive use of the land while offering protection for those who worked it.

9. **Name three ways that feudalism affected the Church of the Middle Ages.**

   Church leaders were part of the feudal system itself, the structure of the Church imitated that of the feudal system, and the view of reality reflected the hierarchical worldview of feudalism.

Institutional Problems and Church Reforms

The close link between secular and religious power leads to forms of corruption that a reform movement and a reforming pope seek to change. Institutional problems do not prevent Christianity from spreading to the remaining non-Christian sections of Europe.

pages
100–103

TROUBLES AND TRIUMPHS

Three Problems That Plagued the Medieval Church

Cluny and the Reform of Monastic Life

Hildebrand—The Reforming Pope

1. This section of the chapter identifies the three major problems resulting from the Church's involvement in the feudal system. It also describes the two major instruments of reform during the period—the reform of monasticism beginning in Cluny, France, and the reforms of Pope Gregory VII. These two movements can help the students appreciate that the gospel message constantly called Christians back to fidelity to the message of Jesus in the particular historical circumstances in which they found themselves. Direct the students to read these sections. Review with them key points made in each section.

2. Then assign a few students to prepare the second **In-Text Activity,** page 103—the role-play of the debate between emperor and pope.

3. Have the remaining students individually complete the first **In-Text Activity** on page 100, and then discuss their responses in small groups.

In-Text Activities

page 100   **FYI**

Using the FYI

The meeting of the eligible cardinals (less than eighty years of age) is called the conclave. After preliminary sessions for the conclave, the cardinals are "sealed in"; that is, the conclave is sealed until a pope is elected in order to prevent outside influences on the decision.

ACTIVITY

Using the Activity

The issues here are not simple, but taken together the suggestions would have helped the Church deal with a myriad of problems. Hindsight is great, but at the time these options may not have been possible or even thought of. Use a contemporary example to help the students see how solutions perceived after the fact may not have been possible or even imagined before or in the midst of a crisis. For example, after the attack on the World Trade Center and the Pentagon, security lapses were identified in hindsight.

page 103   **ACTIVITY**

Using the Activity

End the lesson with the assigned students performing their role-play.

Discuss with your students:

- Members of the Church are always in need of reform and someone like Pope Gregory VII calling for regular reform. What types of reform would be most beneficial for the Church community today?

- Reform of monasticism was very effective in reforming the Church of the time. What instruments would be most effective in bringing about Church reform today?

pages 104–106

Further Christian Expansion

Margaret of Scotland

Further information about Margaret of Scotland is available in books on lives of the saints and on the Internet.

Cyril and Methodius

1. After the students have read these sections, have them summarize the main ideas.

2. Either as a class or in small groups, discuss the **In-Text Discussion** questions found on page 106.

In-Text Activities

page 106

DISCUSSION

Using the Discussion

This discussion may surface a wide variety of opinions. It's important for a teacher to express a tolerance of divergent views while challenging any that appear to be contrary to the Church's teachings or that are divisive rather than unifying in the long run.

ConCept ReviEw —————

Saint Benedict and Saints Cyril and Methodius are co-patron saints of Europe. From what you have studied so far, do you believe that any other people should also share this honor? Why should they?

(For instance, since many Irish monks served as missionaries to Europe, Saint Patrick deserves consideration for converting the Irish. Saint Boniface converted Germanic tribes. Saint Clotilde converted her husband, Clovis, which was an important step toward Christianization of many pre-Christian European groups. Saint Gregory the Great emphasized missionary work and also gave helpful guidelines about how to do it.)

page 106

Review Questions and Answers

1. **What was the difference between the positions of Charlemagne and Pope Nicholas I on Church governance?**

   Charlemagne believed that he ruled the Church and that the pope was to pray for it. Pope Nicholas I believed that the pope ruled the Church and that the emperor was to protect it.

2. **Name three problems that the Church had to face during the early Middle Ages?**

   Three problems facing the Church during the Middle Ages were lay investiture, simony, and lack of fidelity to the vow of celibacy.

3. **How did the Cluny movement help reform Church practices?**

   Cluny provided an example of spiritual life to counteract the immorality that had become commonplace within the Church.

4. **What is a conclave of cardinals?**

   A conclave of cardinals is a gathering of cardinals for the purpose of electing a new pope.

5. **Who was Hildebrand? What action did he take against Emperor Henry IV, and why did he do so?**

   Hildebrand became Pope Gregory VII and instituted many reforms in the Church. He excommunicated Emperor Henry IV for refusing to accept papal control over investiture of Church leaders.

6. **What are the changes called that Pope Gregory VII introduced into the Church?**

   Pope Gregory VII's changes are called the Gregorian reforms.

7. **How did the Concordat of Worms strengthen the position of the pope?**

   The Concordat of Worms gave the pope power to choose bishops and abbots and to invest them with spiritual power.

8. **What contributions to Slavic culture did Saints Cyril and Methodius make?**

   Saints Cyril and Methodius created an alphabet so that the Slavic language could be written as well as spoken.

9. **What form of Christianity did Prince Vladimir of Rus adopt?**

   Prince Vladimir adopted Eastern Christianity as practiced in Constantinople.

The East–West Schism

The growing separation between East and West leads finally to a split between the two sections of the Church in 1054.

pages
107–110

THE EAST-WEST SCHISM

The *Filioque* and Iconoclast Controversies

Sicily—East or West?

EASTERN ORTHODOX AND EASTERN RITE CATHOLICS

1. Before discussing the East–West Schism, ask the students:
   - What is the difference between "unity" and "uniformity"?
   - Give examples of unity with uniformity and unity without uniformity.
   - What types of conflicts can exist when there is apparent unity but not uniformity?

- What must be done to maintain unity when there is not uniformity?

  (For instance, a marriage is an example of unity without uniformity. For a marriage to work, husband and wife must communicate often, be open to different points of view, and seek the welfare of the other. None of these strategies was present in the relationship between the Eastern and Western Churches at the time of the schism.)

2. Use this discussion to lead into discussion of the East–West Schism. Direct the students to read these sections and ask them:

   - What were some of the problems that created tension between the two sections of the Church?

   - What circumstances led to the mutual excommunications issued by leaders of both sections of the Church?

   - How did leaders of other Eastern Churches initially view this mutual excommunication?

   - Why did the crusades cement the schism between the two sections of the Church?

   - What is the difference between Eastern Orthodox and Eastern Rite Catholics?

In-Text Activities

page 108 **ACTIVITY**

Using the Activity

1. You might bring in an icon or a reproduction of an icon. One source of modern icons is Bridge Building Images (www. Bridgebuilding.com).

2. If you invite the students to try their hand at painting an icon, remind them that an icon serves as a window into the divine mystery. While traditional icons hold to ancient styles, they might use contemporary images or themes to express this notion.

3. If any students paint icons, be sure to display them in the classroom or school chapel.

page 109 **FYI**

Using the FYI

If there is an Orthodox church in the area, consider inviting an orthodox staff person to share with the class the Orthodox interpretation of the schism. Have the class prepare questions ahead of time.

page 110 **ACTIVITY**

Using the Activity

Provide time in class for discussion of this experience.

ICONS IN THE EASTERN CHURCH

1. You might want to discuss with your students the role of icons in the Eastern Church. Pope John Paul II wrote about icons in his 1999 "Letter to Artists" He stated:

    "In the East, the art of the icon continued to flourish, obeying theological and aesthetic norms charged with meaning and sustained by the conviction that, in a sense, the icon is a sacrament. By analogy with what occurs in the sacraments, the icon makes present the mystery of the Incarnation in one or other of its aspects. That is why the beauty of the icon can be best appreciated in a church wherein the shadows burning lamps stir infinite flickerings of light." As Pavel Florensky has written: "By the flat light of day, gold is crude, heavy, useless, but by the tremulous light of a lamp or candle it springs to life and glitters in sparks beyond counting—now here, now there, evoking the sense of other lights, not of this earth, which fill the space of heaven." (number 8)

    In the same letter the pope points out that:

    The icon is venerated not for its own sake, but points beyond to the subject which it represents. (number 7)

2. Read aloud these quotes and ask the students:
    - What was the "iconoclast controversy" about?
    - How might icons be misunderstood or misused?
    - What is the rightful way to understand icons?
    - Are there practices in the Western Catholic Church similar to the use of icons in the Eastern Church? If so, what are they?
    - Do people today tend to appreciate icons, or are they more iconoclastic? Explain.

CoNCept RevieW

Pope John Paul II told Eastern Catholics that the best gift they can offer the Church is for them to be true to their own traditions. Discuss with the students how this attitude is different from the attitude of Cardinal Humbert and Patriarch Michael Cerularius.

page 110 ## Review Questions and Answers

1. **Describe the difference in how Eastern and Western Christians viewed their bishops.**

    The Eastern Church saw the role of bishop as that of a father to his particular community but as a brother to all his fellow bishops. Christians in the West saw the pope, the bishop of Rome, as the head of the entire Church.

2. **Explain the *filioque* controversy.**

    After two councils held in the East (Nicaea and Constantinople) agreed upon the Nicene Creed, the Western Church added the phrase "and the Son" to the sentence: *We believe in the Holy Spirit, the Lord, the giver of life, who proceeds from the Father.* Leaders of the Eastern Church disagreed with the wording and also with the process of making the change, namely, without consulting them.

3. **What are icons? What function do they play in the Churches in the East?**

    Icons are highly stylized sacred images popular especially in the Eastern Church. These paintings inspired the faithful and helped a largely illiterate community to better understand their faith.

4. **Explain the iconoclast controversy.**

The iconoclast controversy was disagreement about whether or not icons are acceptable for use in worship. The controversy resulted when an Eastern emperor condemned their existence and use.

5. **What roles did Patriarch Michael Cerularius and Cardinal Humbert play in the break between the Eastern and Western Churches?**

For a few days Patriarch Michael Cerularius refused to meet with Cardinal Humbert, the pope's representative. Cardinal Humbert, who carried with him a decree of excommunication from the pope, laid the proclamation on the altar of Hagia Sophia, thus excommunicating the entire Greek Church. In retaliation, Michael Cerularius excommunicated the pope and the entire Latin Church.

6. **What is the difference between Eastern Orthodox and Eastern Rite Catholic Churches?**

Eastern Orthodox Churches are Churches of the East not in union with the pope. Eastern Rite Catholic Churches are Churches of the East that are in union with the pope.

The Christian Life during Christendom

A variety of activities exhibit the spirit of Christianity during the Middle Ages in Europe.

pages
111–116

MEDIEVAL CHRISTIAN EXPERIENCE

The Pilgrim

The Cathedral

The Theologian

The Knight

1. This section examines four ways that people of the Middle Ages expressed their spirituality: as pilgrim, artist, theologian, and knight. You might divide the students into four groups and assign each group one of these topics, asking them to prepare a multimedia presentation for the class.

2. Spend some time with the entire class on the chart on page 115: Arguments for the Existence of God. Discuss observation examples to help the students grasp each of the arguments or "proofs."

In-Text Activities

page 112   WWW.

Using the www.

See also the CD-ROM, *Exploring the Holy Land,* available from Harcourt Religion Publishers.

WWW.

Using the www.

You might ask the students to identify any Gothic or Romanesque churches in the area.

ACTIVITY

Using the Activity

Some of the students may be willing to share their descriptions with the class. On the other hand, if you first collect and read the papers, you may want to choose one or two to include in class prayer; obtain the writers' permission to do so.

ACTIVITY

Using the Activity

1. There are a variety of films on these topics. *Camelot,* for example, deals with the King Arthur story. The conclusion to *Indiana Jones and the Last Crusade* presents an interesting view of the Holy Grail.

2. Consider a round-table (no pun intended) discussion on this question.

Additional Activities

CHRISTIAN LIFE AS PILGRIMAGE

Handout 5–B, Pilgrimage—Model of the Christian Life, offers some thoughts about the experience of pilgrimage and an assignment designed to give the students an opportunity to reflect upon the theme of pilgrimage.

ERASMUS AND LUTHER ON PILGRIMAGE

1. The text contains quotes from Erasmus and Martin Luther who denied that pilgrimage was spiritually efficacious; the following quotes are on page 112.

   "You could run off to Rome or Compostela and buy up a million indulgences, but in the last analysis there is no better way of reconciling yourself with God than reconciling yourself with your brother."—Erasmus

   ". . . apply the money and effort required for the pilgrimage to fulfilling God's commandments, and to doing works a thousand times better than a pilgrimage, namely, meeting the needs of his family and his poor neighbors."—Martin Luther

2. Read aloud the two quotes and invite comments about whether the students agree or disagree with these more "modern" perspectives on pilgrimage. As part of the discussion, you might point out to the students the following Catholic perspectives on pilgrimage:

   • Our earthly life is a pilgrimage.

   • Our God has been manifest in actual persons who lived in specific places. Incarnational spirituality recognizes the value of visiting these "holy places."

   • The experience of going on a pilgrimage is a spiritual experience as much as reaching the goal is.

- We have reports of Christians going on a pilgrimage from early in the Church's history, and Catholics continue to find pilgrimages to the Holy Land, Rome, Lourdes, and other places to be spiritually enriching.
- The Church does not automatically approve every apparition. While there may be pilgrimages organized to unapproved sites, this should not be seen as Church approval of the apparition.

3. Conclude the discussion by inviting the students to reflect on the following questions:
- If you had the time and resources, where would you go on a pilgrimage?
- How could you prepare yourself and conduct yourself so that it would be a true pilgrimage?

CoNCept ReviEw

Discuss with the students: Four ways of experiencing the Christian life during the Middle Ages were pilgrim, artist, theologian, and knight. What are some ways of experiencing the Christian life today? Explain.

(If the students do not mention "being a student" as a way of experiencing the Christian life, remind them that the life of study and learning has always been an important dimension of the Christian life.)

page 116

Review Questions and Answers

1. **What does it mean to say that a pilgrimage symbolizes the Christian experience?**

   According to the Christian worldview, we are all on a journey from God seeking to make our way back to God.

2. **Name two popular destinations for medieval pilgrims.**

   The most popular destinations for pilgrims were the Holy Land, Rome, and the tombs of martyrs.

3. **What position did Erasmus and Martin Luther hold regarding pilgrimage?**

   Erasmus and Martin Luther believed that people should spend their time helping people rather than going on pilgrimages.

4. **Describe the difference between Romanesque and Gothic architecture.**

   Romanesque buildings have decorative arcades and ornamentation while Gothic buildings have higher walls and expanded space for windows.

5. **What is scholasticism?**

   Scholasticism is the use of reason, specifically Greek philosophy, to explain and organize Christian teachings.

6. **Whose *Summa Theologica* examined Christian beliefs in light of Greek philosophy?**

   Saint Thomas Aquinas wrote *Summa Theologica* in order to examine Christian teachings in light of Greek philosophy.

7. **How did Christian leaders of the Middle Ages Christianize the profession of knighthood?**

   Knights were to uphold morality and fight for the good.

Crusaders and Reformers

European crusaders, with the blessing and encouragement of the Church, set off to restore control of the Holy Lands to Christians. In the process, they wreak havoc on Christians, non-Christians, and ultimately themselves as well. Saint Francis of Assisi and Saint Dominic begin a new form of religious life.

Instruct the students to read the sections on the crusades on pages 117–118. Review key points made in the text and then use the **In-Text Activity** and the **Additional Activity** to discuss their outcome. Point out that European Christians entered into the crusades with good intentions. Their methods ended up in barbarism, indiscriminately killing and plundering whomever they encountered.

pages 117–118

CRUSADERS AND REFORMERS

The Christian Attempt to Win Back the Holy Land

The students may have differing opinions regarding the crusades; surface these in discussion. By using more modern examples, help the students see that the Western world and even the Church have at times continued to exercise poor judgment regarding the Middle East.

In-Text Activities

page 118

ACTIVITY

Using the Activity

The Just War Principles are listed and explained in most justice and peace or morality textbooks. They are summarized here. You might have a student write the principles on the board or overhead, discuss the meaning of each one, and then evaluate the crusades in light of them.

- Just cause*: Does a real and certain injustice exist?
- Right intention: Is justice the intended outcome of the action?
- Legitimate authority: Are recognized leaders following accepted unwritten rules in declaring war and in overseeing how it is carried out?
- Proportionality*: Will the foreseeable goal of the military action outweigh the possible damage caused?
- Reasonable hope of success*: With a fair degree of certainty, are intended results likely to be achieved?
- Noncombatant immunity: Will people not directly involved in fighting be spared becoming victims?
- Last resort*: Have all other means of resolving the conflict been tried?

Joseph Stoutzenberger, *Justice & Peace* (Dubuque, IA: Harcourt Religion Publishers), 245–247.* See also the *Catechism of the Catholic Church,* #2309.

Note: *The Challenge of Peace* (US Bishops) deals with noncombatant immunity in another section and includes comparative justice (balancing the rights of all involved, using the least means possible) in its list of seven criteria.

KNIGHTS—CHRISTIAN WARRIORS?

After the students have read the section on the crusades, write the words *Christian Warriors* on the board or overhead. Ask the students:

- Are these two words incompatible? Why or why not?
- Is there such a thing as a "holy war"? Why do you think that?
- Are there "holy wars" today?
- Should Catholic leaders ever condone warfare?
- Does religious sanctioning of a particular war lead to a more moral use of violence?
- Should soldiers view their profession as a religious duty? Why or why not?

Concept Review

Discuss the crusades in light of the following statement: Yes or no: The crusades were a *good idea* but were *badly executed.*

(One part of this question is whether or not circumstances leading up to the crusades justified the use of violence. If not, then the crusades were not a good idea to begin with. If the crusades were justified in theory, there remains the reality that overall they were carried out in overly destructive ways and resulted in disastrous consequences.)

pages
119–122

The Mendicant Orders—Franciscans and Dominicans

SAINT FRANCIS OF ASSISI

SAINT DOMINIC

With Francis and Dominic, we come to another major development in living the Christian life. Throughout history, Christians have felt an urge to live their faith more intensely. If we are familiar with the story of the mendicant orders, we still may not appreciate what a radical change they represented. For instance, Thomas Aquinas was expected to enter the Benedictine monastery at Monte Casino. When he instead joined the new Dominican order, his parents thought he had entered something of a cult. They wanted for him the prestige of orders in the well-established Benedictine community; the mendicant orders clearly were not about seeking prestige. After the students have read these sections, ask them: Why were the mendicant orders so radical for their time?

(The students may point out that the monastery system had been in place for centuries and the mendicant orders rejected the monastic ideals of living independently and apart from the rest of society. Also, monks typically stayed in one monastery, while the mendicants were known for traveling about. Monks lived a structured, highly regulated lifestyle. The mendicant lifestyle, at least initially, would have seemed free and haphazard. By living in complete poverty, the mendicants also went against the materialism that was common at the time. Finally, the mendicants were something new and demonstrated an excitement and enthusiasm not found in the established forms of religious life.)

page 120   YOUTH NEWS

Using the Youth News

This would be an appropriate time to plan and carry out a class service project, especially one in the areas mentioned in this activity: environmental and right-to-life issues.

Saint Clare of Assisi

Further information about Saint Clare of Assisi is available in books of lives of the saints and on the Internet at **http://www.ewtn.com/library/MARY/CLARA.htm**

---

page 122   **FYI**

Using the FYI

You might ask the students to do a newspaper/Internet search of reactions to this statement by the pope and to share the reactions in a class discussion.

page 123   ACTIVITY

Using the Activity

- Francis: Much has been written in particular about Saint Francis. *Praying with Francis of Assisi* in the Saint Mary's Press *Companions for the Journey* series lists fifteen themes associated with Saint Francis. You might further divide this assignment among individual students or groups of students by assigning the following topics for a written or oral report:

  — The life of Saint Francis of Assisi
  — Stories about Saint Francis of Assisi
  — Themes associated with Saint Francis of Assisi
  — Franciscans in history
  — Franciscans today

- Dominic: See *Praying with Dominic* from Saint Mary's Press. Again, you might further divide this assignment among individual students or groups of students by assigning the following topics for a written or oral report:

  — The life of Saint Dominic

  — Stories about Saint Dominic

  — Themes associated with Saint Dominic

  — Dominicans in history

  — Dominicans today

Ask your students the following question: If you were alive at the time and wanted to enter religious life, would you more likely join: the Benedictines? the Dominicans? the Franciscans? Why?

page 123   ## Review Questions and Answers

1. **What two actions by the Seljuk Turks helped spark the crusades?**

   First, the Seljuk Turks prevented Christians from living in or coming in pilgrimage to the Holy Land. Then they began to attack Constantinople.

2. **What was the intended outcome of the crusades? How successful were the crusades in meeting their objective?**

   The intended outcome of the crusades was to restore Christian control of the Holy Land. This objective was met only briefly following the First Crusade.

3. **What two unofficial crusades took place during the period of the crusades?**

   The two unofficial crusades were the "People's Crusade" and the "Children's Crusade."

4. **How were the mendicant religious communities different from monastic communities?**

   Mendicant communities lived among the rest of society and depended on other people for their needs.

5. **How did Saint Francis of Assisi initially interpret the message, "Repair my church"?**

   Initially, Saint Francis believed that he was to rebuild the chapel where he heard this message.

6. **What is the name of the religious community founded by Saint Francis?**

   Saint Francis's religious community is known as Friars Minor, or "the little brothers."

7. **Against what heresy did Saint Dominic preach? What were the beliefs of this heresy?**

   Saint Dominic preached against Albigensianism which held that all matter was evil.

8. **What is the name of the religious community founded by Saint Dominic?**

   Saint Dominic founded the Order of Preachers, commonly known as the Dominicans.

Chapter Review and Conclusion

REVIEW

1. Ask the students to summarize the main points in the chapter in their own words. Write notes on the board from their contributions. To reinforce their summary, you might want to review the major concepts in this chapter in the teaching manual. Then read the **Conclusion** on page 123.

2. Review the vocabulary in this chapter:

   medieval—pertaining to the Middle Ages (page 93)

   Christendom—the Christian world as dominated by Christianity; used during the Middle Ages to denote Western Europe (page 94)

   Saracens—nomadic Muslim people who raided Mediterranean coastal areas, especially around southern Italy (page 97)

   Magyars—nomadic people from the Eastern frontier (page 97)

   Vikings—a seafaring people who originated in Denmark (page 97)

   feudalism—a social form of interlocking relationships based on the use of land in payment for military services (page 98)

   vassal—in the feudal system, someone who is subject to and under the protection of another person (page 98)

   serf—one who tilled soil in the feudal system and was bound to the will of the landowner (page 98)

   Great Chain of Being—perception of reality as a pyramid from God at the top to inanimate objects at the bottom (page 99)

   lay investiture—the practice of lay persons (such as kings) appointing bishops, priests, abbots, and abbesses (page 100)

   simony—the payment of money in order to be appointed to a Church office (page 100)

   Truce of God—a rule enacted by the medieval Church forbidding warfare during certain holy days of the year (page 101)

   conclave—a meeting of cardinals to elect a pope (page 102)

   Gregorian reforms—a series of reforms under Pope Gregory VII that addressed major problems in the Church (page 102)

   East–West Schism—the official separation of the Eastern (Orthodox) Church from the Western Church; sometimes referred to as the Great Schism (page 107)

   excommunication—a severe ecclesiastical penalty which excludes the offender from taking part in the Eucharist or other sacraments (page 107)

   filioque—Latin term meaning "and the Son" (page 108)

   iconoclast controversy disagreement caused by the Eastern emperor's decision to condemn the use of icons in worship (page 108)

icon—a highly stylized painting venerated in Eastern Christianity (page 108)

idolatry–worship of false gods or of an image of God (page 108)

Eastern Orthodox Churches–Christian Churches with origins in the Eastern Roman Empire that are not in union with the Church centered in Rome (page 110)

Eastern Rite Catholic Churches—Christian Churches whose origins were in the Eastern Roman Empire that are in union with the Church centered in Rome (page 110)

Gothic—a style of architecture developed in northern France that allowed for higher walls and expanded space for windows (page 113)

Romanesque—style of architecture developed in Italy characterized by decorative use of arcades and profuse ornamentation (page 113)

Summa Theologica—Saint Thomas Aquinas's comprehensive systematic examination of Christian theology (page 114)

mendicant—religious communities whose members live among people and rely on the charity of others or work at the lowest-paying jobs available (page 119)

Friars Minor—the community of "little brothers" founded by Saint Francis of Assisi (page 120)

Albigensianism—heresy that believes the physical to be evil and only the spiritual to be good, similar to the beliefs of Manicheism (page 121)

Order of Preachers—the religious community founded by Saint Dominic (page 122)

Inquisition—Church trials established to help curb the spread of heretical doctrines (page 122)

TEST

Give the students the Chapter 5 Test or an alternative assessment. The tests have been placed on the Harcourt Religion Publishers' Web page. This has been done to enable the teacher to customize this material for local needs. First contact Harcourt Religion Publishers' high school consultant at 800-922-7696, ext. 3781 for a user ID and password. Then connect with the Harcourt Religion Publishers' Web site at **www.harcourtreligion.com** to download the information. Collect the tests for grading.

Chapter 5 Test Answers

MULTIPLE CHOICE (1 point each)

1. d	5. a	9. b	13. c	17. c	21. d
2. b	6. b	10. c	14. a	18. a	22. d
3. a	7. a	11. d	15. c	19. c	23. c
4. a	8. a	12. a	16. b	20. a	24. d

MATCHING (1 point each)

1. D	3. E	5. K	7. L	9. C	11. I
2. J	4. A	6. F	8. G	10. B	12. H

IDENTIFICATION (3 points each)

1. Scholasticism—the approach to theology that used reason to explain and organize Christian teachings
2. *Summa Theologica*— Saint Thomas Aquinas's comprehensive systematic examination of Christian theology
3. *Deus vult!*— "God wills it," the motivating cry for the First Crusade
4. The Book of Kells—a finely illustrated manuscript of the Four Gospels in Latin which was produced in the early Middle Ages
5. Great Chain of Being—perception of reality as a pyramid from God at the top to inanimate objects at the bottom
6. Gregorian Reforms—a series of reforms under Pope Gregory VII that addressed major problems in the Church
7. Excommunication—a severe ecclesiastical penalty which excludes the offender from taking part in the Eucharist or other sacraments
8. Romanesque—style of architecture developed in Italy characterized by decorative use of arcades and profuse ornamentation

ESSAYS (5 points each)

1. The Middle Ages in Europe are also known as Christendom because all aspects of life were viewed from a Christian worldview.
2. Charlemagne considered himself to be ruler of the Church, responsible for making and enforcing laws for the Christian world under his care.
3. Feudalism affected the Church in three ways: many Church leaders were also feudal lords, Church structure mimicked feudalism, and feudalism influenced the way Church members viewed all of reality.
4. The East–West Schism was preceded by a controversy over the phrase "and the Son" which was added to the Nicene Creed by the pope and the iconoclast controversy, when the pope sided with the patriarch of Constantinople against the emperor.
5. Christian theology views life itself as a pilgrimage toward heaven.
6. Scholasticism helped to explain Christian beliefs in philosophical terms and helped create great medieval universities.
7. When Seljuk Turks conquered Jerusalem, they prevented Christians from living in the city or from visiting it on pilgrimage. Except for a brief period of time, the crusades failed to achieve their goal, to win back the holy land from the Turks.
8. Mendicants lived as vowed religious among the rest of society. Previous to this time, vowed religious lived apart from the rest of society in monasteries.

Prayer

MUSIC SUGGESTIONS

"Bring Forth the Kingdom" by Marty Haugen from *Gather (Comprehensive)* (GIA).

"Companions on the Journey" by Carey Landry from *Glory & Praise (Comprehensive)* (OCP), *Today's Missal* (OCP).

"Hope at the Crossroads" by Michael Mahler from *Give Your Gifts, the New Songs* (GIA, Harcourt Religion Publishers).

"Prayer of Saint Francis" by Sebastian Temple from *Today's Missal* (OCP), *We Celebrate* (J.S. Paluch Co., Inc.), *Glory & Praise Comprehensive* (OCP).

"We Are Called" by David Haas from *Gather (Comprehensive)* (GIA), *Give Your Gifts, the Songs* (Harcourt Religion Publishers, GIA).

"With You by My Side" by David Haas from *Give Your Gifts, the New Songs* (GIA, Harcourt Religion Publishers).

SCRIPTURE SUGGESTIONS

Job 27:1–11

Romans 8:1–6

Luke 18:18–30

PRAYER

May God the Father who made us bless us.

May God the Son send his healing among us.

May God the Holy Spirit move within us and give us eyes to see with, ears to hear with, and hands that your work might be done.

May we walk and preach the word of God to all.

May the angel of peace watch over us and lead us at last by God's grace to the kingdom.

Saint Dominic

CHAPTER 5 TEST

Name_____ Date_____ Class period_____

Test is made up of questions with suggested point values of 100 points.

Multiple Choice (1 point each)

_____ 1. Some scholars begin the Middle Ages with the year 476 because in that year
   a. Charlemagne was crowned emperor
   b. Gregory the Great became pope
   c. all Northern and Eastern European tribes were Christian
   d. the classical Roman Empire in the West ended

_____ 2. Charlemagne is called the "second Constantine" because he
   a. united the Eastern and Western empires
   b. formed all of Western Europe into one family of faith
   c. designed his own capital city and palace
   d. took control of the empire from his brothers

_____ 3. Charlemagne came from the European group, the
   a. Franks
   b. Visigoths
   c. Lombards
   d. Angles

_____ 4. Charlemagne believed that he
   a. had authority over Church matters
   b. was subject to the pope
   c. ruled over secular affairs; the pope ruled over Church affairs
   d. should consult with the pope when making decisions

_____ 5. After Charlemagne's reign
   a. the empire fell into chaos
   b. a century of peace followed
   c. Muslims overtook France
   d. the English king became emperor

_____ 6. The nomadic Muslims who attacked southern Italy and overtook Rome were the
   a. Magyars
   b. Saracens
   c. Franks
   d. Khazars

_____ 7. In feudalism, a vassal was someone
   a. subject to another
   b. with authority over another
   c. who worked the land
   d. who was a knight

_____ 8. During the Middle Ages Church leaders
   a. were also landowners
   b. lived separate from feudalism
   c. condemned feudalism
   d. were known for simple living

_____ 9. Lay investiture refers to lay people
   a. owning Church land
   b. appointing Church leaders
   c. serving as Church leaders
   d. wearing religious garb

_____ 10. Simony refers to
   a. clergy not practicing celibacy
   b. secular leaders appointing bishops
   c. paying money for a Church office
   d. appointing relatives to Church offices

_____ 11. Cluny is known for
   a. its Gregorian chant
   b. its Gothic cathedral
   c. the Albigensian heresy
   d. the reform of monasticism

_____ 12. According to the Truce of God,
   a. warfare was forbidden on certain days
   b. the pope and emperor shared power
   c. Muslims and Christians ceased fighting
   d. new religious orders were formed

_____ 13. A conclave refers to
   a. a collection of manuscripts
   b. the pope and emperor sharing power
   c. cardinals meeting to elect a pope
   d. the ceiling of a cathedral

_____ 14. The Concordat of Worms determined that
   a. popes would invest bishops with spiritual power; the emperor would invest them with
      their temporal power
   b. the bishops of a country would participate in determining its laws
   c. the pope and emperor would no longer battle each other over control of the empire
   d. local lords would hand over their power to one supreme ruler

The Church and World United

_____ 15. Besides bringing about the conversion of the Slavic people, Saints Cyril and Methodius
   a. ruled the Slavic nation
   b. converted the Vikings
   c. created a Slavic alphabet
   d. destroyed all pre-Christian temples

_____ 16. For his people Prince Vladimir of Rus chose
   a. Western Christianity
   b. Byzantine Christianity
   c. Islam
   d. Judaism

_____ 17. At the time of the East–West Schism, Michael Cerularius was the
   a. representative of the pope
   b. Eastern emperor
   c. Patriarch of Constantinople
   d. Ruler of Sicily

_____ 18. Cardinal Humbert
   a. placed a decree of excommunication on the altar of Hagia Sophia
   b. sent an envoy to bring about a reconciliation between East and West
   c. spoke Greek and was familiar with Eastern Christian practices
   d. represented the Patriarch of Constantinople in negotiations

_____ 19. The _filioque_ controversy had to do with
   a. who was leader of the Church
   b. priests marrying in the Eastern Church
   c. wording of the Nicene Creed
   d. Cardinal Humbert's view of the Eastern Church

_____ 20. The iconoclast controversy had to do with
   a. use of images in worship
   b. disagreements between East and West
   c. use of Latin in the liturgy
   d. whether priests could marry

_____ 21. Eastern Rite Catholics
   a. follow Western styles of worship
   b. are considered heretics by Rome
   c. are members of the Orthodox Church
   d. are in union with Rome

_____ 22. Scholasticism refers to
   a. using philosophy to criticize Christian teachings
   b. viewing reason as more important than faith
   c. studying the Scriptures in monasteries
   d. using reason to explain Christian teachings

_____ 23. Mendicants are known for
    a. living in monasteries
    b. developing farm techniques
    c. relying on charity from others
    d. being the oldest form of religious life

_____ 24. Albigensians believed that
    a. the physical and spiritual are both good
    b. the pope is not the true head of the Church
    c. heretics should be burned at the stake
    d. the physical world is evil

Matching (1 point each)

_____ 1. Francis of Assisi

_____ 2. Abbot Suger

_____ 3. Margaret

_____ 4. William of Aquitaine and Abbot Berno

_____ 5. Thomas Aquinas

_____ 6. Pope Leo III

_____ 7. Michael Cerularius

_____ 8. Hildebrand

_____ 9. Dominic

_____ 10. Clare

_____ 11. Cyril and Methodius

_____ 12. Vladimir

A. Reformed monasticism at Cluny

B. First member of the Order of Poor Ladies

C. Began the Order of Preachers

D. Began the Friars Minor

E. Brought about conversion of Scotland

F. Crowned Charlemagne Holy Roman Emperor

G. Started papal reforms

H. Responsible for conversion of Ukraine

I. Responsible for conversion of Slavs

J. Began Gothic architecture

K. Medieval philosopher and theologian

L. Patriarch of Constantinople

Identification (3 points each)

1. Scholasticism

2. *Summa Theologica*

3. *Deus vult!*

4. The Book of Kells

5. Great Chain of Being

6. Gregorian Reforms

7. Excommunication

8. Romanesque

Essays (5 points each)

1. Why are the Middle Ages in Europe also known as Christendom?

2. How did Charlemagne view his role as Holy Roman Emperor?

3. In what three ways did feudalism affect the Church?

4. What events led up to the East–West Schism?

5. In what way does Christian theology support pilgrimage as a religious activity?

6. What contribution did scholasticism make to the Church?

7. What led up to the crusades? How successful were they in attaining their goal?

8. Why were the mendicant orders a radical innovation for their time?

FEUDALISM AND THE CHURCH

Name_____ Date_____ Class period_____

The following passages from *The Catholic Encyclopedia* (1909 edition) describe some of the effects that feudalism had on the Church of the Middle Ages. Explain in your own words what each passage is saying about the dangers the Church faced from feudalism.

The Church, too, had her place in the feudal system. She too was granted territorial fiefs, became a vassal, possessed immunities. . . . In gratitude kings and emperors endowed her with property; and ecclesiastical property has not infrequently brought evils in its train. The result was disputed elections; younger sons of nobles were intruded into bishoprics, at times even into the papacy.

The cause of this was feudalism, for a system that had its basis on land tenure was bound at last to enslave a Church that possessed great landed possessions. In Germany, for example, three out of the mystically numbered seven electors of the empire were churchmen. There were, besides, several prince-bishops within the empire, and mitered abbots, whose rule was more extended and more powerful than that of many a secular baron.

The Church was in danger of becoming the annex of the State; the pope, of becoming the chaplain of the emperor.

PILGRIMAGE—MODEL OF THE CHRISTIAN LIFE

Name_____ Date_____ Class period_____

A group of pilgrims setting off to visit a holy shrine sounds medieval. However, pilgrimage actually models the Christian life itself. Read over the following accounts of pilgrimage and do one of the following:

- Write a pilgrimage story (real or fictional)
- Describe your life as pilgrimage
- Explain the significance of pilgrimage

Passages are from an anthology by Martin Robinson, *Sacred Places, Pilgrim Paths* (London: HarperCollins, 1997). Page numbers are for the Robinson text.

Pilgrimage is not like tourism, which sets out to see the sights. It has set before it a significant goal, one that has meaning for the traveller but has not been seen. . . . Companions have been invited and the journey will involve risks, hardships and excitement.

Christopher Ellis, *Together On The Way*, 27.

We all go on pilgrimage. It is part of our human yearning to associate places with people we love, with experiences which are precious, with events which are holy, and such places may be imbued with sanctity renewing our dedication, stimulating our devotion, and imparting a sense of healing, holiness, and peace.

Brother Ramon SSF, *The Heart of Prayer*, 17.

One of the most powerful features of early Christianity was its deep sense of the transitoriness of the present age and its eager waiting for the age to come. "Here we have no lasting city, but we are looking for the city that is to come" (Hebrews 13:14). We are only pilgrims on the way to "the Jerusalem above; she is free, and she is our mother" (Galatians 4:25–26). . . . Jesus lived the life of a wanderer and a pilgrim. Born in a manger, rejected by the social structures of security and comfort, Jesus' ministry pervaded throughout by the sense of homelessness. . . . He gathered his disciples, not into a secure and stable home, but to share in his work of an itinerant preacher of the Kingdom to come and a wandering healer of all kinds of sickness.

K. George, *The Silent Roots*, 15.

The pilgrim leaves his home. He is ready to forgo his familiar horizon; he extricates himself from habit, which so easily becomes routine and servitude. He goes off to an "elsewhere! Elsewhere is the Kingdom of God, peace!"

Who can fail to see that this is an opportunity to break away from the apathy of an inert existence from the servitude of sin and the chains of bad habits? An opportunity, for the person who goes out to the Other, to return as "another" person . . .

Francis Bourdeau, "Pilgrimage, Eucharist, Reconciliation," 29.

FROM DISORDER TO BEAUTY AND HOPE

The Road to the Renaissance

A Teacher's Prayer

Dear God, when I find my own life in disorder, remind me that the Church, the people whom you love, also faced difficult times. Keep my students and me on the road to our own renaissance, our own rebirth, discovering you in our lives anew. Amen.

Overview

This chapter begins with a discussion of a dark period in the history of the papacy. For a time, known in history as the Great Western Schism, two men claimed to be pope. Good people sided with one or the other claimant. During this same period the bubonic plague ravaged Europe; this event also had a great effect on the Church. Mysticism, which has always been a part of Christianity, found expression in some of history's most outstanding spiritual personages, even in the midst of the turmoil surrounding them. These were difficult times for Eastern Christianity as well. Constantinople, the longstanding center of Eastern Christianity, fell to the Turks (Muslims) in 1453. Toward the end of this period, the Renaissance blossomed throughout Europe and produced some of Western civilization's greatest works of art.

Major Concepts Covered in This Chapter

1 Introduction

2 The Great Western Schism

3 The Black Death

4 Medieval Mysticism

5 The Changing Geography of Christianity

6 The Renaissance

7 Chapter Review and Conclusion

Introduction

Prayer

pages
124–126

■ **Music Suggestions**

"Ashes" by Tom Conry from *Glory & Praise (Comprehensive)* (OCP), *Gather (Comprehensive)* (GIA).

"Canticle of the Turning" (Irish Traditional) from *Give Your Gifts, the Basics* (GIA, Harcourt Religion Publishers).

"God of Day and God of Darkness" by Marty Haugen from *Today's Missal* (OCP), *We Celebrate* (J.S. Paluch Co., Inc.).

"Hope at the Crossroads" by Michael Mahler from *Give Your Gifts, the New Songs* (GIA, Harcourt Religion Publishers).

"Jesus, Heal Us" by David Haas from *Gather (Comprehensive)* (GIA).

"Lay Your Hands Gently Upon Us" by Carey Landry from *Glory & Praise (Comprehensive)* (OCP).

"Raise Me Up" by Eric Becker from *Give Your Gifts, the New Songs* (GIA, Harcourt Religion Publishers).

"Standin' in the Need of Prayer," spiritual from *Gather (Comprehensive)* (GIA), *Lead Me, Guide Me* (GIA).

■ **Scripture Suggestions**

Isaiah 38:10–16

1 John 2:7–11, 14

Matthew 24:3–14

■ **Prayer**

See student text, page 124.

Overview

pages
124–126

1. Have the students read the **Chapter Overview** and timeline on pages 124–125. Briefly discuss some of the points and events noted.

2. You might want to begin discussion of the period by starting out on a positive note. To do that, direct the students' attention to the quote from Julian of Norwich on page 137. Read aloud the quote and then write on the board or overhead:

   God is —Creator

   —Protector

   —Lover

3. Ask the students to think about whether or not they agree with Julian's sentiments. Give them a few moments to write their thoughts on the Julian quote. Then point out to the students that the author of this quote wrote these words during a period when Europe and Christianity were experiencing many difficulties and tragedies. Nonetheless, this woman whom we know as Julian of Norwich was able to experience God's unsurpassed goodness in the midst of these dark times. She is not the only one of the period who experienced God's love personally and deeply. Now let us look at some of the troubles faced by the Church of the time.

4. Have the students complete the **Before We Begin . . .** activity on page 126. (You might instead assign this activity as homework before beginning the chapter and ask the students to report on their findings.)

The Great Western Schism

For over seventy years, popes reside away from Rome, in Avignon, present-day France. Immediately following this period, two men—one in Rome and one in Avignon—claim to be pope. The Council of Constance resolves this schism when all Church leaders of the West agree on one pope.

pages
127–131

DECLINE OF UNITY

Church-State Conflicts

The Avignon Papacy

Popes and Anti-Popes

Resolving the Schism

1. These sections of the chapter center on the papacy and conflicts surrounding the papacy. Direct the students to read the sections.

2. Write on the board or overhead:
    —Avignon Papacy
    —Great Western Schism

3. Ask the students:
    • Explain the difference between these two periods in Church history.
    • What led up to each event?
    • How was each event resolved?
    • How does the insert about Pope Celestine V help us understand problems facing the papacy at the time?
    • Why did election of Pope Urban VI lead to the schism?

4. Point out that the period of the Avignon papacy was not a time of schism. There was one pope recognized by all Christians. The schism occurred when two men claimed to be pope. Pope Celestine V and Pope Urban VI were validly elected popes, but both proved to be ineffective as pope and were challenged by many other Church leaders. Pope Celestine quickly resigned. In an attempt to oust Pope Urban from the papacy, cardinals elected another man pope, thus beginning the schism.

In-Text Activities

page 127

FYI

Using the FYI

You might ask the students to recall some of the events of the jubilee year 2000 or to interview an adult concerning events he or she recalls. Share these in a class discussion, and discuss the religious significance of each event.

<table>
<tr>
<td>page 130</td>
<td>

Pope Celestine V

Use the information provided as a springboard for a class discussion about the Avignon papacy and the Great Western Schism.

</td>
</tr>
</table>

pages 131–132

Pope or Council—Who Has the Greater Authority?

In-Text Activities

page 131   **DISCUSSION**

Using the Discussion

As we will see beginning in the next chapter, separate nation-states are one of the major characteristics of the modern era. Today with global communications' satellites, the Internet, multi-national corporations, and other nation-transcending resources, an emphasis on separate nations is diminishing. Early on, Christianity proclaimed that its message was not just for Jews and not just for Gentiles but for everyone. Therefore, the Church has been able to be a way of identifying with the human community, not just with a particular nation or section of the world.

<table>
<tr>
<td>page 132</td>
<td>

Saint Catherine of Siena

1. Use the **In-Text Discussion** to expand discussion of this section of text.

2. Further information on Catherine of Siena is available in books of lives of the saints and on the Internet.

</td>
</tr>
</table>

Additional Activities

FACTS ABOUT THE PAPACY

1. Since the papacy is the major concern of this section, it may be helpful for the students to know more about this unique position in the Catholic Church. **Handout 6–A, Facts about the Papacy,** provides the students with some interesting information about popes.

2. As an accompaniment to this handout, you might assign the students to write a report on a pope and make a brief presentation about him to the class.

THE EARTHY WISDOM OF SAINT CATHERINE OF SIENA

Although the experience of God is ultimately indescribable, Christians have regularly used images to speak about God. Catherine of Siena uses wonderfully earthy images when speaking about her experience of God. You might invite the students to think about this medieval woman's descriptions of how God acts in our lives by distributing **Handout 6–B, The Earthy Wisdom of Saint Catherine of Siena,** and allowing them time individually or in small groups to complete the assignments described on the handout.

CONCILIARISM—A DEBATE

1. Review with the students the debate about conciliarism following the Great Western Schism. After determining that the students understand the concept, mention to them that the Church has often grappled with the question of how best to lead the Christian community. For a number of reasons, conciliarism failed.

2. Discuss with the students: What could be the positive and negative results if there were Church governance by regular councils of Church leaders?

3. You might have a few students speak to a leader in a Presbyterian Church, which follows an expanded version of conciliarism. As part of the interview, tell the students to ask what the Presbyterian leader sees as strengths and weaknesses in the form of decision-making used in the Church. (If no Presbyterian Churches are in your area, ask a group of students to read about the way the Presbyterian Church makes decisions. The Internet is one source of information.) Instruct the students who gathered the information to present their findings to the class

Concept Review

In the late 1990s Pope John Paul II asked people to help him determine the best way the pope could be a force for good in the world. Discuss with the students what advice you would give about the types of actions the pope could be doing today.

page 132 ## Review Questions and Answers

1. **What is a jubilee year? When was the first jubilee year held?**

   A jubilee year, first held in 1300, is a special year of prayer and pilgrimages celebrated by the Catholic Church every fifty years.

2. **What action by the English and French kings created a conflict with Pope Boniface VIII? What was the pope's response?**

   The two kings made laws stating that clergy were to pay taxes. In response, Pope Boniface VIII issued a papal bull stating that all rulers are subject to the pope.

3. **To what does the term *Babylonian Captivity of the Papacy* refer?**

   Babylonian Captivity of the Papacy refers to the seventy years when popes resided in Avignon rather than in Rome.

4. **What two saints were instrumental in convincing the pope to return to Rome?**

   Saints Catherine of Siena and Bridget of Sweden helped convince the reigning pope to return to Rome.

5. **What action by the majority of cardinals at the time brought on the Great Western Schism?**

   After electing Pope Urban VI, all cardinals except one met in northern Italy and "elected" another man to be pope. He took up residence in Avignon.

6. **How was the Great Western Schism resolved?**

   The Council of Constance gained resignations from two men claiming to be pope and had a third claimant sent into exile. In 1417 the council declared the papal throne empty. Cardinals then elected Pope Martin V who was universally recognized as the one pope.

7. **How did the pope elected in 1958 resolve the question of the status of the earlier so-called Pope John XXIII?**

Giuseppe Roncalli took the name Pope John XXIII for himself, thus proclaiming that the earlier John XXIII was not a legitimate pope.

8. **What position on Church authority is held by conciliarism?**

Conciliarism is the belief that Church councils have greater authority than the pope does.

The Black Death

The bubonic plague devastates Europe and causes problems for the Church.

pages 133–135

THE BLACK DEATH

The Impact on the Church and Religious Life

The focus of this topic for a Church history course is the ways that the plague affected members of the Church and Church affairs. After the students have read the sections, use either the **In-Text Activity** or the **Handout** activity to provide them with an opportunity to reflect on the Church and the plague.

In-Text Activities

page 133 **WWW.**

page 135 **ACTIVITY**

Using the Activity

The students may want to focus on images for death. However, encourage them to think about the role that the Church and members of the Church can play in the face of a horrible situation such as that caused by the plague. Relate the topic to more recent situations of tragedy, and compare the role of the Church now with how it might have been then.

Additional Activities

THE BLACK DEATH AND CHRISTIAN LIFE

Handout 6–C, The Black Death and Christian Life, can be used to help the students consider how the plague altered the quality of sacramental celebrations and other Church practices. Distribute the handout and allow the students, either individually or as groups, to write responses to the questions raised. Use the questionnaire to discuss how Christians of the time responded to the devastation that surrounded them.

Concept Review

Discuss with the students what it must have been like to lose over a third of a community's population in a short period of time.

Review Questions and Answers

1. **As a result of the plague, what was the death toll in Europe?**

   As a result of the plague, over one-third of Europe's population died.

2. **What effect did the plague have on the quality of the celebration of the Mass and sacraments in Europe?**

   Since young, inexperienced men often took over as priests, they typically performed the Mass and sacraments inadequately, with a combination of poor Latin and superstitious gestures.

3. **What group underwent persecution because they were blamed for the plague?**

   In a number of localities, Christians blamed Jews for the plague and persecuted them.

Medieval Mysticism

Mystics achieve depths of spirituality and add greatly to the literature on Christian spirituality.

pages
136–137

MEDIEVAL MYSTICISM
A Mystic Describes God's Love

1. Mysticism is a theme that runs throughout Church history. Direct the students to read the two sections on medieval mysticism and Julian's description of God's love.

2. Then ask the students:

   • Does it make a difference whether or not someone believes in God? If so, what difference does it make?

   • Does it make a difference whether or not someone believes in a loving God? If so, what difference does it make?

3. After discussing these questions, ask the students: What are ways that we know the God of Christianity?

   (Even if this question has been raised in the past, it is important to relate this question to mysticism.)

4. The students may note that we come to know God through creation and through the community of believers (parents, friends, fellow parishioners and community members, other Christians throughout the world today). We also know what God is like through Scripture and Tradition. However, mystics are people who come to know God through *direct experience*. Christian mystics move from *knowledge* about God as revealed in Scripture, Tradition, and the Christian community, to *experience* of the living God. In a sense, mystics are living reminders of God's love revealed in Scripture, Tradition, and the Christian community.

5. Follow up this discussion by assigning the **In-Text Activity,** which can be done in small groups. Then use the Additional Activity to help the students understand the place of mysticism in the Christian life.

page 137   ## ACTIVITY

Using the Activity

1. Consider the sacraments, retreats for youth, youth conferences and rallies, spiritual direction, service, devotions, and so on.

2. Provide time for volunteers to share their creative expressions.

Additional Activities

FOUR STAGES OF LOVE, FOUR STAGES OF MYSTICISM

1. Saint Bernard of Clairvaux (1090–1153) offers a clear description of how Christians are drawn to mysticism. The description is found on **Handout 6–D, Four Stages of Love, Four Stages of Mysticism.** Distribute the handout and ask the students to describe the difference between "knowing about" someone and actually "knowing" someone.

   (We can know about an actor or a sports figure whom we have never met. We *know* people with whom we are intimate and share our lives.)

2. Then read aloud from the handout Saint Bernard's description of the four stages of love. Invite the students to write up responses to the questions on the handout. The students can then share their responses in pairs, in small groups, or as a class. Point out to the students that Christian faith is lifeless without knowing God, not simply knowing about God.

Concept Review

Discuss with the students:

- What is mysticism?
- What role do mystics play in the life of the Christian community?
- What is there in Christianity, especially in Catholicism, that leads so many people to mysticism?
- Does Catholicism today still have the power to draw people to true knowledge of God (mysticism)? If so, what is there in Catholicism today that promotes mysticism?
- Should Church leaders emphasize mysticism more than they do? Why or why not?

page 137   ## Review Questions and Answers

1. **What role does mysticism play in religion?**

   Mystics seek to experience God.

2. **Describe Meister Eckhart's negative theology.**

   Eckhart's negative theology reminds us that God completely surpasses any image or concept that we might have of him.

3. **How did Julian use the image of a hazelnut to describe her relationship with God?**

   Julian pointed out that, just as God creates, loves, and preserves a hazelnut, so God creates, loves, and preserves people.

Joan of Arc—Maid of Orleans

Point out to the students that the Joan of Arc story has fascinated people ever since her time. It demonstrates how sainthood and living the Christian life can take many forms. Being a teenager, being a young girl who led troops in battle, being a Christian who fought for one Christian ruler against another, being someone who denied her "voices" and then changed her statement—none of this prevented the Church from recognizing Joan's sanctity.

The Changing Geography of Christianity

After the fall of Constantinople, Russian leaders see their country as the Third Rome and as the new center of Orthodox Christianity. Under Isabella and Ferdinand, Christianity is restored as the official religion of all of Spain.

pages
139–141

EVER-CHANGING GEOGRAPHY

The Fall of Constantinople

The Restoration of Christianity to Spain and Its Introduction to the New World

1. This section looks at two events that occurred in the fifteenth century that changed the geography of Christianity: the fall of Constantinople and the Restoration of Christian rule to Spain. Both involved Muslims. Begin by asking the students to share their impressions of Muslims. Be sure to explain that mainline Muslims have an emphasis on peace; it is fringe radicals who are responsible for an often misguided emphasis on holy war.

2. Direct the students to read the section on the fall of Constantinople and discuss why the Union of Florence was rejected by most Eastern Christians. You might assign a group of the students to research the Council of Florence and report to the class on its reception by Eastern Christians. You might also assign the students to research the Russian Orthodox Church, especially its ascendancy following the fall of Constantinople.

3. Many students may have heard about the Spanish Inquisition without knowing all that it entailed. Even scholars disagree about the severity of the Inquisition and the role of Church leaders in carrying it out. The period following the restoration of Christian rule over Spain was not one of tolerance, and Jews and Muslims suffered under the Inquisition. Assign another group of the students to research the Spanish Inquisition and prepare a report for the class about it.

4. After the students have read the section, discuss with them how the Inquisition was carried out and why the way it was done, especially in Spain, often violated Christian principles.

page 141   ACTIVITY

Using the Activity

This activity suggests that circumstances caused paranoia and xenophobia to increase during certain periods, such as the early fifties in the U.S. when fear of Communism was widespread, the late sixties when anti-government protests were great, and the period following the terrorist attacks of September 11, 2001. In order to help them understand the societal atmosphere underlying the Spanish Inquisition, the activity asks the students to think about possible sources of societal paranoia and xenophobia today. Again, when it comes to religious groups, clarify the distinction between religions such as Islam (which preaches love and peace) and groups claiming to be part of Islam who preach hate and violence.

CoNCept ReViEw

Ask the students:

• What was your understanding of the Spanish Inquisition before this lesson?

• Has your understanding of it changed in any way because of your study of it? If so, how?

page 141   **Review Questions and Answers**

1. **What crisis led Eastern leaders to seek union with the Western Church?**

   Eastern leaders sought union with the Western Church when the Turks threatened to overtake Constantinople.

2. **What was the Union of Florence? Why did it fail to hold?**

   The Union of Florence was an agreement of union between Eastern and Western Church leaders. It failed to hold because many Eastern Christians intensely disliked Western Christians, mainly because of their behavior during the crusades.

3. **How and when did the Roman Empire end?**

   The Roman Empire ended when Constantinople fell to the Turks in 1453.

4. **Which country saw itself as inheriting the legacy of Rome after the fall of Constantinople?**

   After the fall of Constantinople, Russia saw itself as the Third Rome.

5. **How did Isabella and Ferdinand go about insuring the Christianization of their nation?**

   Isabella and Ferdinand called for the conversion or expulsion of non-Christians in Spain.

6. **What discovery in 1492 opened new lands to Christianity?**

   Columbus discovered the Americas in 1492, leading to a flurry of missionary activity in this New World.

The Renaissance

A rebirth of culture reflecting the spirit of classical Greece and Rome begins in Italy and spreads throughout Europe.

pages
142–143

THE RENAISSANCE

1. You might use this section to discuss with the students Christian works of art. Assign the students to read the section on the Renaissance and then assign the **In-Text Activity.**

2. If possible, make available examples of Christian visual art and ask the students to write about one work of art that they believe conveys a sense of the sacred. Invite the students to explain their choices.

In-Text Activities

page 142 **FYI**

page 143 **YOUTH NEWS**

Using the Youth News

Ask the students to share information regarding the arts in the school and in the larger community. Post dates for concerts and plays. Borrow student art from the art department to hang in the classroom.

ACTIVITY

Using the Activity

Take time in class to share the students' findings for these activities.

Additional Activities

GUEST LECTURE ON RENAISSANCE ART

You might invite an art teacher or a representative from a local museum or art school to speak about Renaissance art, especially about religious themes in Renaissance art. If possible, ask the guest speaker to bring slides of representative art.

TEACHERS OF THE ARTS

Invite teachers from the school's departments of art, drama, literature, and music to share their understanding of the relationship between religion and the arts. Ask them to explain as well the programs they sponsor, both within the school schedule and as extracurriculars.

CONCEPT REVIEW

Discuss with the students:

- During the Renaissance, art typically dealt with religious themes. Do you believe that there is an affinity between art and Christianity? If so, what is the nature of that affinity?

- Would you like to see the Church and individual Christians support the arts to a greater degree? Why or why not?

- A saying from the Hindu tradition reads, "If I had two loaves of bread, I would sell one and buy flowers." What does the saying imply about the importance of art and beauty? Do you agree with the message of the saying?

Dissenting Opinions during the Renaissance

1. The last section of the chapter leads into the next chapter on the Reformation. Direct the students to read the section.

2. Then write on the board or overhead the names:
   —John Wyclif
   —John Hus
   —Savonarola

   Ask the students:
   • What message did each of these figures preach?
   • What challenge did each of them present to the Church of the time?

CoNCept RevieW

Use the above questions as a review of the section. Tell the students that these three figures anticipate the Reformation, which will be the topic of the next chapter.

Review Questions and Answers

1. **What and when was the Renaissance?**

   The Renaissance was a rebirth of interest in classical Greek and Roman culture that lasted in Western Europe approximately from the fourteenth to the sixteenth centuries.

2. **Where did the Renaissance begin?**

   The Renaissance began in Italy where stability and commerce fostered such a rebirth.

3. **Who is the model for the "Renaissance man"?**

   Leonardo da Vinci, who was a scientist, inventor, artist, and all-around scholar, modeled the "Renaissance man"—that is, someone skilled and knowledgeable in a number of areas.

4. **Name two creations of Michelangelo.**

   Michelangelo sculpted the statue of David in Florence and *La Pietà* in Saint Peter's Basilica. He also painted the ceiling of the Sistine Chapel.

5. **What two positions did John Wyclif hold that would later be advocated by Protestants?**

   John Wyclif proposed that Scripture is more important than Tradition for Christian teaching and that all Christians together are the Church, with no ruler except Jesus.

6. **What was the focus of the sermons of John Hus?**

   John Hus criticized conditions in the Church and called upon it to return to the poverty and simplicity of the Gospels.

7. **What happened that turned the people of Florence against Savonarola?**

   When Savonarola attacked the pope, the pope responded by placing an interdict on Florence, denying the people of the city the Mass and sacraments. Because of the interdict, the people of Florence turned against Savonarola.

Chapter Review and Conclusion

REVIEW

1. Ask the students to summarize the main points in the chapter using their own words. Write notes on the board from their contributions. To reinforce their summary, you might want to review the major concepts in this chapter in the teaching manual. Then read the **Conclusion** on page 145.

2. Review the vocabulary in this chapter:

> **jubilee year**—a special year of prayer and pilgrimage in the Catholic Church that takes place every fifty years; also called a holy year (page 127)
>
> **papal bull**—a formal decree by a pope sealed with a round leaden seal (in Latin, *bulla*) (page 127)
>
> **Babylonian Captivity of the Papacy**—period during which the pope resided in Avignon, (France) in the Kingdom of Naples (page 128)
>
> **Great Western Schism**—the period from 1378 to 1417 during which two and then three rival people claimed papal authority (page 129)
>
> **conciliarism**—belief that Church councils have greater authority than the pope (page 131)
>
> **Black Death**—popular name for the bubonic plague, so named because body parts turned black from lack of blood (page 133)
>
> **mysticism**—the highest expression of Christian prayer—communion with God (page 136)
>
> **negative theology**—belief that God can never be known by the intellect (page 136)
>
> **showing**—Julian of Norwich's term for her mystical encounters with Christ (page 137)
>
> **Union of Florence**—a short-lived agreement between leaders of Eastern and Western Christianity on certain doctrines of faith (page 139)
>
> **Spanish Inquisition**—the process in Spain for identifying and punishing non-Christians and those said to be heretics (page 140)
>
> *conversos*—Jews and Muslims who converted to Christianity, either willingly or unwillingly, following the Christian takeover of Spain (page 141)
>
> **humanism**—during the Renaissance, an emphasis on the human in intellectual and artistic activity (page 142)
>
> *La Pietà*—Michelangelo's statue of Mary holding the crucified Jesus (page 143)
>
> **interdict**—prohibition against celebrating sacraments in a particular area (page 144)

TEST

Give the students the Chapter 6 Test or an alternative assessment. The tests have been placed on the Harcourt Religion Publishers' Web page. This has been done to enable the teacher to customize this material for local needs. First contact Harcourt Religion Publishers' high school consultant at 800-922-7696, ext. 3781 for a user ID and password. Then connect with the Harcourt Religion Publishers' Web site at **www.harcourtreligion.com** to download the information. Collect the tests for grading.

Chapter 6 Test Answers

MULTIPLE CHOICE (1 point each)

1. c	4. a	7. b	10. a	13. c	16. d
2. a	5. b	8. a	11. c	14. b	17. c
3. d	6. a	9. c	12. b	15. a	18. b

MATCHING (2 points each)

Set 1			Set 2		
1. C	3. B	5. D	1. D	3. F	5. B
2. E	4. A	6. F	2. C	4. A	6. E

IDENTIFICATION (3 points each)

1. Papal Bull *Unam Sanctam*—statement issued by Pope Boniface VIII in 1302, stating that all rulers are subject to the pope and that it was "necessary for salvation" for every human to be subject to the pope

2. Avignon Papacy—period of seventy years during which the popes resided in the town of Avignon in the kingdom of Naples

3. Anti-popes—men who called themselves pope but resided in Avignon during the thirty-eight years of the Great Schism; not recognized as valid popes

4. Great Western Schism—the period from 1378 to 1417 during which two and then three rival people claimed papal authority

5. Conciliarism—belief that Church councils have greater authority than the pope

6. Mysticism—the highest expression of Christian prayer—communion with God

7. Negative Theology—belief that God can never be known by the intellect

8. Union of Florence—a short-lived agreement between leaders of Eastern and Western Christianity on certain doctrines of faith

9. Spanish Inquisition—the process in Spain for identifying and punishing non-Christians and those said to be heretics

10. *Conversos*—Jews and Muslims who converted to Christianity, either willingly or unwillingly, following the Christian takeover of Spain

11. Interdict—prohibition against celebrating sacraments in a particular area

ESSAYS (5 points each)

1. Prior to the Great Western Schism the pope had lived away from Rome, in Avignon, which is in modern-day France. An aging pope was convinced to return to Rome, but soon died. Cardinals, most of whom were French, elected an Italian to replace him. However, many Church leaders came to dislike the new pope's autocratic style. A number of cardinals elected as "pope" another man, who took up residence in Avignon. The Great Western Schism refers to the period when two men claimed to be pope. A Church council resolved the schism.

2. The Black Death caused the death of many Church leaders. It also led to a focus on death and the afterlife among Church members. Many people turned to superstition or sought scapegoats in response to the plague.

3. Medieval mystics experienced a strong, tangible sense of communion with God.

4. The Spanish Inquisition began as Christian rulers were reclaiming control of Spain from Muslims. The Inquisition refers to trials, overseen by Church authorities, determining whether or not converts to Christianity from Judaism or Islam were sincere in their beliefs. The Inquisition created an atmosphere of fear and suspicion among people. It also led to numerous abuses, since people could accuse others of attacking Christianity either from within or from outside the Church.

5. The spirit of the Renaissance was one of glorying in the human as exemplified in the classical Greek and Roman era.

Prayer

Music Suggestions

"All Things New" by Rory Cooney from *Give Your Gifts, the Basics* (GIA, Harcourt Religion Publishers).

"Follow the Light" by Richard Putori and Christopher Dutkiewicz from *Give Your Gifts, the New Songs* (GIA, Harcourt Religion Publishers).

"Givin' Back the Gifts" by Larry Schexnaydre and Rhett Glindmeyer from *Give Your Gifts, the New Songs* (GIA, Harcourt Religion Publishers).

"How Can I Keep From Singing" Quaker Song from *Today's Missal* (OCP), *Gather (Comprehensive)* (GIA), *Glory & Praise (Comprehensive)* (OCP).

"Join in the Dance" by Dan Schutte from *Today's Missal* (OCP).

"Joyfully Singing" by The Dameans from *Give Your Gifts, the Songs* (GIA, Harcourt Religion Publishers).

"Let Us Go Rejoicing" by Jeanne Cotter from *Give Your Gifts, the Songs* (GIA, Harcourt Religion Publishers).

"Lord of the Dance," Shaker Song from *Gather* (GIA), *Today's Missal* (OCP).

Scripture Suggestions

Psalm 150

1 John 3:18–24

Luke 14:16–23

Prayer

Come, my Light, and illumine my darkness.
Come, my Life, and revive me from death.
Come, my Physician, and heal my wounds.
Come, Flame of divine love, and burn up the thorns of my sins,
    kindling my heart with the flame of your love.
Come, my King, sit upon the throne of my heart and reign there.
For you alone are my King and my Lord.

Saint Dimitrii of Rostov

CHAPTER 6 TEST

Name_____ Date_____ Class period_____

Test is made up of questions with suggested values totaling 100 points.

Multiple Choice (1 point each)

_____ 1. Christians flocked to Rome in 1300 because
   a. an unpopular pope was about to be elected
   b. two men claimed to be pope
   c. the first jubilee year was taking place
   d. Saint Peter's Basilica was completed

_____ 2. Avignon was a city in
   a. the kingdom of Naples in modern-day France
   b. English territory in modern-day France
   c. the Papal States in modern-day Italy
   d. the Holy Roman Empire in modern-day Germany

_____ 3. Petrarch equated the Avignon papacy to
   a. the Tower of Babel
   b. the Exodus
   c. David and Goliath
   d. the Babylonian Captivity

_____ 4. Someone who helped bring about the return of the pope to Rome was
   a. Catherine of Siena
   b. Roger of Geneva
   c. King Philip IV
   d. Pope Celestine V

_____ 5. Immediately before resolution of the Great Western Schism, _____ men claimed to be pope.
   a. two
   b. three
   c. four
   d. five

_____ 6. The Great Western Schism was resolved by
   a. a Church council
   b. the people of Rome
   c. military intervention
   d. the Black Death

_____ 7. The bubonic plague began by way of
     a. knights returning from the crusades
     b. rats aboard ships
     c. untreated drinking water
     d. medieval medical practices

_____ 8. The Black Death received its name because of
     a. body parts turning black from lack of blood
     b. the image of death as the grim reaper
     c. burial shrouds used to dispose of the dead
     d. a plague mentioned in the Bible

_____ 9. One group blamed for the Black Death were
     a. priests
     b. doctors
     c. Jews
     d. Protestants

_____ 10. One problem facing the Church because of the Black Death was
     a. the decline of monasticism
     b. the death of a talented pope
     c. priests and nuns marrying
     d. missionaries dying in faraway lands

_____ 11. Mysticism refers to knowing God through
     a. reading Scriptures
     b. reciting prayers
     c. direct experience
     d. devotion to saints

_____ 12. The message Julian of Norwich received from her vision of a hazelnut was that
     a. we are worth very little
     b. God loves us
     c. nuts grow into trees
     d. nature is beautiful

_____ 13. Joan of Arc died by being
     a. beheaded
     b. left to die in prison
     c. burned at the stake
     d. killed in battle

_____ 14. In 1439 Eastern Christians sent delegates to the West because
     a. the plague had caused devastation
     b. Ottoman Turks surrounded Constantinople
     c. they wanted a united Christianity
     d. the pope had offered them help

_____ 15. The Renaissance began in
  a. Italy
  b. Germany
  c. France
  d. Spain

_____ 16. John Wyclif anticipated Protestantism by proposing that
  a. sacraments should be eliminated
  b. the Bible contains falsehoods
  c. the pope alone should decide Church matters
  d. Scripture is more important than Tradition

_____ 17. After the fall of Constantinople, the country that saw itself as the Third Rome was
  a. Italy
  b. China
  c. Russia
  d. Germany

_____ 18. The model "Renaissance man"—artist, inventor, and all-around scholar—was
  a. Michelangelo
  b. Leonardo da Vinci
  c. Raphael
  d. Fra Angelico

Matching (2 points each)

SET 1

_____ 1. Torquemada	A. Teenager who led troops	
_____ 2. Meister Eckhart	B. Wrote "showings" describing mystical experiences	
_____ 3. Julian of Norwich	C. Oversaw Spanish Inquisition	
_____ 4. Joan of Arc	D. Urged the pope to reside in Rome	
_____ 5. Bridget of Sweden	E. Dominican preacher who wrote about mysticism	
_____ 6. Savonarola	F. Called for Church reform in Florence	

SET 2

_____ 1. *Unam Sanctam*	A. We can never fully comprehend God	
_____ 2. Union of Florence	B. Converted to Christianity	
_____ 3. Interdict	C. Temporary resolution to East–West Schism	
_____ 4. Negative theology	D. Secular rulers are subject to the pope	
_____ 5. *Conversos*	E. Classical Greek and Roman influence	
_____ 6. Humanism	F. Refusal to administer sacraments	

From Disorder to Beauty and Hope

Identification (3 points each)

1. Papal Bull *Unam Sanctam*—

2. Avignon Papacy—

3. Anti-popes—

4. Great Western Schism—

5. Conciliarism—

6. Mysticism—

7. Negative Theology—

8. Union of Florence—

9. Spanish Inquisition—

10. *Conversos*—

11. Interdict—

Essays (5 points each)

1. Name the factors that led up to the Great Western Schism. Explain how the schism was resolved.

2. Describe two ways that the Black Death affected the Church and two responses that people had to the Black Death.

3. From the point of view of a medieval mystic, describe mysticism.

4. What was the Spanish Inquisition? What events created the atmosphere leading up to the Inquisition?

5. Describe the spirit of the Renaissance.

FACTS ABOUT THE PAPACY

Name_____ Date_____ Class period_____

The papacy has been around for many centuries. It is not surprising, therefore, that many customs have developed related to this important office. Here is some information about the papacy that you may not have known.

TITLES FOR THE POPE
- **His Holiness the Pope**
- **The Bishop of Rome**
- **The Vicar of Jesus Christ**
- **Successor of Saint Peter**
- **Prince of the Apostles**
- **Supreme Pontiff**
- **Archbishop and Metropolitan of the Roman Province**
- **Primate of Italy**
- **Patriarch of the West**
- **Sovereign of the State of Vatican City**
- **Servant of the Servants of God**

Including John Paul II, there have been 266 popes. Seventy-eight are recognized as saints, and ten have been declared Blessed.

NATIONALITIES OF THE POPES

215	Italians (77 born in Rome)	2	Spanish
14	French	2	Africans
11	Greeks	1	Galilean
6	Germans	1	Dutch
6	Syrians	1	Portuguese
3	Sicilians	1	English
2	Sardinians	1	Polish

Pope Pius IX reigned the longest—from June 16, 1846, to February 7, 1878 (over 31 years).

Pope Urban VII had the shortest reign—from September 15 to September 27, 1590 (12 days).

Name_____ Date_____ Class period_____

WHY DOES THE POPE WEAR WHITE?

In 1566 a Dominican friar was elected Pope Pius V. He continued wearing his white Dominican habit, and from that time on popes have worn white robes. Beginning with Pope Pius VI (1775–1799), popes began wearing a white skullcap called a *zucchetto*. Beginning in the Middle Ages, popes also wore special red slippers with gold crosses embroidered on them. Up until the time of Pope John XXIII (1958–1962), clergy knelt and kissed the cross as a sign of respect. Pope John Paul II, elected pope in 1978, does not wear these "Shoes of the Fisherman" and instead prefers loafers and tennis shoes.

WHY DO POPES CHANGE THEIR NAMES?

In 535 a priest named Mercury was elected pope. He did not think his name, that of a Roman god, appropriate for a pope. He therefore took the name Pope John II. He was the first pope to change his name since Simon had become Peter. However, changing names did not become customary until 1009 when a bishop named Pietro was elected. Out of respect to Saint Peter, he took the name Pope Sergius V. From then on with two exceptions, popes chose new names.

OTHER FACTS

- Before the Polish Pope John Paul II, the last non-Italian pope was Adrian VI (1522–1523), who was Dutch.
- Pope Urban VI (1378) was the last non-cardinal elected pope. Following his election the Great Western Schism began.
- In the eleventh century, Pope Benedict IX was pope three different times.
- The last pope declared a saint was Pope Pius X (1903–1914). In 2000, Pope Pius IX and Pope John XXIII were declared Blessed.

On official papal documents, "p.p." is written behind the pope's name.
It means "Pastor of Pastors."

THE EARTHLY WISDOM OF SAINT CATHERINE OF SIENA

Name_____ Date_____ Class period_____

Catherine of Siena was the twenty-fourth of twenty-five children. Her father wanted her to marry when she turned fifteen, but Catherine had already decided that she wanted to give her life to God in some other fashion. Angry at his daughter for refusing to marry, Catherine's father dismissed the family maid and required Catherine to take care of all the household chores. Experiences such as this Cinderella story give Catherine's letters and other writings an earthy feel to them. Explain the earthy images Catherine uses in each of these passages. Then try your hand at writing about the experience of God using an image from your own experience or worldview.

O sweet Lamb roasted by the fire of divine charity on the stake of the cross! O most delightful food, full of joy, happiness and consolation. There is nothing lacking in you, because for the soul that truly serves you, you become her table, food and waiter. We see well that the Father is the table and bed where the soul can rest. We see the Word, his only Son, who is given to you as food, with so much fire of love. Who brings it to you? The waiter is the Holy Spirit. Because of the great love he has for us, he is not satisfied that we are served by others, but he himself wants to be the waiter. (pages 30–31)

In this life [we] can have nothing but the crumbs that fall from the dinner table as in Canaan. The crumbs are the grace that we receive from the Lord's table. But when we shall be in everlasting life where we will taste God and see him face to face, then we will have the food of the table. (page 32)

If you had a burning lamp and all the world came to you for light, the light of your lamp would not be diminished by sharing it, yet each person who shared it would have the whole light. (page 44)

The one who has made of herself a garden of self-knowledge is strong against the entire world, because she is conformed and made one with the supreme strength. She truly begins in this life to enjoy a foretaste of eternal life. She rules the world. (page 60)

I write you with desire to see you with such light and knowledge that you will see what you need to cut off and what not to release. For whoever does not cut, always remains bound, and whoever does not flee, always remains caught. (page 91)

We are pilgrims . . . [the Word Incarnate] has accompanied us on our pilgrimage and given himself to us as food to make us run bravely. (page 110)

Quotes are from Giuliana Cavallini, *Things Visible and Invisible:
Images in the Spirituality of Saint Catherine of Siena* (New York: Alba House, 1996).

THE BLACK DEATH AND THE CHURCH

Name_____ Date_____ Class period_____

During the plague, people tried anything to ward off the suffering and death caused by it. At times, Christians reverted to pre-Christian superstitions or used Christian practices as if they were magic. Matters were not helped by the large death toll. When leaders and educated persons died, people were left to their own resources. The quality of sacramental life diminished as untrained priests attempted to carry on the work of the Church.

   Use the following questions to think about how Christians of the time responded to the plague, and how people today might respond.

1. Describe some of the ways that people responded to the Black Death during the time that it ravaged Europe.

2. When the bubonic plague struck Western Europe, killing over a third of its population, the continent had been Christian-dominated for around a thousand years. Did their Christian faith make a difference in how people experienced and responded to the plague? How might their response to the plague have been different if Christianity had never entered Europe?

3. Do people tend to become more or less religious during an event such as the Black Death? What forms does religion tend to take? What aspects of religion tend to become emphasized?

4. If an outbreak of an unknown and incurable disease plagued our world today, what are some ways that people might respond? How would their response be similar to or different from that of people in the Middle Ages? Would religion become more or less important in most people's lives?

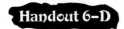

FOUR STAGES OF LOVE, FOUR STAGES OF MYSTICISM

Name_____ Date_____ Class period_____

Saint Bernard of Clairvaux was a monk who wrote *On the Love of God*. In that work he describes what he sees as stages leading up to mystical experience. Read his description of the stages and then answer the questions that follow.

What are the four stages of love?

- First, we love ourselves for our own sake. Since we are unspiritual and worldly, we cannot be interested in anything that does not relate to ourselves.

- Second, when we begin to see that we cannot get along by ourselves, we begin to seek God for our own sakes. We love God, but only for our own interests.

- Third, if we begin to worship God and come into his presence repeatedly by meditating, reading, praying, and obeying, little by little we come to know God through experience. By tasting how sweet the Lord is, we begin to love God, not for our own sake, but for himself.

- I am not certain that the fourth stage of love, in which we love ourselves only for the sake of God, may be perfectly attained in this life. But whenever it happens, we experience the joy of the Lord and forget ourselves in a wonderful way. We are, for those moments, of one mind and one spirit with God.

> Quoted in *Breakfast with the Saints*, selected by LaVonne Neff
> [Ann Arbor, MI: Servant Publications, 1996], 23.

1. Do these stages apply to love between two people? Explain.

2. Is this an accurate description of how people tend to come to love of God? Explain.

3. Do you see yourself anywhere along these stages of love? Explain.

CHAPTER SEVEN

CHALLENGE AND RESPONSE
The Church in Disunity

A Teacher's Prayer

Loving God, help my students appreciate that your Spirit continues to be present even when members of your Church argue and disagree. May we come to learn how harsh words can lead to harsh actions but that your desire is for all people to be one in Christ Jesus. Amen.

Overview

This chapter limits itself to the sixteenth century, when the Reformation transformed Western Christianity into the denominational Christian world that exists today. While the focus of the chapter and the course is the history of the Catholic Church, necessarily the text describes key concepts of Protestantism against Catholicism.

Major Concepts Covered in This Chapter

① **Introduction**

② **The Reformation Story**

③ **Causes of the Reformation**

④ **Protestant and Catholic Theological Differences**

⑤ **The Catholic Reformation**

⑥ **New Religious Orders**

⑦ **Chapter Review and Conclusion**

Introduction

Prayer

pages
146–148

■ **Music Suggestions**

"Change Our Hearts" by Rory Cooney from *Glory & Praise (Comprehensive)* (OCP), *Gather (Comprehensive)* (GIA), *Today's Missal* (OCP).

"Church of God" by Margaret Daly from *Gather (Comprehensive)* (GIA), *Glory & Praise (Comprehensive)* (OCP), *Today's Missal* (OCP).

"Hope at the Crossroads" by Michael Mahler from *Give Your Gifts, the New Songs* (GIA, Harcourt Religion Publishers).

"One in His Name" by Larry Schexnaydre and Kenny Braud from *Give Your Gifts, the New Songs* (GIA, Harcourt Religion Publishers).

"One Spirit, One Church" by Kevin Keil from *Today's Missal* (OCP).

"Song of the Body of Christ"/ "Canción del Cuerpo de Cristo" by David Haas, Spanish Trans. by Donna Peña, from *Gather (Comprehensive)* (GIA), *Today's Missal* (OCP).

"With You by My Side" by David Haas from *Give Your Gifts, the New Songs* (GIA, Harcourt Religion Publishers).

■ **Scripture Suggestions**

Baruch 3:9, 13–14

Colossians 3:12–14 (page 146)

Matthew 7:15–20

■ **Prayer**

God our Father,
source of unity and love,
make your faithful people one in heart
and mind
that your Church may live in harmony;
be steadfast in its profession of faith,
and secure in unity.
We ask this through our Lord Jesus Christ,
your Son,
who lives and reigns with you and the
Holy Spirit,
one God, for ever and ever.
Amen.

Opening Prayer for
Promoting Harmony, #42.

pages
146–148

Overview

1. Have the students read the **Chapter Overview** and timeline on pages 146–147. Briefly discuss some of the points and events noted.

2. Have the students complete the **Before We Begin . . .** activity on page 148. (You might instead assign this activity as homework before beginning the chapter and ask the students to report on their findings.)

The Reformation Story

After Martin Luther challenges the interpretation of certain practices in 1517, by the middle of the sixteenth century developments lead to a split in the Western Church.

pages
148–152

THE PROTESTANT REFORMATION

Protestantism Develops

Luther's Ninety-Five Theses—The Reformation Begins

LUTHER ON INDULGENCES

Church Teaching on Indulgences

1. If you are not familiar with the story of events leading up to the Protestant-Catholic split, read about it in a Church history book that provides greater detail than this present text can include.

2. After the students have read about the Reformation, you might review with them events that led to Protestantism becoming a separate and distinct entity. Use the following questions in discussing these events:

   - What were the ninety-five theses? What role did they play in leading the way to the Protestant movement? How did the pope's representative respond to Martin Luther's concerns?

   - What are indulgences? What was happening in 1517 that made indulgences a controversial issue? How might the teaching on indulgences be misinterpreted?

   - What role did the following people play leading up to a Protestant-Catholic split: Archbishop Albrecht, John Tetzel, Pope Leo X, Duke Frederick of Saxony, Emperor Charles V?

   - What was the Peasants' Revolt? How did such revolts add to the atmosphere of rebellion and intolerance that existed at the time?

   - What action by Luther before the Diet of Worms cemented his position against Church authority?

   - What decision called the Peace of Augsburg finalized a Lutheran-Catholic split?

In-Text Activities

page 150   **FYI**

   Using the FYI

See the following **Additional Activity** and **Handout 7–A.**

Additional Activities

A SAMPLING OF LUTHER'S NINETY-FIVE THESES

Some of Martin Luther's theses on indulgences are included in the text on page 151. **Handout 7–A, A Sampling of Luther's Ninety-Five Theses,** includes several other theses. After reading the theses, the students are asked to summarize three key beliefs of Luther. Follow up with a large group discussion of the beliefs summarized by the students.

POSTERS ON REFORMATION FIGURES

1. **Handout 7–B, Figures of the Reformation,** lists twenty-four persons related to religious developments during the volatile sixteenth century. Most of them are mentioned in the chapter. Before the classes on the Reformation period, you might ask the students to make posters of the various Reformation-era figures as described on the handout. To avoid duplication, pass around a sheet on which the students can sign their name and one of the figures. The students should research their particular figure and prepare a poster about the person.

2. Designate a day on which the students should bring in their posters and hang them around the room. Invite the students to walk around the room to learn about the various figures. Tell them that they will be responsible for explaining the importance of at least three of the persons on the posters. (You might include such a question in an end-of-chapter test.) Keep the posters up and refer to them as you discuss the Reformation.

   Note: If you are not familiar with Sebastian Castellio (1515–1563), he is an interesting figure who exemplifies the conflicts of the time. In 1540 Castellio witnessed the execution of three Lutherans for heresy in Catholic France. He was so shaken that he went to Switzerland and joined the Calvinists there. In Geneva he found that Calvin was executing people who disagreed with his teachings as well. Castellio left Geneva and anonymously wrote a book against killing people for their beliefs. The Reformation was not a time for tolerance among religions. Even today many wars are fought between religious groups. As we will see, the Catholic Church approved a document on religious liberty during its Second Vatican Council four hundred years later stating that people should not be persecuted for their religious beliefs.

Concept Review

1. Discuss with the students:

   - Do you think that anyone at the time anticipated that there would be separate and divided Churches as a result of decisions made during the first half of the sixteenth century? Why or why not?

   - Do you think that anyone at the time wanted a divided Church? Why or why not?

2. Remind the students that many educated Christians saw a need for reform of the Church. They did not intend to create a divided Church. This was true for Martin Luther as well. To support this position, read aloud to your students the following statement by historian Karl Steck:

   The split of Western Christendom into at least two major groups, which we take for granted, was indeed in the offing, but it became a permanent reality only after Luther's death. . . . At all events Luther wrote only for Catholics, and it was Catholics who felt attracted or repelled by his findings, by his new understanding of Christianity. . . . Luther never envisaged the Christianity split up into "confessions" that we know today (and view as perfectly natural), and he would scarcely have approved it.

   Alfred Lapple, *The Catholic Church: A Brief History*
   (New York: Paulist Press, 1982), 62–63.

Review Questions and Answers

1. **How was Western Christianity changed as a result of the Reformation?**

   As a result of the Reformation, European Christianity went from being a united Church to being fragmented into Catholicism and various Protestant denominations.

2. **What action by Martin Luther led the way to the Reformation? What was he protesting?**

   In 1517 Martin Luther wrote a German bishop protesting in particular the selling of indulgences then occurring in Germany.

3. **Name three factors that helped enflame Luther's protest.**

   Luther's protest was enflamed by the taxation in which Church leaders were involved, by the fact that money was being taken out of Germany to finance projects in Rome, and by the perception that Church leaders were corrupt and decadent.

4. **How did the papal representative initially respond to charges against Luther?**

   The papal representative initially condemned Luther for questioning the pope's authority.

THE BREAK WITH CATHOLICISM

Peasants' Revolt

Use the vocabulary words on these two pages to initiate an oral, class summary of each section of text.

In-Text Activities

ACTIVITY

Using the Activity

It may be necessary to distinguish between teachings and practices that cannot change and those that can. In other words, just because someone objects to a teaching or practice doesn't mean that it will or can change. On the other hand, there is a hierarchy of truths in the Church, and not all teachings and practices will remain as they are today. For example, the way the Sacrament of Reconciliation has been celebrated has varied over the centuries.

Additional Activities

WHY LUTHER?

Martin Luther is such a key figure in the history of Christianity that he deserves study. Much has been written about him, his personal life, and his beliefs. **Handout 7–C, Martin Luther—Reformer and Rebel,** lists four qualities possessed by Luther that made him a natural candidate for the role he played. You might ask the students to find information about Luther and to list characteristics about him that would support his role as a reformer and a rebel. (If you think the students need some direction in this assignment, distribute the handout first. Otherwise, allow the students to arrive at their own list of characteristics.) Invite the students to report on their research; make a class list of Luther's qualities.

CoNCepT ReViEw

Discuss with the students the following statement: The Reformation was about economic, political, and social issues as much as it was about religious issues.

(A number of conditions at the time precipitated the Reformation. For instance, the pope had to make decisions between upsetting the emperor, whose aunt Catherine was the wife of Henry VIII of England, and upsetting King Henry—a political concern. German princes did not want the Spanish emperor or the Italian pope dictating how to deal with the popular German scholar, Martin Luther—again, a political concern. The revolts by German peasants struck fear into many European leaders—a social and economic concern. The growing power of the middle classes was also a social and economic concern. Religious life was not separate from economic, political, and social life of the time. Thus, a combination of these factors, along with the doctrinal arguments, led to the Reformation. Also, change resulting from the Reformation was not confined to religious change.)

Review Questions and Answers

1. **What happened at the Diet of Worms?**

   At the Diet of Worms Martin Luther was asked to deny his teachings as being heretical. He said that in conscience he could not.

2. **What was the Peasants' Revolt? How did Luther respond to it?**

   The Peasants' Revolt was a series of bloody uprisings by German peasants in the early 1520s. Luther denounced the peasants for their actions and called upon the German nobility to do whatever was necessary to stop the peasants.

3. **When did *Protestant* become the popular term for those who rejected Catholicism?**

   At the second Diet of Speyer, some Catholic representatives called for reversing earlier concessions to Luther and his followers and for carrying out prosecution of Luther as a heretic. Those who "protested" these decisions received the name "Protestants."

4. **What decision was reached at the Peace of Augsburg?**

   At the Peace of Augsburg an imperial assembly called by the emperor decided that local rulers would determine the religion for their citizens, either Catholicism or Lutheranism.

pages 155–156

SPREAD OF PROTESTANTISM

The Reformation in France and Spain

King Henry VIII and the Anglican Church

1. Direct the students to read the section on the Reformation in France and Spain. Ask them: Why did France and Spain remain primarily Catholic countries during and following the Reformation? (Review questions 1 and 2 address this topic.)

2. The students may already have information to share on Henry VIII and the Church of England. Have the studenats do some sharing of this information before reading the section. Then correct any inaccuracies first presented.

page 156　**FYI**

Using the FYI

- Many people find the story of Henry VIII to be fascinating. A number of films have been made about him, his wives, and his daughter Elizabeth. One of the best films on the religious crisis of the time is *A Man for All Seasons*, based on the play by Robert Bolt. The story centers on Thomas More's conflict with Henry VIII about Henry's claim to head the Church in England. You may consider showing at least a portion of the film to the students.

- Remind the students that the Reformation in England was different from the Reformation in Germany. In Germany, Luther had a number of theological differences with standard Catholic beliefs. In England, King Henry's primary theological difference with the pope was about who heads the Church in England—the pope or the king?) Only later did English citizens leaning toward Protestantism succeed in "purifying" the English or Anglican Church of some of its Catholic beliefs and practices.

Additional Activities

ENGLISH PURITANS

People in the United States know about the Puritans because they were one of the first English groups to arrive in the New World seeking religious freedom. However, they also exhibit how the Protestant movement saw itself as a "purification" of a corrupt Catholicism. **Handout 7–D, The Puritans,** allows the students to think about the Puritans in this light. Distribute the handout to the students and ask them to answer the questions in small groups. You might also have one group research the Puritans and prepare a presentation to the class about them.

CoNCept Review

Ask the students: If you lived in Europe during the sixteenth century, in which country would you want to live? Why?

page 156　**Review Questions and Answers**

1. **Give two reasons why Protestantism did not become strong in France.**

   Two reasons why Protestantism did not become strong in France were that (1) the civil government there exercised greater control over internal Church affairs, and also that (2) Catholic scholars at French universities were able to effectively refute Protestant teachings.

2. **Name three factors that helped keep Spain Catholic.**

   Three factors that helped keep Spain Catholic were: (1) Church reforms initiated by Queen Isabella, (2) the Inquisition, and (3) exceptional spiritual figures in Spain at the time.

3. **What title did the pope give King Henry VIII of England? Why?**

The pope named Henry VIII "Defender of the Faith" for his strong stand against Protestantism.

4. **Why did Henry VIII want to divorce Catherine of Aragon?**

With his wife Catherine, Henry had a daughter but no male children who lived beyond infancy. He wanted to marry his mistress in the hope of securing a male successor to the throne.

5. **Who were the Puritans?**

Puritans were English Protestants who wanted to "purify" the Church of England of Catholic ways. When subject to persecution, many Puritans went to Holland and later to North America.

TWO PROTESTANT REFORMERS

pages 157–159

Heroes of the Reformation

1. This section of the chapter clarifies why Protestantism is best understood as a movement. Interestingly, Luther himself rejected Reformed Christianity as led by Zwingli and Calvin. Reformed Christianity moved the Protestant movement well beyond what Luther called for. To give the students a visual image of Protestantism as a movement away from certain characteristics of the Catholicism of the time, as the students are reading the section draw a horizontal line on the board or overhead. On one end of the line draw a vertical line and write "Catholicism" above it. Draw another vertical line a few inches along the horizontal line and write "Anglicanism" above it. Third, draw another vertical line a few more inches along the horizontal line and write "Lutheranism" above it. Finally, a few more inches along draw another vertical line and write "Reformed Christianity" above it.

2. When the students have finished reading the section, ask them:
   - Why is Protestantism best viewed as a movement?
   - What role did Zwingli and Calvin play in the movement?
   - What key idea related to this section of text was promoted by each of the following persons: Erasmus, Thomas More, and Philip Melancthon?

page 158   FYI

Using the FYI

The "Declaration on Religious Freedom" was promulgated on December 7, 1965. John Courtney Murray SJ wrote the following about the document:

> *[The Declaration's] content is properly doctrinal. In particular, three doctrinal tenets are declared: the ethical doctrine of religious freedom as a human right (personal and collectively); a political doctrine with regard to the functions and limits of government in matters religious; and the theological doctrine of the freedom of the Church as the fundamental principle in what concerns the relations between the Church and the socio-political order. . . . taken in conjunction with the Pastoral Constitution on the Church in the Modern World, the Declaration opens a new era in the relations between the People of God and the People Temporal . . . The Declaration has opened the way toward new confidence in ecumenical relationships, and a new straightforwardness in relationships between the Church and the world.*

DISCUSSION

Using the Discussion

The Catholic understanding of predestination differs from that of Calvin. The Catholic Church understands predestination as the eternal and gracious decree of God by which we are saved. Since humans have free will, they must accept the salvation that God offers in love. Calvin, on the other hand, taught that God predestined some people to salvation and predestined some others to damnation. The Council of Trent condemned this double predestination.

ACTIVITY

Using the Activity

Have the students use the Internet or, with your guidance, contact a local congregation for information on each of the groups listed in the second activity. Internet suggestions:

Anabaptists: **www.bibleviews.com**—Mennonite-Anabaptist beliefs; www.anabaptist.org—links to Mennonites and Amish

Methodists: **www.umc.org**—official site of the United Methodist Church; www.confessingumc.org—beliefs

Quakers: www.quaker.org—numerous links; **www.fgcquaker.org**—Friends General Conference is one of three umbrella organizations.

Presbyterians: **www.pcanet.org**—site for the Presbyterian Church in America; www.epc.org—the Evangelical Presbyterian Church

CONCEPT REVIEW

Discuss with the students: The text refers to "Heroes of the Reformation." What kind of heroes would have been most effective during this period? Why?

Review Questions and Answers

1. **What type of governance did Ulrich Zwingli institute in Switzerland?**

   Ulrich Zwingli instituted a theocracy in Switzerland, meaning that religious leaders served as the governors of all aspects of societal life.

2. **What term came to be applied to those people who went beyond Luther in their rejection of Catholic beliefs and practices?**

   A term for Protestants who went beyond Luther in their rejection of Catholic beliefs is Reformed Christians.

3. **What is a Presbyterian form of leadership?**

   Presbyterian leadership means leadership by a group of elders.

4. **What is predestination?**

   Predestination, according to Calvin, is the belief that certain people are destined for damnation and others are destined for salvation. People can do nothing to alter this fate.

5. **Who was John Knox?**

   John Knox introduced Presbyterianism to Scotland.

Causes of the Reformation

Multiple factors create an atmosphere that makes the Reformation both possible and likely. In some ways this section takes a step back in time to immediately before the Reformation. However, it actually describes in greater depth the atmosphere existing at the time of the Reformation.

pages 160–163 ## CAUSES OF THE REFORMATION

Before they read the section, point out to the students: If Martin Luther had lived even seventy years earlier (say, before the printing press), his protests probably would not have led to a split in the Church. Many factors conspired to make the Reformation possible besides the actions of a few men. Read the text to discover some of them.

In-Text Activities

page 163 ### ACTIVITY

Using the Activity

After the students have read the section, instruct them to complete the **In-Text Activity** individually. After a few minutes, divide the class into small groups and direct the groups to come to a consensus on their rankings and to be prepared to defend and explain their rankings.

Discuss with the students the following statement: The Reformation era produced an atmosphere conducive to a split in Western Christianity. Today an atmosphere exists that is conducive to greater cooperation and unity among religions.

(For example, fifty years ago Catholics were discouraged from entering Protestant churches. Today, the pope and Catholic bishops, priests, and laypersons participate in prayer services not only with other Christians, but with leaders of other religions as well. Also, representatives from various religions come together to seek common ground among themselves. These examples represent an atmosphere that is much different from the atmosphere that existed in Christianity for the first four hundred years after the Reformation.)

page 163

Review Questions and Answers

1. **Give an example of the extravagant lifestyle of Church leaders at the time of the Reformation.**

   One Reformation-era pope spent a good deal of money on extravagant weddings for his children and grandchildren. The Church sometimes operated as a royal court with a great deal of luxury and pomp. Ornate buildings and extensive art collections were common.

2. **Why did many Church leaders have little training in or sensitivity for spiritual matters?**

   At the time of the Reformation, bishops and abbots often gained their title because their families bought the offices for them. Lower clergy often had little theological training.

3. **What was the state of popular religion at the time of the Reformation?**

   Popular religion at the time of the Reformation was often tinged with superstition and fear of the devil.

4. **On the one hand, Protestant reformers embraced the spirit of the Renaissance; on the other hand, they reacted against it. Explain.**

   Protestant reformers embraced the Renaissance notion of appealing to the authority of their own beliefs. On the other hand, they renounced the ornate buildings, the money spent on art, and the extensive reliance on non-Christian (classical Greek and Roman) sources for truth.

5. **What impact did nationalism, the discovery of new lands, and the printing press have on the Reformation?**

   Nationalism led to increased fragmentation in Europe and helped the Reformation to spread one locality at a time with diminished interference from transnational entities such as the Church. With the discovery of new lands, Europeans also became more open to new ideas and the possibility of living elsewhere. The printing press made it possible to spread revolutionary ideas far and wide.

6. **What Lutheran teaching did the German middle class embrace?**

   Luther's attack on corruption among Church leaders and his teaching that everyone is equal in the sight of God appealed to the German middle class who were angry at taxation by Church leaders and were asserting their power more and more against the old order exemplified by the Church.

Protestant and Catholic Theological Differences

A Protestant theology emerges that manifests fundamental differences from traditional Catholic theology, especially regarding Scripture, justification, and priesthood. This section lists three differences between traditional Protestant and Catholic teachings.

pages 164–165

DIFFERENCES IN TEACHINGS
Scripture Alone or Scripture and Tradition?

1. Alert the students that religions are not static. That is, Catholics and Protestants have come closer together in recent decades as groups within each tradition have examined their beliefs over against those of the other group. Nonetheless, it is important for the students to realize that there are different points of view between Catholicism and Protestantism that have existed from the time of the Reformation. Three major differences are discussed in the text:
   - Scripture Alone or Scripture and Tradition? (pages 164–165)
   - Faith Alone or Faith and Good Works? (page 166)
   - The Priesthood of All Believers or a Separate Priesthood? (page 168)

2. Before beginning each of these sections, ask the students to share their thoughts on what the problem was.

In-Text Activities

page 165 YOUTH NEWS

Using the Youth News

You might suggest that the students develop a plan for reading a chapter or psalm each day, once they have decided where they want to start. Perhaps once a week you could schedule ten or fifteen minutes of class time for the students to gather in fixed small groups (faith-sharing groups) to share what they are reading and how the reading is affecting them.

DISCUSSION

Using the Discussion

The Catholic Church still makes use of Greek categories to explain the Real Presence of Christ in the Eucharist. The Catechism defines the Real Presence as the unique, true presence of Christ in the Eucharist under the species or appearances of bread and wine (see #s1376–1377). In *The Real Presence of Jesus Christ in the Sacrament of the Eucharist* (2001), the U.S. bishops explain the belief by making use of Greek philosophical terms, referring to the Catechism numbers noted here: "in the Church's traditional theological language, in the act of consecration during the Eucharist the 'substance' of the bread and wine is changed by the power of the Holy Spirit into the 'substance' of the Body and Blood of Jesus Christ. At the same time, the 'accidents' or appearances of bread and wine remain . . . what appears to be bread and wine in every way (at the level of 'accidents' or physical attributes—that is, what can be seen, touched, tasted, or measured) in fact is now the Body and Blood of Christ (at the level of 'substance' or deepest reality). This change at the level of substance from bread and wine into the Body and Blood of Christ is called 'transubstantiation.'" (#3, page 7)

Additional Activities

LITERAL VERSUS CONTEXTUAL INTERPRETATIONS OF SCRIPTURE

1. Since the Protestant tradition has emphasized *sola scriptura* as Catholicism has not, the debate about how to interpret Scripture has been more problematic for some Protestants than for Catholics. If your students have not addressed the difference between a literal and a contextual (or historical-critical) interpretation of Scripture, you might explain and discuss the differences at this time.

2. Explain to the students that *sola scriptura* does not necessarily imply a literal interpretation of Scripture. The question remains: How should we interpret Scripture? Those who read Scripture literally look for meaning in the text alone and do not use historical-critical tools that have been developed over the past century or so. This is frequently the approach of fundamentalist groups. A contextual interpretation of Scripture looks to the text as well as the context in which the text was written to interpret it.

   - **Literal**—take the words of Scripture at face value according to their literalistic meaning without regard for context or historical or scientific inaccuracies

   - **Contextual or historical-critical**—accepts human as well as divine authorship, and therefore recognizes differences in style, vocabulary, and growth in religious insights; incorporates language studies and historical and archaeological discoveries into the translation process and into the interpretation

3. After explaining the two approaches to Scripture interpretation, discuss the following questions.

   - In what ways is a literal interpretation of Scripture problematic?

     (A literal interpretation is problematic because it runs the risk of misinterpretation. For instance, a story intended to be fictional could be understood as historically true. The story of Jonah, for instance, has characteristics of moral tales from the time. Thus, it quite likely was not intended to be taken literally.)

   - In what ways is a contextual or historical-critical interpretation of Scripture problematic?

     A contextual or historical-critical approach to Scripture is problematic because, for some people, it could call into question the very foundation of Scripture as God's word. That is, we must be careful to avoid the same problem that literalism suffers from—a generalizing where the opposite is called for. Just because some parts of Scripture are not literally true, that doesn't mean no parts of Scripture are literally true. It is one thing to call the account of Jonah in the fish a fictional tale; it is quite another to call the resurrection fiction.

   - Which approach to Scripture appeals more to you? Why? (Make clear that a purely literal interpretation of every part of the Bible is not the official Catholic approach to Scripture.)

Discuss with the students the following questions:

- What reasons might have led Luther to emphasize Scripture to the exclusion of Christian Tradition?

  (Luther appealed to Scripture, as well as his personal conscience, as the basis upon which to disagree with Church leaders of the time. Similarly, U.S. citizens who disagree with current government policies might appeal to the Constitution of the United States for confirmation of their views. Just as the Constitution of the United States is part of the nation's tradition and not above or apart from it, so Scripture is part of the Tradition of the Church.)

- How would you describe the relationship between Scripture and the Church?

  (Catholicism views Scripture as the inspired word of God. It looks upon Scripture interpretation dynamically. That is, Christian Tradition, the historical Christian community, and the magisterium are channels of Revelation along with Scripture.)

page 166 | **Faith Alone or Faith and Good Works?**

1. If the students are not aware of the animosity that existed between many Catholics and many Protestants until the 1960s and Vatican Council II, point it out to them. The question of justification was a major disagreement between the two traditions. More recently, it has received greater clarification both within Catholicism and within a number of Protestant circles. As mentioned in the text, Lutheran and Catholic scholars have found no substantial disagreement on the question.

2. Direct the students to read the text on page 166 and to explain the conflict surrounding the question of justification. Then read aloud **In-Text Activity #1** and ask for comments.

In-Text Activities

page 166 | ACTIVITY

Using the Activity

1. If possible come to a near consensus on this activity.

CoNCept RevíEw

Use **In-Text Activity #2** as a review of this concept. Read James 2:14–26 to begin the discussion of this question. Read Romans 3:21–28 to the students. Reading these two passages together may help the students see the need for biblical scholarship and some official guidance in the interpretation of Scripture. Private interpretation obviously has pitfalls when it comes to passages that seem to be in contradiction.

Saint Margaret Clitherow

THE PRIESTHOOD OF ALL BELIEVERS OR A SEPARATE PRIESTHOOD?

1. Direct the students to read pages 167–168. Mention to them that, prior to Vatican Council II, priests were sometimes put on a pedestal within the Catholic community. Since Vatican Council II, with the increased emphasis on the role of lay people, the perspective on priests has changed as well. They are certainly respected as leaders, but they are also seen as members and leaders of a Christian community that is worthy and honorable and, indeed, a sign of the kingdom of God.

2. To illustrate how strongly Catholics traditionally viewed their priests and work of priests, direct the students to read the story of Saint Margaret Clitherow. When they have finished reading her story, ask the students: Besides compassion for another human, why would this woman risk torture and death to conceal priests as she did? What is it about priesthood that makes priests so special and important to Catholicism?

3. Emphasize the fact that the Church distinguishes between—but honors both— the priesthood of the faithful, which includes all the baptized, and the ministerial priesthood of deacons, priests, and bishops.

In-Text Activities

ACTIVITY

Using the Activity

1. Provide the diocesan directory for the students (check with the school office or with a parish or the diocesan center). If the priests are members of a religious community, collect the notes with the names on the envelopes, and ask a community member to help with finding addresses.

2. Encourage the students to especially reflect on the common priesthood of the faithful. You might check out these paragraphs in the Catechism: #s 784, 941, 1119, 1141, 1143, 1268, 1273, 1546–1547, 1591.

CoNCept RevieW

Discuss with the students:

• Film directors often use Catholic priests to portray spiritual power. (For instance, movies about World War II often show a priest saying Mass in a war zone or hearing confessions on the battlefield. This is true even though at the time there were many more Protestant chaplains than Catholic chaplains.) Why do you think a director would use a priest rather than a Protestant minister to provide a snapshot of spirituality?

• How are priesthood, and priests in general, viewed within the Catholic community today?

• Do you believe that Catholic perspectives on priesthood have changed over the past century? If so, how?

Review Questions and Answers

1. **What does the Protestant principle *sola scriptura* mean? What is the traditional Catholic position on this principle?**

   Sola scriptura means "Scripture alone." Protestantism looks to the Bible alone as source of truth, while Catholicism looks to both Scripture and the Tradition of the Church.

2. **Explain what justification by faith means in Catholicism. In Lutheranism.**

   Catholicism refers to God's gracious act of rendering a person holy and justification by faith. Since Catholicism views people as members of a community, the Church and sacraments play a role in that justification. In Lutheranism, justification tends to be viewed as a divine gift given to individual persons who recognize that they can do nothing to merit such a gift.

3. **What is the difference between the Catholic and the Lutheran position on priesthood?**

   Protestantism speaks only of the "priesthood of all Christians" whereas Catholicism includes a separate and distinct role for specially ordained priests.

The Catholic Reformation

Reform of the Catholic Church centered around the Council of Trent. By clarifying Catholic teaching in precise terms, often over against what Protestants were teaching, it strengthened the separation between Catholicism and Protestantism. In doing so, it also led to some unintended results. For instance, following Trent it at least appeared that Catholics were discouraged from reading the Bible, while Protestantism was in many ways completely based upon the Bible. It took four hundred years after Trent before Catholicism returned to a strong emphasis on Scripture and some Protestants to a better appreciation of the importance of Tradition.

pages 169–171

THE CATHOLIC REFORMATION

The Council of Trent

SAINT CHARLES BORROMEO—APPLYING THE COUNCIL OF TRENT

Direct the students to read these sections on pages 169–171 and then pose the following questions:

- Where was Trent? Why was this city chosen for a Church council?

  (The pope chose Trent because it was in German territory. He didn't want the impression to be that it was to be an Italian affair; rather, it was a universal Church gathering. Nonetheless, most bishops who attended were Italian—partially because of the difficulty bishops from other countries had getting to Trent, given the heated atmosphere in Europe at the time.)

- How did the council go about reforming the Church?

  (The council approached reform in two ways: it dealt with clarifying doctrine and then based Church reforms on these doctrines. In many ways, Trent defined its teachings specifically against Protestant attacks on Catholic teaching.)

- Why was Saint Charles Borromeo an important figure in the Church reform of the time?

  (Charles Borromeo is a good model of applying Trent's reforms on the local level.)

page 170   **FYI**

Using the FYI

- If possible borrow a sacramentary to bring to class for the students' perusal.
- A revised sacramentary was published around the year 2000 and implemented after the approval of national adaptations to the *General Instruction of the Roman Missal*.

ACTIVITY

Using the Activity

1. You might have the students vote (anonymously and in writing) on each issue before and after the debates.

2. Be sure those on either side of each issue present at least three good arguments for their case.

Additional Activities

THE IMPORTANCE OF SEMINARY TRAINING

A major instrument of reform instituted by the Council of Trent was creation of a formal seminary program for the education and training of priests.

1. Invite a seminarian to your class and ask him to describe the program offered at his seminary.

2. Following his presentation, ask the students:

   - What would it be like if there were no such formal training process for priests?
   - What would you recommend to be part of seminary training today?

CoNCept ReviEw

Discuss with the students the following statement: If the Council of Trent had begun in 1500 instead of in 1545, the Protestant Reformation would not have happened.

(While this statement is pure speculation, it does encourage the students to think about the many factors involved in the Reformation. Trent brought both clarification of doctrine and real Church reform. If it had taken place before the animosity that grew during events of the previous half-century, Luther might not have ended up outside of the Catholic communion and Luther's ideas might have received a hearing in the Church. What would have become of the movement known as Reformed Christianity is also speculation.)

Saint Charles Borromeo—Applying the Council of Trent

Have a small group of students research Saint Charles Borromeo in the library and on the Internet and make a presentation to the class, followed by a group discussion.

Review Questions and Answers

1. **What were the two main goals of the Council of Trent?**

   The two main goals of the Council of Trent were to address abuses in the Church and to clarify Catholic teaching to meet the Protestant challenges.

2. **What three things were bishops instructed to do by the Council of Trent?**

   Bishops were instructed to reside in their diocese, to meet with their clergy regularly, and to visit the parishes in their diocese.

3. **How was priestly life to change after the Council of Trent?**

   The council reaffirmed celibacy for priests, instructed priests to wear distinctive garb, and instituted seminaries for formally training priests.

4. **The Council of Trent clarified Catholic teachings. Why was this a reforming step?**

   Before the council, problems often arose because beliefs were misunderstood or misrepresented.

5. **What does it mean to say that the spirit of the teachings at the Council of Trent was legalistic and critical?**

   The Council of Trent clarified Church teaching and practice against the attacks of Protestantism. Therefore, it stated its teachings as specific legal statements critical of what it considered erroneous Protestant beliefs.

6. **What role did Saint Charles Borromeo play in relation to the Council of Trent?**

   Saint Charles Borromeo was an active participant in the Council of Trent. However, he is especially known for applying the council to his particular diocese.

New Religious Orders

New religious orders and the saintly dedication of many Catholics set new directions for the Catholic Church. This section looks at two phenomena following on the heels of the Reformation: the many spiritual giants in Europe at the time, the creation of the Jesuits and their influence.

pages 172–173 ## CATHOLIC SPIRITUALITY
The Society of Jesus

Direct the students to read this section. Then talk through the chart on Jesuit Spirituality on page 173.

page 173 ### ACTIVITY

Using the Activity

1. Provide a reflective atmosphere and Bibles for this activity; consider using the school chapel, or, if the weather is good, a quiet space outdoors.

2. Suggest books on the lives of the saints. The most extensive is the twelve volume *Butler's Lives of the Saints* published by Liturgical Press. See also *Jesuit Saints & Martyrs : Short Biographies of the Saints, Blessed, Venerables, and Servants of God of the Society of Jesus* by Joseph N. Tylenda (Chicago: Loyola Press, 1998). The Internet will likely also provide background; search for "Jesuit saints" as a start.

Additional Activities

THE JESUITS TODAY

Assign a group of the students to research modern-day Jesuits. Information on their numbers, their history, their ministry, their extensive volunteer program, and their institutions can be found on the Internet. Direct the students doing the research to share their information with the class.

Concept Review

Discuss with the students the following question: How might the experience of Ignatius of Loyola as a soldier have influenced the Society of Jesus that he founded?

pages 174–176

Two Catholic Visionaries

Saint Philip Neri—The text points out that Philip Neri frequently employed humor to express or make light of his spirituality. Discuss with the students how humor can play a role in:

- spirituality in general
- their own spirituality

Saint Angela Merici—More information about Saint Angela Merici can be found in books on lives of the saints and on the Internet.

page 175 ## The Mystics

Assign the students to read pages 174–176. Summarize by listing key points from the lives of Philip Neri, Angela Merici, and Teresa of Ávila.

In-Text Activities

page 176 ### ACTIVITY

Using the Activity

Provide time for the students to share their poems or songs with the class. Be sure they know ahead of time that they will be asked to share.

PHILIP NERI AND SPIRITUAL HUMOR

Assign a student who has exhibited a sense of humor in class to read more about Philip Neri and to report to the class on the saint's other expressions of humor and lightheartedness.

JOHN OF THE CROSS ON GOD'S LOVE

Handout 7–E, John of the Cross on God's Love, offers quotes from the great Reformation-era Spanish mystic. It is important for the students to realize that Christian spirituality remained strong despite the bitterness and conflicts of the Reformation. Distribute the handout and ask the students to read over the quotes found there. Invite them to write a response to the question on the handout.

Concept Review

Discuss: Who among the spiritual figures mentioned in this section do you find most appealing? Why?

page 176   ## Review Questions and Answers

1. **What incident led to Saint Ignatius Loyola's spiritual quest?**

    Ignatius Loyola was a soldier who spent a year recuperating in a castle. During that time he read about Jesus and the saints, especially the martyrs, and was drawn to their courage.

2. **Name four contributions that Ignatius and the Society of Jesus made to Catholicism.**

    Founded by Ignatius Loyola, the Society of Jesus developed a set of spiritual exercises, established many educational institutions throughout the world, helped hold off the spread of Protestantism, and served as missionaries in non-Christian lands.

3. **What was unique about the spirituality of Saint Philip Neri?**

    Saint Philip Neri was often playful in his spirituality.

4. **What innovation did Saint Angela Merici make to women's way of living the Christian life?**

    Women who joined Saint Angela Merici did not live in convents; rather, they lived among people who were in need, in particular, poor girls.

5. **Name two groups who helped foster Catholic spirituality during the Reformation period.**

    Two groups who fostered Catholic spirituality during the Reformation period were the Jesuits and mystics.

6. **What two Spanish Carmelite saints became Doctors of the Church for their writings on mysticism?**

    Saints Teresa of Ávila and John of the Cross became Doctors of the Church for their mystical writings.

Chapter Review and Conclusion

REVIEW

1. Ask the students to summarize the main points in the chapter using their own words. Write notes on the board from their contributions. To reinforce their summary, you might want to review the major concepts in this chapter in the teaching manual. Then read the **Conclusion** on page 177.

2. Review the vocabulary in this chapter:

> **Reformation**—political and religious event beginning in the sixteenth century that resulted in the division of Western Christianity into Catholic and Protestant faiths (page 149)
>
> **ninety-five theses**—Martin Luther's statement of principles regarding penance and the abuse of indulgences (page 149)
>
> **indulgences**—the remission before God of the temporal punishment due to sin whose guilt has already been forgiven (page 149)
>
> ***Exsurge Domine*** and ***Decet Romanum Pontificem***—papal decrees excommunicating Martin Luther (page 153)
>
> **Diet of Worms**—meeting of the leadership of the Holy Roman Empire during which Luther refused to recant his beliefs (page 153)
>
> **Peasants' Revolt**—a series of uprisings by German peasants against their landowners (page 154)
>
> **Peace of Augsburg**—allowed each prince to decide the religion of his subjects (page 154)
>
> **Huguenots**—members of the French Reformed community (page 155)
>
> **Edict of Nantes**—document granting some rights to Huguenots (page 155)
>
> **theocracy**—form of government in which religious leaders are the secular leaders as well (page 157)
>
> **Reformed Christianity**—Protestant Churches emerging in Europe from the Reformation and following primarily the teachings of Zwingli and John Calvin (page 157)
>
> **Presbyterianism**—a Protestant religion characterized by governance by a group of elders and traditionally Calvinistic in doctrine (page 158)
>
> **predestination**—belief that God has selected some people for hell and others for heaven regardless of any personal actions or merit (page 158)
>
> **laypeople**—members of the Church who are not ordained clergy or members of a religious order (page 161)
>
> ***sola scriptura***—Protestant belief that the Bible is the sole source of religious truth (page 164)

justification by faith—God's gracious act of rendering a sinful human to be holy and endowed with grace (in Catholic and Orthodox doctrines) or as acceptable to God (Lutheran) (page 166)

Council of Trent—post-Reformation meeting of the world's Catholic bishops to reform the Church and clarify Catholic teaching (page 169)

spiritual exercises—a thirty-day program of spiritual practices developed by Saint Ignatius Loyola (page 172)

TEST

Give the students the Chapter 7 Test or an alternative assessment. The tests have been placed on the Harcourt Religion Publishers' Web page. This has been done to enable the teacher to customize this material for local needs. First contact Harcourt Religion Publishers' high school consultant at 800-922-7696, ext. 3781 for a user ID and password. Then connect with the Harcourt Religion Publishers' Web site at **www.harcourtreligion.com** to download the information. Collect the tests for grading.

Chapter 7 Test Answers

MATCHING (1 point each)

Set 1		Set 2		Set 3	
1. D	5. B	1. C	5. A	1. A	4. B
2. C	6. E	2. D	6. G	2. F	5. C
3. A	7. G	3. F	7. E	3. E	6. D
4. F		4. B			

MULTIPLE CHOICE (2 points each)

1. a	5. b	9. d	13. b	16. b	19. c
2. d	6. a	10. b	14. a	17. c	20. a
3. b	7. a	11. a	15. b	18. b	
4. c	8. b	12. d			

IDENTIFICATION (5 points each)

1. Theocracy—form of government in which religious leaders are the effectively secular leaders as well

2. Predestination—belief that God has selected some people for hell and others for heaven regardless of any personal actions or merit

3. Justification by faith—God's gracious act of rendering a sinful human to be holy and endowed with grace (in Catholic and Orthodox doctrines) or as acceptable to God (Lutheran)

ESSAYS (5 points each)

1. The Catholic Church believes that a "treasury of merit" is available to people through the good works of Christ and the saints. The Church refers to this treasury as indulgences.

2. The following factors led to the Reformation: the extravagant lifestyle of Church leaders at the time, certain questionable Church practices such as the buying and selling of Church offices, poorly trained and uneducated lower clergy, the spirit of the Renaissance, the rise of nationalism, the printing press, and the rise of the middle class. (Students should be expected to name and explain three of the above.)

3. (a) Protestantism emphasizes Scripture alone as the source of teachings; Catholicism combines Scripture with Tradition. (b) Protestantism emphasizes faith alone leading to justification before God; Catholicism emphasizes faith and good works. (c) Protestantism emphasizes the priesthood of all believers; Catholicism recognizes a separate priesthood serving a unique function in the Church.

4. The Council of Trent reformed the Church by initiating more formal training and education of priests, by calling for greater care in selection of cardinals, by instructing bishops to live in and actively serve their dioceses, and by clarifying Church teaching.

5. The Society of Jesus was a group of men who underwent intense spiritual training and education. Through their educational projects they were able to counter the teachings of Protestant reformers.

Prayer

MUSIC SUGGESTIONS

"Gather Your People" by Bob Hurd from *Today's Missal* (OCP).

"Healer of Our Every Ill" by Marty Haugen from *Gather (Comprehensive)* (GIA).

"I Say 'Yes,' Lord" / "Digo 'Sí,' Señor," by Marty Haugen and Donna Peña from *Gather (Comprehensive)* (GIA), *Give Your Gifts, the Songs* (Harcourt Religion Publishers, GIA).

"One Bread, One Body" by John Foley from *Today's Missal* (OCP), *Glory & Praise (Comprehensive)* (OCP), *Gather (Comprehensive)* (GIA), *Lead Me, Guide Me* (GIA), *Today's Missal* (OCP).

"Send Down the Fire" by Marty Haugen from *Give Your Gifts, the Basics* (GIA, Harcourt Religion Publishers).

"Standin' in the Need of Prayer," spiritual from *Gather (Comprehensive)* (GIA), *Lead Me, Guide Me* (GIA).

"We Are Many Parts" by Marty Haugen from *Gather (Comprehensive)* (GIA), *We Celebrate* (J.S. Paluch Co., Inc.), *Today's Missal* (OCP).

SCRIPTURE SUGGESTIONS

Deuteronomy 30:1–5

1 Corinthians 12:12–20

John 17:1–2, 6, 16–26

PRAYER

Almighty and eternal God,
you gather the scattered sheep
and watch over those you have gathered.
Look kindly on all who follow Jesus, your Son.
You have marked them with the seal of one baptism,
Now make them one in the fullness of faith
and unite them in the bond of love.
We ask this through Christ our Lord. Amen.

Prayer for Unity, *A Book of Prayers* (Washington, DC: ICEL, 1982),
based on the opening prayer from the votive Mass for Christian Unity.

CHAPTER 7 TEST

Name_____ Date_____ Class period_____

Test is made up of questions with suggested values totaling 100 points.

Matching (1 point each)

SET 1

_____ 1. Ninety-Five Theses

_____ 2. Diet of Worms

_____ 3. *cuius regio, eius religio*

_____ 4. Edict of Nantes

_____ 5. *sola scriptura*

_____ 6. Council of Trent

_____ 7. Erasmus

A. People in a particular area are to accept the religion of their ruler.

B. The Bible is the only guide to truth.

C. Meeting condemning Luther

D. Luther's list of complaints

E. Catholic Reformation

F. French Protestants given some rights

G. Dutch humanist who remained Catholic

SET 2

_____ 1. Margaret Clitherow

_____ 2. Thomas More

_____ 3. John of the Cross

_____ 4. Charles Borromeo

_____ 5. Philip Melancthon

_____ 6. Philip Neri

_____ 7. Angela Merici

A. Lutheran scholar

B. One leader at the Council of Trent

C. Executed for hiding priests

D. Refused to acknowledge Henry VIII as head of the Church of England

E. Educated poor girls

F. Mystic who wrote poetry

G. Second Apostle of Rome

SET 3

_____ 1. Ignatius of Loyola

_____ 2. Queen Elizabeth

_____ 3. John Calvin

_____ 4. Teresa of Ávila

_____ 5. John Knox

_____ 6. Ulrich Zwingli

A. Founder of the Jesuits

B. Reformed Carmelites

C. Introduced Presbyterianism into Scotland

D. Introduced Reformation ideas into Switzerland

E. Frenchman who emphasized predestination

F. Moved England toward Protestantism

Multiple Choice (2 points each)

_____ 1. A factor leading to the Reformation that is NOT listed in the text is
   a. increased involvement of women in the Church
   b. invention of the printing press
   c. discovery of new lands
   d. increased spirit of nationalism

_____ 2. By writing to Archbishop Albrecht of Mainz, Martin Luther hoped to
   a. publicly announce his separation from the Church
   b. enlist the archbishop's support against the pope
   c. seek forgiveness for sins he had committed
   d. spark scholarly debate about Church practices

_____ 3. In his letter to Archbishop Albrecht, Martin Luther addressed in particular Church practices related to
   a. the Mass
   b. indulgences
   c. naming saints
   d. priesthood

_____ 4. Half of the money raised by Archbishop Albrecht was intended for
   a. Martin Luther's religious order
   b. sending missionaries to the New World
   c. construction of Saint Peter's Basilica
   d. care of the poor and sick in Rome

_____ 5. Archbishop Albrecht responded to Luther's letter by
   a. recommending Luther to be a bishop
   b. accusing Luther of "new teachings"
   c. appointing Luther to be a university professor
   d. promising to work for change in the Church

_____ 6. Luther originally believed that, if the pope knew how the selling of indulgences was being carried out, the pope would
   a. condemn the practice
   b. resign the papacy
   c. condemn Luther
   d. make Luther bishop

_____ 7. At the Diet of Worms, Luther said that he
   a. could not in conscience deny his beliefs
   b. would meet with the pope in Rome
   c. merely intended to spark scholarly debate
   d. would publicize his ideas using the printing press

_____ 8. After the Diet of Worms, Duke Frederick of Germany
   a. led a search for Luther
   b. protected Luther in his castle
   c. left the Catholic Church
   d. signed a death warrant for Luther

_____ 9. In the end, Luther's response to the Peasants' Revolt was
   a. support for their cause
   b. an essay on the rights of peasants
   c. a call for democracy in Germany
   d. rejection of the peasants' actions

_____ 10. The resolution reached at the Peace of Augsburg stated that
   a. Lutheranism was condemned in Germany
   b. the prince of each state would select its religion
   c. the pope alone is the head of the Church
   d. Bibles should be printed in the language of the people

_____ 11. Huguenots were
   a. French Protestants
   b. French noblemen
   c. Germans living in France
   d. decrees condemning Luther

_____ 12. In Spain, Queen Isabella
   a. sided with the Protestants
   b. fought against the Inquisition
   c. converted from Judaism
   d. instigated Church reforms

_____ 13. During the time of the Reformation, Spain
   a. was controlled by Muslims
   b. remained largely Catholic
   c. joined the Protestant movement
   d. provided safe haven for Protestants

_____ 14. The first wife of King Henry VIII of England was
   a. Catherine of Aragon
   b. Anne Boleyn
   c. Queen Elizabeth
   d. Mary, Queen of Scotland

_____ 15. Henry VIII petitioned the pope to
   a. recognize him as head of the English Church
   b. annul his first marriage so that he might marry someone else
   c. prevent the spread of Protestantism in England
   d. recognize English claims in the New World

_____ 16. Presbyterian forms of Christianity believed in
   a. remaining close to Catholicism
   b. leadership by elders
   c. women priests
   d. more than seven sacraments

_____ 17. Saint Charles Borromeo is known for
   a. traveling to the New World
   b. becoming pope at a young age
   c. applying the Council of Trent
   d. criticizing the pope of the time

_____ 18. Saint Ignatius Loyola spent his early life as a
   a. monk
   b. soldier
   c. missionary
   d. merchant

_____ 19. A group that played a major role in the Catholic Reformation was the
   a. Benedictines
   b. Augustinians
   c. Jesuits
   d. Trinitarians

_____ 20. The reform group founded by Saint Teresa of Ávila was the
   a. discalced Carmelites
   b. Franciscans
   c. Presbyterians
   d. Ursulines

Identification (5 points each)

1. Theocracy—

2. Predestination—

3. Justification by faith—

Essays (5 points each)

1. Explain Catholic teaching on indulgences.

2. Name three factors that led to the Reformation. Explain how each one helped to bring about the Reformation.

3. Explain three major differences between Catholic and Protestant theology.

4. Describe two ways that the Council of Trent attempted to reform the Church.

5. Describe the role that the Society of Jesus played during the Reformation era.

A Sampling of Luther's Ninety-Five Theses

Name_____ Date_____ Class period_____

Following are several theses of Martin Luther. Many of those on indulgences are included on page 151 of the text.

1. Our Lord and Master Jesus Christ, in saying "Repent ye," etc., intended that the whole life of believers should be penitence.

5. The pope has neither the will nor the power to remit any penalties, except those which he has imposed by his own authority, or by that of the canons.

6. The pope has no power to remit any guilt, except by declaring and warranting it to have been remitted by God; or at most by remitting cases reserved for himself; in which cases, if his power were despised, guilt would certainly remain.

37. Every true Christian, whether living or dead, has a share in all the benefits of Christ and of the Church given him by God, even without letters of pardon.

40. True contrition seeks and loves punishment; while the ampleness of pardons relaxes it, and causes men to hate it, or at least gives occasion for them to do so.

43. Christians should be taught that he who gives to a poor man, or lends to a needy man, does better than if he bought pardons.

44. Because, by a work of charity, charity increases and the man becomes better; while, by means of pardons, he does not become better, but only freer from punishment.

50. Christians should be taught that, if the pope were acquainted with the exactions of the preachers of pardons, he would prefer that the Basilica of St. Peter should be burnt to ashes, than that it should be built up with the skin, flesh, and bones of his sheep.

51. Christians should be taught that, as it would be the duty, so it would be the wish of the pope, even to sell, if necessary, the Basilica of St. Peter, and to give of his own money to very many of those from whom the preachers of pardons extract money.

59. St. Lawrence said that the treasures of the Church are the poor of the Church, but he spoke according to the use of the word in his time.

62. The true treasure of the Church is the Holy Gospel of the glory and grace of God.

81. This license in the preaching of pardons makes it no easy thing, even for learned men, to protect the reverence due to the pope against the calumnies, or, at all events, the keen questionings of the laity.

93. Blessed be all those prophets who say to the people of Christ, "The cross, the cross," and there is no cross!

94. Christians should be exhorted to strive to follow Christ their Head through pains, deaths, and hells.

95. And thus trust to enter heaven through many tribulations, rather than in the security of peace.

From the *Grolier Multimedia Encyclopedia*, 1996 Edition.
Copyright 1996 by Grolier Incorporated. Reprinted with permission.

Chapter Seven

Name_____ Date_____ Class period_____

Summarize three key beliefs of Luther:

1.

2.

3.

FIGURES OF THE REFORMATION

Name_____ Date_____ Class period_____

A wonderful cast of characters people the Reformation era. Sign up for one of the following people and create a poster highlighting the role that he or she played in the religious development of the sixteenth century.

Martin Luther	Pope Leo X
Erasmus	Thomas More
Queen Elizabeth I	King Henry VIII of England
John Calvin	John Knox
Philip Melancthon	George Fox
Teresa of Ávila	John of the Cross
Isabella & Ferdinand of Spain	Ulrich Zwingli
Emperor Charles V	Catherine of Aragon
Mary, Queen of Scots	Sebastian Castellio
Ignatius Loyola	Margaret Clitherow
Menno Simons	King Henry IV of France
Pope Paul III	Torquemada
Charles Borromeo	John Tetzel

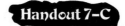

MARTIN LUTHER—REFORMER AND REBEL

Name_____ Date_____ Class period_____

What was it about Martin Luther that made him the key figure in the split that occurred in Western Christianity that we know as the Reformation? Here are four answers to this question. Read about Luther to find out other aspects of his character and his times that help explain his position as a man capable of dividing the Church.

Scripture Scholar—Luther taught and studied the Scriptures. He wanted people to read Scripture and to refer to it directly as *the* source of truth. Unwittingly, his emphasis on Scripture deemphasized Christian tradition and the authority of Church leaders to guide the faithful in understanding Scripture.

German—Luther was German during a time of increasing nationalism. Many people of the time believed that the old system, in which the emperor and the pope ultimately could dictate the fate of Europe, continued to be operative. When a German prince saved Luther from punishment at the hands of the (Spanish) emperor as directed by the (Italian) pope, it became clear that a new world of nation-states was emerging, making different religions for different places possible.

Guilt-Ridden in His Youth—Luther described battling with a great sense of being a sinner during his youth. Luther tried "following the rules" scrupulously as a way to make things right with God. This only made matters worse for him. Christians who sense their sinfulness at the depth of their being often also experience God's love for them in spite of their sinfulness. They realize that nothing they can do will save them; only God can save them. This experience led Luther to question the way many Christians of his time seemed to go about trying to gain God's favor through their own actions and also to a superstitious degree. This type of questioning became a starting point for much Protestant thinking.

A "Modern Man" in a Medieval World—Luther lived during a transition period, from a medieval mindset to a modern mindset. Feudalism was dying out. The middle class was on the ascendancy. Instead of a separate religious life, family life and working in "the world" were considered models for the spiritual life. People were beginning to see themselves more as separate individuals than as members of an integrated community. A number of characteristics of the Protestant movement anticipated the transition to the modern world.

THE PURITANS

Name_____ Date_____ Class period_____

1. Puritans left England and arrived in the New World in 1620. What was the religious climate like in England and in Europe at the time that helped to shape the group?

2. What did the Puritans hope to purify?

3. What impurities were they particularly concerned about? Why?

4. How did they hope to purify themselves and their world?

5. Why was North America a particularly appropriate place for this religion?

6. Do you think that their experience in North America shaped the religion of the Puritans? If so, how?

7. Are there remnants of Puritanism in the U.S. cultural and religious landscape today? If so, how is it manifest?

JOHN OF THE CROSS ON GOD'S LOVE

Name_____ Date_____ Class period_____

During the sixteenth century, while so many Christians in Europe were battling over teachings and practices, a Spaniard wrote about the inner depths of persons where God is at home. It is almost as if God says through this man, John of the Cross, "Don't forget what is essential—that I love you always." Here are some passages from his writings. Choose one of the passages and describe how you might apply it to your own life.

If you are seeking after God, you may be sure of this: God is seeking you much more. He is the Lover, and you are His beloved. (page 26)

And the more we allow love to enter, the more we grow to love others with our whole will—even when they treat us miserably. In fact, God's aim is to change us from within so that it is the easiest thing for us to act in love at these times, whether we are overwhelmed with feeling for a person or not. (page 30)

I want to show you a marvel, a spiritual truth that will help you to understand the ways of God which the worldly-minded cannot understand: The love of God is never idle, though our weak flesh often believes that He has forgotten us. We think the proof of His abandonment is that He allows unlovely things to happen to us. This is not so. But we misunderstand the way His love works.

    God's purpose is to so enkindle us in love that we are full of life, and full of delight. But first, in order to penetrate into our souls, it is necessary for love to wound. (page 33)

God is alive and present in the very substance of the soul—even the soul of the world's greatest sinner. This primal kind of union exists between God and every creature. For it is God alone who preserves their very being, and if He breaks this bond their life ceases at once. (page 63)

Examine your heart. Do you carry secret ill-will toward those who misunderstand you? Perhaps they are the very ones whom God has sent to expose your pride. (page 79)

Remember that He may use anyone at all—however unwitting they may be—to teach us and direct us on our way. (page 148)

Do not let your "eye" be drawn by the false "beacon lamps"—of wealth, or position, or fame, or possessions. Be vigilant over your will and desires, for these are the corrupt forces that dwell within, and keep you from living free. (page 43)

So this is the marvel: God's slightest touch could utterly annihilate—yet His only desire is to embrace us, with a love that knows no limits at all. . . . Never doubt that this is God's will for you. Never doubt that He is able to lift your soul to so high a state. (page 164)

Used with permission from *You Set My Spirit Free* by David Hazard, 1994, Bethany House Publishers. All rights reserved.

SACRED OR SECULAR?
Rationalism Confronts the Catholic Church

A Teacher's Prayer

Jesus, may my students and I find joy in simple things and the freedom to express our faith in you with deep feelings. May we discover a Catholic faith that is reasonable, emotionally moving, and profoundly exciting. Amen.

Overview

Two innovations associated with the modern world are its emphasis on science as the leading avenue to truth and the transformation of the world into clearly delineated nation-states. These modern points of emphasis challenged all religions. However, Western Christianity, both Catholic and Protestant communities, faced these changes before other religious groups. The primary focus of this chapter is how the Catholic Church dealt with the challenges of the increasingly secular and nationalistic modern age.

Major Concepts Covered in This Chapter

① **Introduction**

② **The Enlightenment**

③ **Political Change and the Church**

④ **Catholicism during the Baroque Era**

⑤ **World Catholicism during the Baroque Era**

⑥ **Chapter Review and Conclusion**

Introduction

Prayer

pages
178–180

- **Music Suggestions**

    "All Things New" by Rory Cooney from *Give Your Gifts, the Basics* (GIA, Harcourt Religion Publishers).

    "Follow the Light" by Richard Putori and Christopher Dutkiewicz from *Give Your Gifts, the New Songs* (GIA, Harcourt Religion Publishers).

    "Hope at the Crossroads" by Michael Mahler from *Give Your Gifts, the New Songs* (GIA, Harcourt Religion Publishers).

    "Let There Be Peace on Earth" by Sy Miller/Jill Jackson from *Gather (Comprehensive)* (GIA), *We Celebrate* (J.S. Paluch Co., Inc.), *Glory & Praise (Comprehensive)* (OCP), *Today's Missal* (OCP).

    "Now" by Rory Cooney from *Give Your Gifts, the Songs* (GIA, Harcourt Religion Publishers).

    "Send Down the Fire" by Marty Haugen from *Give Your Gifts, the Basics* (GIA, Harcourt Religion Publishers).

    "Sign Me Up" by Kevin Yancy and Jerome Metcalfe from *Lead Me, Guide Me* (GIA).

    "The Cry of the Poor" by John Foley from *Today's Missal* (OCP), *Glory & Praise (Comprehensive)* (OCP).

- **Scripture Suggestions**

    Ezekiel 18:30–32

    Revelation 21:1–7

    Matthew 28:16–20

- **Prayer**

    See the prayer on page 178.

pages
178–180

Overview

1. Have the students read the **Chapter Overview** and timeline on pages 178–179. Briefly discuss some of the points and events noted.

2. Have the students complete the **Before We Begin . . .** activity on page 180. (You might instead assign this activity as homework before beginning the chapter and ask the students to report on their findings.) Discuss the questions.

MAJOR
2
CONCEPTS

The Enlightenment

The Enlightenment presents new challenges for the Catholic Church.

pages
181–183

THE CHURCH AND SCIENCE

Galileo, Science, and the Catholic Church

1. The students may already know that Church leaders and Galileo reached an impasse around the question of heliocentric versus geocentric views of the universe. Before they read the section, you might ask the students what they know of Galileo's story. After they have shared their knowledge of the story, direct the students to read pages 181–183.

2. Then ask the students: How does Galileo's experience represent a turning point for Western Christianity?

   (Galileo appealed to direct experience rather than scholastic categories. Galileo saw the Church as having a role in truth-seeking, but he held to the results of his scientific investigations even when condemned by Church courts. Galileo represented the new excitement that advances in science and technology brought with them. Following after Galileo, science takes on a privileged position in the pursuit of truth.)

In-Text Activities

page 183

ACTIVITY

Using the Activity

1. You might discuss ways in which the Church presently uses science and technology. There are areas in which a scientific "advancement" is contrary to the moral law: cloning, *in vitro* fertilization, weapons of mass destruction, and so on. In these cases, the Church speaks out against these misuses of human creativity, and this is part of the mission of the Church.

2. Provide time for the students to share the results of their work.

CoNCept ReVieW

Discuss with the students:

- Is science supportive of, in opposition to, or indifferent to religious faith? Explain.
- If someone believed that science and religion are by nature enemies, upon what basis would he or she make this claim?
- Do you believe that the Catholic Church supports scientific progress? Should it at all times? Sometimes? How might the Catholic Church promote genuine scientific progress even more?

pages
184–185

Characteristics of the New Age of Science

This section lists seven characteristics of deism. After the students have read the section, ask them the following question in order to emphasize the difference between a deistic and a Christian understanding of God: How would a mystic, a John of the Cross or Catherine of Siena, respond to deism?

(Both of these saints experienced God's active presence in their lives personally and in the world around them. Deists would view this understanding of God as an affront to human reason, which should depend on nothing except itself in seeking truth.)

Chapter Eight

page 185   **FYI**

Using the FYI

You might share the following quote from Thomas Paine to explain how he and other deists felt:

> *Every person, of whatever religious denomination he may be, is a DEIST in the first article of his Creed. Deism, from the Latin word Deus, God, is the belief of a God, and this belief is the first article of every man's creed.*
>
> *It is on this article, universally consented to by all mankind, that the Deist builds his church, and here he rests . . . when the divine gift of reason begins to expand itself in the mind and calls man to reflection, he then reads and contemplates God and His works, and not in the books pretending to be revelation. The creation is the Bible of the true believer in God. Everything in this vast volume inspires him with sublime ideas of the Creator.*

DISCUSSION

Using the Discussion

During discussion of the question, "Might people think of you as a deist," take note whether the students are unwitting deists. That is, do they believe in God but fail to see this belief as of central importance to them? Would people observe that the students' belief in a personal God is evident in their lives? A God who exists but who does not get involved in the world nor act to bring about salvation is a deistic conception of God.

ACTIVITY

Using the Activity

- The students might best do this activity by first checking the Catechism regarding the topics they list; make copies of the Catechism available for that purpose.

- If a topic is not addressed in the Catechism, the students might consult a theology teacher at a Catholic college or university or a teacher of Catholicism at another college or university. Make arrangements for this consultation, or invite such a teacher in for a class.

Additional Activities

pages
186–187

VINCENT VAN GOGH CONFRONTS A DEISTIC CONCEPTION OF GOD

Handout 8–A, An Artist Speaks of the Importance of God, gives the students an opportunity to write their thoughts about a deistic notion of God versus an active and involved God. Distribute the handout, read aloud the quote, and give the students five minutes to write their reflections on the passage from van Gogh. After that time, invite the students to share their responses in pairs or as a class.

CONCEPT REVIEW

Discuss with the students: The Enlightenment, ushering in an "age of science," began around the seventeenth century. (That is, science gained a privileged position as a source of truth.) Do you think that we live as much, more, or not as much in an "age of science" today? Why or why not?

The Catholic Response to Rationalism and Deism

Have the students read the section on pages 186–187 and do the **In-Text Activity.**

In-Text Activities

ACTIVITY

Using the Activity

Butler's Lives of the Saints, twelve volumes (Collegeville, MN: Liturgical Press), is a great resource for this activity. It is likely more up to date than the following Internet sites:

www.catholic-forum.com/saints/indexsnt.htm

http://saints.catholic.org/stsindex.html

www.cin.org/saints.html

http://users.erols.com/saintpat/ss/ss-index.htm

FYI

Using the FYI

The glossary of the second edition of the *Catechism of the Catholic Church* defines Mary's assumption in this way: The dogma which recognized the Blessed Virgin Mary's singular participation in her Son's Resurrection by which she was taken up body and soul into heavenly glory, when the course of her earthly life was finished. (See #966; note that the definition does not tell us whether Mary died or not, as this has never been definitively stated.)

ACTIVITY

Using the Activity

Refer to the quote by Pierre Bayle on page 188; this quotation gives the students an appreciation of some common ground even between believers and atheists. Discuss what might be some values shared by believers and atheists. Then discuss what Christians might have to offer the world regarding these values.

Additional Activities

ENLIGHTENMENT THINKERS

An **In-Text Activity** invites the students to learn about some of the officially recognized saints of the Enlightenment period. You might assign some students to research major Enlightenment thinkers as well. Ask the students to report on:

- What is this person's view of religion and Christianity?
- What is this person's relationship to the Church?
- What are key teachings of this person in relationship to Enlightenment ideas?

Some thinkers for the students to research are:

- Galileo
- Voltaire
- Descartes
- Diderot
- Francis Bacon
- Montaigne
- Pascal

You might note that most of these thinkers were faithful sons of the Church. Descartes, for instance, had been educated by Jesuits since he was eight years old and thought that his ideas would fit well in a Jesuit educational program. Galileo's daughter, with whom he maintained regular correspondence until his death, spent her life as a cloistered nun.

FAITH AND SCIENCE ON THE INTERNET

1. The following web site provides information and opinions about the Catholic Church and science: **http://www/cco.caltech.edu/-newman/sci-faith.html**. Instruct the students to access this site and use information found there to prepare a case for or against the following statement: The Catholic Church is pro-science.

2. Also, ask the students to take note of the most recent issues being raised on this or other relevant web sites.

CoNCept ReViEw

Elicit from the students their response to the following statements:

- Atheism (denying that there is God) or agnosticism (not taking a stand about whether or not there is God) reflects a more scientific viewpoint than theism (believing in God).

- The more educated people become, the more likely they are to become either atheists or agnostics.

- A trend toward increased atheism and agnosticism began a few centuries ago and will continue into the future. In the future, most people will consider a religion such as Christianity to be simply a remnant from the distant past.

(None of these statements are true. The students should be able to offer evidence that contradicts each statement.)

page 188   **Review Questions and Answers**

1. **What instrument did Galileo create that helped him in his astronomical investigations?**

   Galileo invented a telescope, which made available astronomical information not available to others of the time.

2. **What is the difference between a geocentric and a heliocentric system?**

   Someone who believes in a geocentric system believes that the earth is the center of the universe instead of a solar system centered around the sun, a heliocentric system.

3. **What three reasons did the Inquisition give for condemning Galileo's position?**

   The Inquisition objected that Galileo offered no firm proof for his position, it appeared to contradict certain statements in the Bible, and it could present a danger to the faith of common people if they were exposed to it.

4. **What three issues facing the Church does Galileo's story illustrate?**

First, since the time of the great medieval thinkers, Catholicism had sided with scholastic philosophy as its window into the truths of the natural world. Second, at the time many people considered the Bible to be literally true. Third, Galileo's story represents a shift in the role Catholic Church authorities would play in the pursuit of truth.

5. **What perspective on truth seeking did Descartes and Bacon advocate?**

Enlightenment thinkers Descartes and Bacon believed that inductive reasoning, beginning with observable phenomena, was the best approach to truth-seeking.

6. **According to Kant, what was the spirit of the Enlightenment?**

Kant said that the spirit of the Enlightenment was having the courage to rely on one's own understanding for knowledge.

7. **What position on Christianity did most Enlightenment thinkers hold?**

Most Enlightenment thinkers did not reject Christianity. Instead they found it to be in agreement with reason.

8. **What is rationalism?**

Rationalism believes that all truth claims should be held up to scrutiny by science, reason, and the five senses.

9. **How do deists perceive God?**

The God of the deists, in its extreme, is a passive, uninvolved God who began the universe and then left it alone.

10. **In what three ways did the Catholic Church respond to rationalism and deism?**

The Catholic Church responded to the challenges of the Enlightenment by emphasizing scholasticism, by promoting popular devotions that had an emotional bent to them, and by strengthening the moral and spiritual authority of the pope.

Political Change and the Church

Political changes in Europe result in the pope and the Church having less of a political role but an increased role in faith and morals. Along with its emphasis on science, a major characteristic of the modern era is the division of the world into clearly defined nation-states. (The text mentions that, even though we may take such a division for granted, the world was not so divided before modern times.) Church leaders, who viewed the Church as being over and above such divisions, had to navigate this new arrangement. By 1870, the pope went from being a European monarch as well as head of the universal Church to being primarily a moral and spiritual leader who possessed only indirect influence in the world's political affairs.

pages
189–191
AN AGE OF NATION-STATES
National Churches Versus the Universal Church

1. Instruct the students to read pages 189–191.

2. After the students have read these sections, use the **In-Text Activity** to discuss the atmosphere (Is it more globally oriented or nation-centered?) that exists in the world today compared to that which existed in the early eighteenth century.

(A number of factors are at work in the world today that easily transcend national boundaries, such as multinational corporations, the Internet, and the fight against terrorism.)

In-Text Activities

page 189   **DISCUSSION**

Using the Discussion

Discussion of these topics will most likely lead the students to conclude that there is a move toward de-emphasizing nation-states and emphasizing global cooperation. The problems that exist in the world today are probably a good indication of areas that separate nations and set them against each other.

page 190

> ## Christina, Queen of Sweden
>
> Direct the students to read the insert about Christina, Queen of Sweden, and then assign a few students to research Christina's role in bringing about the Treaty of Westphalia, her attempts to regain the throne, and her work for the poor in Rome. Then have the students share the information with the class.

In-Text Activities

page 191   **FYI**

ACTIVITY

Using the Activity

- This information can be found in a variety of sources, such as:

    The Catholic Source Book by Rev. Peter Klein (Dubuque, IA: Harcourt Religion Publishers, 1999).

    The Catholic Encyclopedia by Robert C. Broderick (Huntington, IN: Our Sunday Visitor).

    The HarperCollins Encyclopedia of Catholicism, Richard P. McBrien, general editor (New York: HarperCollins, 1995).

- For your information, here are the popes of the twentieth century and the dates of their reigns:

Leo XIII, 1878–1903	John XXIII, 1958–1963
Pius X, 1903–1914	Paul VI, 1963–1978
Benedict XV, 1914–1922	John Paul I, about one month of 1978
Pius XI, 1922–1939	
Pius XII, 1939–1958	John Paul II, 1978–

CoNCept RevIEw

Draw the students' attention to the Four Gallican Articles issued by King Louis XIV of France; they are found on page 190. Discuss with the students:

- Why would the pope of the time object to each of these?
- Has the Church more recently moved toward accepting any of these articles in any way? If so, explain.

The Impact of the French Revolution

Napoleon and the Concordat with the Pope

1. Direct the students to read these sections of the text.
2. Write the following terms on the board. Review with the students the significance of each term.

- Monarch
- Thirty Years War
- Peace of Westphalia
- Gallicanism
- French Revolution
- Reign of Terror
- Napoleon's concordat
- Ultramontanism
- Cardinal Consalvi

3. Then invite the students to discuss the **In-Text Activity** on page 194.

Cardinal Ercole Consalvi

Ask for a volunteer to read aloud the text concerning Cardinal Ercole Consalvi. After the students have heard the story, initiate a classroom discussion regarding Napoleon's punishment of fobidding the cardinals to wear any sign that they were cardinals.

In-Text Activities

Discussion

Using the Discussion

Those students defending the statement might bring to the discussion examples from the Gospels, Letters, and the Acts of the Apostles that show or teach the Christian understanding of freedom, equality, and fraternity.

Additional Activities

The Martyrs of Compiègne

Exhibited tragically in the story of sixteen Carmelite nuns guillotined during the French reign of terror under Robespierre is the confrontation between (1) a rationalism and a nationalism that are misused and (2) Catholicism. **Handout 8–B, The Martyrs of Compiègne,** briefly tells their story and invites the students to respond to it using some creative form. Discuss with the students why religious life was viewed as irrational and uncivil in that cultural milieu.

Concept Review

Discuss with the students the pros and cons of the pope signing agreements with heads of state.

Pope Pius IX—The First Modern Pope

1. To introduce this section, ask the students: What difference would it make if your school's chaplain or campus minister were also the principal and disciplinarian?

   (Typically, a chaplain is not responsible for administrative decision-making or disciplinary responsibilities. Typically, that is, a chaplain is not directly involved in the political power or the practical matters of a school. For centuries, popes had to balance their spiritual leadership with their responsibilities as ruler of the Papal States.)

2. Point out to the students that a situation such as the one described in the question existed on a grand scale for the papacy up until 1870. Until that time, popes were both heads of state and spiritual leaders. With the fall of the Papal States, Pope Pius IX lost his status as head of a large nation.

3. Direct the students to read this section and elicit from them why Pius IX is the first modern pope.

   (From his time on, popes were viewed as moral and spiritual leaders almost exclusively, not primarily as heads of state.)

In-Text Activities

FYI

Using the FYI

The definition of infallibility in the student text is taken from the glossary of the *Catechism of the Catholic Church,* second edition; see #891. The usual way in which the bishops in union with the pope would teach infallibly is through an ecumenical council. Be sure the students understand that the pope and the bishops usually teach without invoking infallibility; that kind of teaching is referred to as the ordinary magisterium.

Concept Review

1. Invite the students to imagine what it must have felt like for Pope Pius IX when he lost political control of the Papal States. Then ask them:
   - If you had been Pius IX, how would you have reacted?
   - What view of change and progress would you hold after this experience?
   - What would you focus your attention on after the experience?

2. Point out that Pius IX became very conservative politically after losing the Papal States and focused his attention on personal morality and spirituality, and less on matters of state.

Review Questions and Answers

1. **What is the difference between a feudal king and a monarch?**

   Under feudalism, kings functioned as the first among equals who ruled under the authority of the emperor. Monarchs saw themselves as the one and only ruler of a nation.

2. **What three outcomes of the Peace of Westphalia strengthened the modern nation-state system in Europe?**

   With the Peace of Westphalia, the empire was reduced to being one nation among many, the pope's complaints about certain tenets in the treaty went unheeded, and religious lines were sharply drawn in Europe.

3. **What is Gallicanism?**

Gallicanism was a movement proposing that national rulers have authority over Church governance in their country.

4. **What did European monarchs do to maintain a weakened papacy?**

In order to ensure that the papacy would be politically weak, monarchs influenced their bishops to elect weak popes.

5. **What impact did the suppression of the Jesuits have on Catholic education?**

When the Jesuits were suppressed, many of the best Catholic educational institutions lost their power to defend Catholicism against challenges from other sources.

6. **What event is celebrated as the official beginning of the French Revolution?**

On July 14, 1789, citizens of Paris attacked the Bastille prison and set its prisoners free. Because this act marked the beginning of the involvement of the common people in the revolution, Bastille Day is celebrated as the official beginning of the French Revolution.

7. **What effect did the French Revolution have on the Catholic Church?**

The Church in France was associated with the nobility, and many clergy suffered under the Reign of Terror. Thus, for decades after the revolution, Church leaders were fearful of ideas and movements that reflected a revolutionary spirit.

8. **Why did Napoleon's concordat with the pope support Ultramontanism?**

According to the concordat, Napoleon would appoint bishops, but the pope would approve the appointments. By making this agreement directly with the pope, Napoleon validated the pope as the spiritual head of the Church, even in France.

9. **When was the "age of Metternich"? Why is it so called?**

Prince Metternich of Austria oversaw Europe's return to a pre-revolutionary monarchical system. Metternich's ideas dominated Europe until 1858, and so the period is known as "the age of Metternich."

10. **What event occurred in 1870 that led Pope Pius IX to declare himself to be "the prisoner of the Vatican"? What was he protesting by taking this title?**

In 1870 the Italian general Garibaldi overtook Rome and declared it the capital of a united Italy under King Victor Emmanuel, thus ending the Papal States and the pope's position as ruler of a large nation. Pope Pius IX protested this act by declaring himself a prisoner.

11. **Why is Pope Pius IX considered to be the first modern pope?**

Pope Pius IX was the first pope to be solely a moral and spiritual leader of the Church rather than both head of the Church and ruler of a large nation, the Papal States.

12. **When was the first Vatican Council? What doctrine did it proclaim?**

Vatican Council I took place in 1870 and proclaimed the infallibility of the pope.

ENGLAND AND IRELAND

pages 196–197

> ### Three Leaders of the Church in England
>
> Instruct the students to read and summarize the sections on pages 196–197.

Chapter Eight

page 197 ACTIVITY

Using the Activity

The situation in Northern Ireland has been turbulent for centuries. Help the students see that an intertwining of religion and politics in this case has been a factor in producing continual strife. You might extend the activity to present-day conflicts in which people of one religion or one sect of a religion battle people of another religion or sect. Such conflicts are especially difficult when both sides firmly believe God is with them.

Additional Activities

THE CHURCH IN IRELAND

For the most part, the text leaves out discussion of Christianity in Ireland after the time of Patrick and the monastic movement there. Some students may wish to examine Irish Catholicism in greater depth. A number of resources are available that describe Irish or Celtic spirituality. You may assign the students to research and report on historical developments in Irish Catholicism or examples of Irish spirituality. Suggestions:

Listening for the Heartbeat of God: Celtic Spirituality by J. Philip Newell (Mahwah, NJ: Paulist Press, 1997).

The Book of Creation: An Introduction to Celtic Spirituality by J. Philip Newell (Mahwah, NJ: Paulist Press, 1999).

Celtic Spirituality by Oliver Davies and Thomas O'Loughlin (Mahwah, NJ: Paulist Press, 1999).

Discovering Celtic Christianity: Its Roots, Relationships, and Relevance by Bruce R. Pullen (Illustrator) (Mystic, CT: Twenty-Third Publications, 1999).

The Music of What Happens: Celtic Spirituality by John J. O Rordain (Winona, MN: Saint Mary's Press, 1997).

The Spirituality of the Celtic Saints by Richard J. Woods (Maryknoll, NY: Orbis Books, 2000).

THE OXFORD MOVEMENT

The Oxford Movement in England deserves further examination by the students since it represents an attempt to make the Anglican Church more Catholic, partially in response to some of the liberal Enlightenment and Protestant ideas that were popular at the time. Some leaders of the movement even converted to Catholicism—most notably, John Henry Newman. Divide the following topics among the students in small groups, assigning them to research and report on their topic to the rest of the class:

- The Oxford Movement
- Members of the movement other than John Henry Newman
- The life of John Henry Newman
- The writings and teachings of John Henry Newman
- Newman's developing relationship with the Catholic Church

GERARD MANLEY HOPKINS—POET OF THE OXFORD MOVEMENT

One person who converted from Anglicanism to Catholicism under the influence of the Oxford Movement made his mark as one of the great poets of the English language. You might invite an English teacher to speak to the class about the poetry of Gerard Manley Hopkins, or simply ask the students to find a poem of his (readily available on the Internet) and to describe imagery he uses to speak about his faith. For instance, he beautifully describes the lure of the Christian doctrines of the resurrection and the incarnation in these words:

> . . . Enough! The Resurrection,
> A heart's-clarion! Away grief's gasping, joyless days, dejection.
>   Across my foundering deck shone
> A beacon, an eternal beam. Flesh fade and mortal trash
> Fall to the residuary worm; world's wildfire, leave but ash:
>   In a flash, at a trumpet crash,
> I am all at once what Christ is, since he was what I am. . . .

"That Nature is a Heraclitean Fire and of the Comfort of the Resurrection"

CoNCept ReViEw

If examined in depth, the following question would require more background than the text provides. However, discussion of this question points out that the lines between Catholic and Protestant are not as clearly drawn as an uncritical observation might conclude. The Oxford Movement in England represents the allure of Catholicism in the modern world. Lead the students in a discussion of the following question related to the Oxford Movement: The Anglican/Episcopalian Church: Is it more Catholic or more Protestant?

(The best answer is "both." As mentioned in the previous chapter, some Anglicans saw their break with Rome to be merely a political one, while other Anglicans moved the Church of England more toward Protestantism. Anglicanism/Episcopalianism continues to live with this conflict today. The Oxford Movement was a move toward stressing Catholic elements in the Anglican Church— so much so that many of its members left the Anglican Church altogether and joined the Catholic Church. In the United States a group of Episcopalians have formed the Anglican Catholic Church, moving even closer to many of the practices and beliefs of the Catholic Church, while rejecting some of the more "liberal" elements of the Episcopalian Church.)

Review Questions and Answers

page 197

1. **What was the Oxford Movement?**

   The Oxford Movement refers to a movement during the 1800s when some of the brightest Anglican churchmen in England joined the Catholic Church.

2. **John Henry Newman concluded that the true Church should be centered upon what institution?**

   Through his studies on early Christianity, Newman concluded that the true Church should be centered on the papacy.

3. **What effect did the Glorious Revolution have on English-Irish relations?**

   The Glorious Revolution refers to the ouster of the Catholic King James II of England when the English throne was given to the Protestant William and Mary of Orange. When James used Ireland as a base for attempting to regain the throne, English-Irish tensions deepened.

202

Chapter Eight

4. Why are Protestants in Northern Ireland known as *Orangemen?*

Protestants supported William of Orange against the Catholic James II in the battle over the English throne in 1688. Irish Catholics called William's supporters "Orangemen."

Catholicism during the Baroque Era

Dedicated Catholics give themselves to new ways of living the Christian life and to a baroque style of spirituality. In general, baroque spirituality was the dominant expression of Catholic spirituality for four hundred years—from the time following the Reformation to the changes of Vatican II. Baroque spirituality was vastly different from the rationalistic, scientific spirit of the age. In many ways, popular perspectives continue to equate Catholic spirituality with baroque spirituality, and baroque spiritual practices continue in the Church. (Sometimes such practices as novenas and Forty-Hours Devotions are given a more contemporary interpretation as well.) Use the information that the text provides to help the students understand the Baroque in art and worship. After that, they can discuss this spirituality's strengths and possible exaggerations.

page 198   ## A CHANGING WORLD

The Baroque in Art and Worship

Have the students read and summarize page 198.

Additional Activities

PRAYER TO THE SACRED HEART—AN EXAMPLE OF BAROQUE SPIRITUALITY

1. To give the students an example of baroque spirituality, you might slowly read aloud the prayer to the Sacred Heart of Jesus formalized by Pope Pius XI in 1925. Ask the students to write down images that they hear in the prayer during your reading.

   Most sweet Jesus, Redeemer of the human race, look down upon us humbly prostrate before Thine altar. We are Thine, and Thine we wish to be; but to be more surely united with Thee, behold, each of us freely consecrates himself today to Thy most Sacred Heart. Many, indeed, have never known Thee; many, too, despising Thy precepts, have rejected Thee. Have mercy on them all, most merciful Jesus, and draw them to Thy Sacred Heart. Be thou King, O Lord, not only of the faithful who have never forsaken Thee, but also of the prodigal children who have abandoned Thee; grant that they may quickly return to their Father's house, lest they die of wretchedness and hunger. Be thou King of those whom heresy holds in error or discord keeps aloof; call them back to the harbor of truth and the unity of faith, so that soon there may be but one fold and one Shepherd. Grant, O Lord, to Thy Church assurance of freedom and immunity from harm; give peace and order to all nations, and make the earth resound from pole to pole with one cry: Praise to the divine Heart that wrought our salvation; to it be glory and honor forever. Amen.

   The Catholic Source Book, Peter Klein (Dubuque, IA:
   Harcourt Religion Publishers, 1999), 376.

2. Following the reading, invite the students to write down what they perceive to be the spirit of the prayer.

3. Then discuss with them the images in the prayer and the message of the prayer.

CONCEPT REVIEW

Review with the students characteristics of baroque spirituality. Discuss: Why do you think this type of spirituality was so popular during the so-called "age of science"?

(The students may note that a more emotional, sensual spirituality gave balance to the rationalistic spirit of the age. Also, the scientific starting point of holding everything up to questioning and doubt can undermine faith when overdone, leaving many people seeking ways to quench their spiritual thirst. Also, as science progressed, it became more elitist-the realm of a select group of educated people. The sensual images of the baroque appealed to people on a more fundamental, human level.)

pages 199–201

Varieties of Spiritual Life

Along with its baroque spirituality, Catholicism of this age is noted for its many members who expressed their faith by dedicating their lives to serving others. Giving ourselves for others continues to be an expectation for and a characteristic of Catholics today. Ask the students to read the section, and then ask them to explain ways they might live the spirituality exemplified by each of the people mentioned.

(Saint Bendict Joseph Labre stands out from the other figures since he was not one who helped people in need. Rather, he seems to have modeled what we today would call a "needy person." It's important for the students to realize that within Catholicism there are a variety of ways to have God's presence in the world shine through.)

In-Text Activities

page 199

YOUTH NEWS

Using the Youth News

If your school sponsors service opportunities, direct the students into areas for which they are suited. Making service a requirement for the course is perfectly acceptable; all of us need practice and encouragement in this area. Later, memories of these activities may prompt these students to make service a part of their everyday life.

page 201

WWW.

Using the www.

1. The diocesan vocations office may be able to supply you with additional print and audiovisual information on communities centered in the area. Consider a visit to a motherhouse or center of a religious order.

2. Set aside time for the students to share their findings with the class.

ACTIVITY

Using the Activity

These activities are quite personal and lend themselves to journaling that will not be shared. Let the students know ahead of time if their work will be shared.

CONCEPT REVIEW

Discuss with the students the following question: If it is to be true to its name, must a Catholic school place an emphasis on serving others? Explain.

World Catholicism during the Baroque Era

An earlier chapter examined evangelization, spreading the gospel message, or the Church's missionary activity. This section addresses the fact that the Church made further inroads into non-European countries. An important issue is the degree of accommodation that the Church—for so long enmeshed with European culture—could accept. This concern emerged as missionaries entered India and the Far East. Instruct the students to read the sections on pages 202–206.

pages
202–206

Catholic Missionaries to Foreign Lands

CHRISTIANITY IN CHINA AND ITS NEIGHBORS

INDIA—MISSIONARIES DISCOVER AN ANCIENT CHRISTIAN COMMUNITY

1. An important issue underlying this section is the accommodationist controversy. That is, to what degree should those who spread the faith adapt its message and practices to the culture in which they are working? The text provides a number of examples of people who attempted to make Christianity not just a European religion but a truly world religion. Have the students read pages 202–206.

2. After the students have read the section, discuss accommodationism with the students. Point out that the issue continues to face the Church today. When the students understand what the accommodationist controversy entails, ask them: How is accommodationism an issue for the Church today?

   (For instance, can elements of traditional Native American cultures or Latino and African American cultures be incorporated into the Mass and sacraments? Should popular music be allowed in Catholic wedding ceremonies? Should a Mass for teens look and sound any different from a Mass for adults or young children?)

3. In discussion summarize the work and results of each of the people discussed in this section.

page 204

Saint Paul Miki and Companions

More information about Saint Paul Miki and his companions is available in books on lives of the saints and on the Internet.

In-Text Activities

page 206

ACTIVITY

Using the Activity

Consider incorporating modern examples into this discussion. Check recent Catholic newspapers and magazines for people and situations to share with the class, or make this an assignment or class project.

POPE PAUL VI ON EVANGELIZATION

In 1975 in the document *On Evangelization in the Modern World,* Pope Paul VI wrote an important statement about evangelization. If you have not addressed this issue earlier, you can use **Handout 8–C, Pope Paul VI on Evangelization,** to provide the students an opportunity to examine how Church leaders see the Church's role in evangelization.

SAINT VINCENT DE PAUL SOCIETY

Invite a member of the Saint Vincent de Paul Society to speak to the class about the work of the organization. In many communities this group quietly serves those in need without fanfare. If it is not possible to schedule a speaker, check with the diocesan offices for information about the group.

Concept Review

Discuss with the students the following two statements:

- Catholicism is enriched by adopting characteristics of non-Christian cultures.
- Catholicism is watered down and diluted by adopting characteristics of non-Christian cultures.

page 206

Review Questions and Answers

1. **Describe a baroque style of spirituality.**

   Baroque spirituality emphasizes feelings and sentimentality.

2. **What experience led Vincent de Paul to become involved in service to people who were poor?**

   After a peasant who was near death asked Vincent to hear his confession, the man thanked Vincent for giving him the opportunity to confess his sins before dying. Vincent realized that his priesthood should be used to serve those in need.

3. **What group was founded by Louise de Marillac?**

   Under the guidance of Vincent de Paul, Louise de Marillac founded the Daughters of Charity, a group of women dedicated to helping poor people full time.

4. **What did Francis de Sales emphasize in his spirituality?**

   Francis de Sales emphasized developing good habits in everyday life. Each person should practice spirituality according to the life that he or she lives.

5. **Why was Benedict Joseph Labre considered a saint?**

   Benedict Joseph Labre was a vagabond who ended up living homeless on the streets of Rome. After he died on the steps of a Roman church, people began to speak about his sanctity.

6. **What changes did John Baptist de La Salle introduce into education?**

   John Baptist de La Salle is patron saint of teachers because he introduced the practices of teaching the students in their own language, in groups rather than individually, and according to a set schedule of classes.

7. **Who was Matteo Ricci, and what is an accommodationist approach to missionary work?**

   Matteo Ricci was a Jesuit missionary in China who mastered Chinese language and literature and who adopted upper-class Chinese manners. An accommodationist approach to missionary work incorporates elements from a particular culture into the teachings and practices of the faith, for example, Matteo Ricci's acceptance of certain traditional Chinese beliefs and rituals into Christianity.

8. **Who were the Christians of Saint Thomas?**

   The Christians of Saint Thomas were a group of Christians in India who trace their ancestry back to the first century and the missionary work of the apostle Thomas.

9. **How did Francis Xavier help Indian converts to Christianity remember the basic prayers and creeds of the faith?**

   Francis Xavier wrote basic prayers and the creed in simple rhymes that were easy to remember and recite so that Indian converts could learn Christian beliefs and practices.

10. **What approach did Roberto de Nobili use in his missionary work?**

    Roberto de Nobili lived like a Brahmin, a holy man of India, in an attempt to explain Christianity to the people in terms of their traditional spirituality.

Chapter Review and Conclusion

REVIEW

1. Ask the students to summarize the main points in the chapter using their own words. Write notes on the board from their contributions. To reinforce their summary, you might want to review the major concepts in this chapter in the teaching manual. Then read the **Conclusion** on page 207.

2. Review the vocabulary in this chapter:

   heliocentric—belief that the earth and other planets revolve around the sun (page 181)

   geocentric—belief that the sun revolves around the earth (page 181)

   scholasticism—a method of intellectual inquiry dominant in western Christian civilization from the Middle Ages until the seventeenth century, and into the twentieth century among Catholic scholars (page 183)

   Enlightenment—the seventeenth- and eighteenth-century movement in Europe during which reason and science held a privileged position as sources of truth (page 184)

   rationalism—a theory that nothing is true unless founded on scientifically demonstrable proofs based solely on reason and the five senses; condemned by the First Vatican Council (page 185)

   deism—belief that God created the world and then left it to run according to natural laws (page 185)

   infallible—incapable of error in defining doctrines involving faith or morals (page 188)

monarch—head of a nation-state who claims to have complete authority in its governance (page 189)

Thirty Years War—war over religious, dynastic, and territorial issues which involved most European nations but was fought mainly in Germany (page 189)

Gallicanism—a movement originating among the French Catholic clergy based on national rulers having authority for Church governance in their country (page 190)

Reign of Terror—period during the French Revolution when nobility and many clergy were executed by French revolutionary leaders (page 192)

condordat—an agreement between the pope and a head of state identifying the role that each would play in Church governance in that country (page 193)

Ultramontanism—belief, often in an exaggerated form, that the pope alone has ultimate authority for Church governance in all countries (page 193)

infallibility—the gift of the Holy Spirit to the Church whereby either the pope or bishops in union with him can definitively proclaim a doctrine of faith or morals for the belief of the faithful (page 195)

baroque—a style of art, architecture, and spirituality that emphasizes feelings and sentimentality (page 198)

accommodation—the practice of incorporating beliefs and practices from local cultures into Christianity (page 203)

Christians of Saint Thomas—Indian Christians who trace their origins to the first century (page 204)

Brahmins—in the traditional Indian caste system, members of the priestly caste (page 206)

TEST

Give the students the Chapter 8 Test or an alternative assessment. The tests have been placed on the Harcourt Religion Publishers' Web page. This has been done to enable the teacher to customize this material for local needs. First contact Harcourt Religion Publishers' high school consultant at 800-922-7696, ext. 3781 for a user ID and password. Then connect with the Harcourt Religion Publishers' Web site at **www.harcourtreligion.com** to download the information. Collect the tests for grading.

Chapter 8 Test Answers

MULTIPLE CHOICE (1 point each)

1. d	6. b	10. d	14. a	18. b
2. c	7. b	11. b	15. d	19. a
3. a	8. b	12. a	16. a	20. c
4. b	9. b	13. c	17. c	21. a
5. d				

MATCHING (1 point each)

Set 1	Set 2		Set 3
1. C	1. G	6. D	1. B
2. D	2. F	7. H	2. D
3. B	3. I	8. A	3. A
4. A	4. E	9. C	4. C
5. E	5. B	10. J	

ESSAYS (10 points each)

1. The spirit of the Enlightenment was one of emphasizing scientific inquiry as the source of truth. In response, Catholics tended to emphasize scholasticism in truth-seeking, popular devotions that appealed to the emotions, and the authority of the pope.

2. Gallicanism refers to emphasizing the role of national leaders in Church governance. Ultra montanism refers to emphasizing the role of the pope in Church governance.

3. The spirit of the age of Metternich was one of emphasizing the role of national monarchs in Europe. This emphasis was a reaction to the chaos and destruction of the French Revolution and the age of Napoleon.

4. Pope Pius IX can be considered the first modern pope because he was the first pope since the time of Charlemagne who was primarily a moral and spiritual leader and not also the head of a large country.

5. Baroque spirituality emphasizes sentimentality and feelings in religious expression, such as devotion to the Sacred Heart of Jesus.

6. Accommodation refers to incorporating elements from local culture into Christianity. Matteo Ricci imitated Chinese scholars and incorporated traditional Chinese beliefs and practices into Christianity. Roberto de Nobili lived like a "Roman Brahmin" in India. On the other hand, many missionaries who worked among the lower classes in mission countries tended to minimize or reject accommodation to local culture.

Prayer

MUSIC SUGGESTIONS

"Amazing Grace," Traditional from *Gather (Comprehensive)* (GIA), *Glory & Praise (Comprehensive)* (OCP), *Today's Missal* (OCP), *We Celebrate* (J.S. Paluch Co., Inc.), *Lead Me, Guide Me* (GIA).

"Givin' Back the Gifts" by Larry Schexnaydre and Rhett Glindmeyer from *Give Your Gifts, the New Songs* (GIA, Harcourt Religion Publishers).

"Lead Me, Lord," by John Becker from *Today's Missal* (OCP).

"Live in the Light" by Michael Mahler from *Give Your Gifts, the New Songs* (GIA, Harcourt Religion Publishers).

"Path of Life" by M. Balhoff, D. Ducote, G. Daigle from *Glory & Praise (Comprehensive)* (OCP).

"Service" by The Dameans from *Glory & Praise (Comprehensive)* (OCP).

"Standin' in the Need of Prayer," Spiritual from *Gather (Comprehensive)* (GIA), *Lead Me, Guide Me* (GIA).

"The Harvest of Justice" by David Haas from *Gather (Comprehensive)* (GIA).

SCRIPTURE SUGGESTIONS

Jeremiah 22:13–16

James 1:19–27

Matthew 25:31–46

PRAYER

*O give thanks to the L*ORD*, for he is good;*
for his steadfast love endures forever.
*Let the redeemed of the L*ORD *say so,*
those he redeemed from trouble
and gathered in from the lands,
from the east and from the west,
from the north and from the south.
Some wandered in desert wastes,
finding no way to an inhabited town;
hungry and thirsty,
their soul fainted within them.
Then they cried to the LORD *in their trouble,*
and he delivered them from their distress;
he led them by a straight way,
until they reached an inhabited town.
*Let them thank the L*ORD *for his steadfast love,*
for his wonderful works to humankind.
For he satisfies the thirsty,
and the hungry he fills with good things.

Psalm 107:1–9

CHAPTER 8 TEST

Name_____ Date_____ Class period_____

Test is made up of questions with suggested values totaling 100 points.

Multiple Choice (1 point each)

_____ 1. To arrive at truth, Galileo used
    a. the Bible
    b. scholastic philosophy
    c. consensus
    d. direct observation

_____ 2. A geocentric view of the universe proposes that
    a. the earth began with volcanic eruptions
    b. the universe began with a "big bang"
    c. the sun and stars revolve around the earth
    d. God created the world in seven days

_____ 3. The Church court hearing Galileo's case ordered him to
    a. stop speaking or writing about his theory
    b. instruct Church leaders about the new science
    c. do further research into his theories
    d. report to the court in a year about his findings

_____ 4. Scholasticism used deductive reasoning, meaning that
    a. truth comes from direct experience
    b. general principles and logical deduction from those principles
    c. religion alone leads to truth
    d. everyone has his or her own perspective

_____ 5. According to a literal reading of the Bible's Book of Joshua,
    a. someone lived in a fish for three days
    b. the earth was created in seven days
    c. God appeared in a fiery chariot
    d. the sun stood still for a day

_____ 6. The Enlightenment emphasized
    a. Scripture and Tradition
    b. reason and science
    c. intuition and meditation
    d. prayer and sacraments

_____ 7. Deists believe that
   a. there is no God
   b. God is not actively involved in the world
   c. praying to God brings personal insights
   d. science has corrupted religion

_____ 8. One reaction within the Catholic Church to rationalism was
   a. the encouraging of Bible reading
   b. an emphasis on scholasticism
   c. sponsorship of scientific study
   d. establishing a papal astronomy commission

_____ 9. Following the Peace of Westphalia ending the Thirty Years War, the pope
   a. no longer ruled the Papal States
   b. became a minor voice in politics
   c. accepted Protestants as fellow Christians
   d. supported the Irish against the English

_____ 10. In order to ensure that the pope had little power, European monarchs
   a. supported a "two pope" system for the Church
   b. elected their own bishops and cardinals
   c. refused to recognize the Papal States as a nation
   d. influenced their bishops to elect weak men as popes

_____ 11. The event recognized as the beginning of the French Revolution was
   a. the death of King Louis XVI and his family
   b. Parisians freeing prisoners in the Bastille
   c. the end of the Reign of Terror
   d. Napoleon's crowning himself emperor

_____ 12. A concordat was
   a. an agreement between Napoleon and the pope
   b. Napoleon's decree granting freedom of religion
   c. the pope's condemnation of Napoleon
   d. a treaty between Napoleon and Russia

_____ 13. Pope Pius IX called himself "prisoner of the Vatican" because
   a. he felt Catholics were disregarding his teachings
   b. wars in Europe prevented him from traveling freely
   c. he was protesting his loss of the Papal States
   d. he proclaimed the pope to be infallible

_____ 14. A principal teaching of Vatican Council I was
   a. the infallibility of the pope
   b. the approval of evolution
   c. the seven sacraments
   d. the condemnation of Protestantism

_____ 15. The Oxford Movement promoted
   a. the education of Catholics
   b. seminary training at an early age
   c. Protestantism in England
   d. Catholicism in the Church of England

_____ 16. Saint Francis de Sales is known for encouraging people to
   a. develop good habits in their daily lives
   b. encourage one child to enter religious life
   c. think of themselves as "Christian soldiers"
   d. serve as missionaries in other lands

_____ 17. Saint Vincent de Paul focused his priesthood on service when he
   a. realized that he had been adopted
   b. was rejected at court for being a commoner
   c. heard the confession of a peasant
   d. read the Gospel story of the Good Samaritan

_____ 18. Saint John Baptist de La Salle is patron saint of
   a. social workers
   b. teachers
   c. hospital workers
   d. infants

_____ 19. The Christians of Saint Thomas were
   a. Indian Christians who trace their origins back to the first century
   b. Laypeople who engaged in missionary work in Asia
   c. Japanese Catholics who were crucified for accepting foreign beliefs
   d. Catholics who lived on islands in Southeast Asia

_____ 20. The saint recognized as both the apostle to India and the apostle to Japan is
   a. Francis de Sales
   b. Matteo Ricci
   c. Francis Xavier
   d. Paul Miki

_____ 21. Jesuit missionaries to China proposed that the ancient Chinese sage Confucius was
   a. not viewed as a god and therefore could continue to be revered by Christians
   b. an early Christian who kept his true religion a secret during his lifetime
   c. someone whose teachings were contradictory to Christianity
   d. an early missionary who had converted a few Chinese to Christianity

Matching (1 point each)

SET 1

_____ 1. Copernicus

_____ 2. Galileo

_____ 3. Descartes

_____ 4. Aristotle

_____ 5. Francis Bacon

A. a philosopher upon whom scholasticism is based

B. "I think; therefore, I am"

C. first modern to propose heliocentrism

D. used telescope for astronomical studies

E. used inductive reasoning; based nothing on authority

SET 2

_____ 1. Bernadette Soubirous

_____ 2. Cardinal Ercole Consalvi

_____ 3. John Henry Newman

_____ 4. Vincent de Paul

_____ 5. Louise de Marillac

_____ 6. Francis de Sales

_____ 7. Benedict Joseph Labre

_____ 8. John Baptiste de La Salle

_____ 9. Julie Billiart

_____ 10. Christina of Sweden

A. taught homeless boys

B. organized women to work with the poor, founded Daughters of Charity

C. risked life during French Revolution

D. advocate of "everyday spirituality"

E. realized priesthood should be service to the poor

F. refused to recognize Napoleon's marriage

G. received apparitions of the Blessed Mother

H. homeless beggar

I. member of the Oxford Movement

J. converted to Catholicism, abdicating her throne

SET 3

_____ 1. Francis Xavier

_____ 2. Roberto de Nobili

_____ 3. Paul Miki

_____ 4. Matteo Ricci

A. Japanese convert to Catholicism and martyr

B. used simple rhymes to teach the creed

C. studied the Chinese classics

D. lived like a Brahmin in India

Essays (10 points each)

1. Describe the spirit of the Enlightenment. Name three trends that developed within Catholicism in response to the challenge of the Enlightenment.

2. Explain the difference between Gallicanism and Ultra montanism.

3. What was the spirit of the age of Metternich? What developments led to this spirit?

4. Why is Pope Pius IX considered the first modern pope?

5. Describe and give an example of baroque spirituality.

6. Describe the controversy surrounding accommodation in mission work. Explain how one missionary adapted Catholicism to local culture.

AN ARTIST SPEAKS OF THE IMPORTANCE OF GOD

Name_____ Date_____ Class period_____

The nineteenth-century Dutch painter Vincent van Gogh wrote of the importance of a living, caring, involved God in the following words:

You must not be astonished when, even at the risk of your taking me for a fanatic, I tell you that in order to love, I think it absolutely necessary to believe in God . . . ; to me, to believe in God is to feel that there is a God, not dead or stuffed but alive, urging us to love again with irresistible force—that is my opinion.

Quoted in *Season of New Beginnings* by Mitch Finley (Mineola, NY: Resurrection Press, 1996), 19.

Write your thoughts on his opinion in the spaces provided.

• What is van Gogh's reaction to a deistic notion of God?

• Why do you think that, given the climate of his time, van Gogh feared his opinion might label him a fanatic? Do you think his opinion would be viewed as fanatical by most people today?

• Do you agree with van Gogh? Why? What difference might agreeing with van Gogh make in a person's life?

THE MARTYRS OF COMPIÈGNE

Name_____ Date_____ Class period_____

In 1784, revolutionary forces controlled France and conducted a "reign of terror" against enemies of the state. In July of that year, sixteen Carmelite nuns were guillotined, convicted of crimes against the state. Most of the people, who had been cheering the deaths of members of the nobility before this time, watched in silence as these women who were from the common people themselves sang hymns praising God until the very moment of their death. Within ten days, the government toppled and its "reign of terror" ended.

Why would Carmelite nuns, who live a cloistered life of prayer, be considered "anti-revolutionary" and subversive of the state? In a sense, contemplative religious life was an affront to two prevailing doctrines of the time—reason and nationalism. The nuns vowed obedience to God alone. To rationalists and nationalists, their lifestyle was irrational and impractical. (If they had been teaching or serving those who are poor, then their religious vows might make sense to rationalists and nationalists, but simply to dedicate their lives to prayer was not "reasonable.")

When the nuns were first called before the courts, the case against them was stated in these terms:

Religious orders are the most scandalous violation of [the rights of man]. In a moment of fleeting fervor, a young adolescent pronounces an oath to recognize henceforth neither father nor family, never to be a spouse, never a citizen; he submits his will to the will of another, his soul to the soul of another; he renounces all liberty at an age when he could not relinquish the most modest possessions; his oath is a civil suicide.

Quoted in Terrye Newkirk, *The Mantle of Elijah*
(Washington, DC: Institute of Carmelite Studies, 1995), 26.

In other words, being a nun was "uncivil" behavior in the eyes of revolutionary France. Representatives of the court had interviewed the nuns separately and in private, believing that if given the chance they would admit that they had been kidnapped into joining such a strange community and wasting their time in silence and prayer. All the nuns remained loyal to their vows and their community, even when it meant death.

Those who have written, or in one case composed an opera, about the martyrs of Compiègne believe that the story of these nuns contains important messages for people of the modern era.

• What do you think those messages are?

• When asked to respond to the charges against her, one of the nuns handed over a poem that she had written. Choose a form of expression to illustrate a theme from her story.

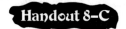

POPE PAUL VI ON EVANGELIZATION

Name_____ Date_____ Class period_____

In 1975, Pope Paul VI wrote *On Evangelization in the Modern World* in which he says that "She [the Church] exists in order to evangelize" (number 14). For each of the following statements from that document, explain how its message could have been applied to the Christian missionary activity that took place in the sixteenth and seventeenth centuries in the Far East and then to possible missionary activity today.

The Church is an evangelizer, but she begins by being evangelized herself. (number 15)

[The Church exists] *to preach and teach,*
to be the channel of the gift of grace,
to reconcile sinners with God,
and to perpetuate Christ's sacrifice in the Mass,
which is the memorial of his death and glorious Resurrection. (number 14)

The Gospel, and therefore evangelization, are certainly not identical with culture, and they are independent in regards to all cultures. Nevertheless, the Kingdom which the Gospel proclaims is lived by men who are profoundly linked to a culture, and the building up of the Kingdom cannot avoid borrowing the elements of human culture or cultures. (number 20)

The Church respects and esteems . . . non-Christian religions because they are the living expression of the soul of vast groups of people. They carry within them the echo of thousands of years of searching for God, a quest which is incomplete but often made with great sincerity and righteousness of heart. They possess an impressive patrimony of deeply religious texts. They have taught generations of people how to pray. They are impregnated with innumerable "seeds of the Word" and can constitute a true "preparation for the Gospel." (number 53)

CHAPTER NINE

MOSAIC OF UNITY AND DIVERSITY
The Church in the Americas

A Teacher's Prayer

Mary, Mother of the Americas, who appeared to the Indian peasant Juan Diego, watch over our northern and southern continents. Help my students to find your Son in the great mosaic of people who make the Americas their home. Amen.

Overview

The chapter is divided into a study of the Spanish, French, and then English presence in America during the early centuries of European colonization. The section on the English presence is further divided into the colonial period and the half-century or so after Independence. The **Before We Begin . . .** activity can serve as a research assignment to be completed during study of the chapter and be reported on after the material in the chapter has been discussed.

Major Concepts Covered in This Chapter

① Introduction

② Spanish America

③ French America

④ English America

⑤ Catholicism in the Early United States

⑥ Chapter Review and Conclusion

Introduction

Prayer

pages
208–209

- **Music Suggestions**

  "All the Ends of the Earth" by Bob Dufford from *Gather (Comprehensive)* (GIA), *Lead Me, Guide Me* (GIA), *Today's Missal* (OCP), *Glory & Praise Comprehensive* (OCP).

  "Canticle of the Turning" (Irish Traditional) from *Give Your Gifts, the Basics* (GIA, Harcourt Religion Publishers).

  "Come, All You People" by Alexander Gondo from *Give Your Gifts, the Basics* (GIA, Harcourt Religion Publishers).

  "Gather Us In" by Marty Haugen from *Gather (Comprehensive)* (GIA), *Glory & Praise (Comprehensive)* (OCP), *Today's Missal* (OCP), *We Celebrate* (J.S. Paluch Co., Inc.).

  "God, in the Planning" by John Bell, traditional Irish tune, from *Gather Comprehensive* (GIA).

  "Seed Scattered and Sown" by Dan Feiten from *Today's Missal* (OCP).

  "We Are the Light of the World" by Jean Anthony Greif from *Glory & Praise* 2, *Today's Missal* (OCP).

- **Scripture Suggestions**

  Proverbs 8:1–4, 20

  Acts 17:22–28

  Luke 9:1–6

- **Prayer**

  See the prayer on page 208.

pages
208–209

Overview

Have the students read the **Chapter Overview** and timeline on pages 208–209. Briefly discuss some of the points and events noted.

Spanish America

Spanish explorers, missionaries, and settlers created a Catholic New Spain from southern South America to Northern California. As the text indicates, the arrival of the Spanish in America caused a "collision of cultures" during which the cultures and people of the many Native American groups suffered drastically. The first part of the chapter's treatment of the Spanish presence in the Americas describes the suffering it caused. The second part describes attempts on the part of missionaries to reduce suffering and to bring spiritual and material benefits to Native Americans. It is important for the students to realize that the clash of cultures was unavoidable. That is, much damage occurred to Native American populations because Europeans arrived on the shores of the Americas; however, Spanish treatment of Native Americans was not unavoidable, and generally speaking, much of that treatment was barbarous. Once the two worlds met, many missionaries tried to make the meeting fruitful for Native Americans.

A Collision of Cultures

Catholicism in Spanish America

Mistreatment of the Native Americans

The Conquistadores and the Search for Gold

pages 210–214

1. Direct the students to read the text on pages 210–214. In discussion, briefly summarize each section.
2. Take note of the map on page 211. Determine the present names of the areas indicated.

In-Text Activities

page 212

WWW.

Using the www.

1. Set aside class time for the students to share some of their findings.
2. Make a list of the ten best sites, and give copies of the lists to the students.

ACTIVITY

Using the Activity

1. Give the students the opportunity to share their reports in small groups or in the large group.
2. If any traditional Native Americans live in the area, consider having one or more of them address the class, especially on their religious beliefs and practices.

Additional Activities

NATIVE AMERICAN CULTURE; SPANISH CULTURE

Either in conjunction with the **In-Text Activity** or separately, you might allow the students an opportunity to think about the way Spanish culture transformed Native American cultures. Assign one group of the students to research and report on native cultures before the arrival of the Spanish and another group to describe life in the California missions under the Franciscans. Discuss with the students:

- How was Native American culture changed under Spanish rule?
- What do you think it would have been like to be a Native American experiencing such change?
- What alternatives were available to the Spanish in their treatment of Native Americans—even by those among the Spanish who had the best intentions?
- What alternatives were available to Native Americans in terms of how they responded to the Spanish?

INDIAN MASCOTS—CONTINUING EXPLOITATION?

One issue that encapsulates the ongoing concern of Native Americans about their place in the dominant American culture is that of team mascots. The U.S. Commission on Civil Rights addressed the issue in 2001. To stimulate discussion about the topic you might distribute **Handout 9–A, Native American Images and Team Names—Exploitation Continues?** The students might also access additional statements on the topic that are posted on the Internet. The handout instructs the students to list the reasons why the commission is against the use of Indian mascots. Since the topic may evoke quick responses on the part of the students, it is important for them to understand the commission's reasoning before they come to a position. You might point out the following information during discussion of this issue:

- There are currently three million Native Americans in the U.S.
- 515 groups live on 300 reservations, rancheros, and colonies.
- Unemployment rates on the average reservation range from 60 to 90 percent.
- Native American youth have a higher suicide rate than the youth of any other ethnic group.
- Average life span among Native Americans is 47, compared to 76 for whites.

CoNCept RevIEw

Discuss with the students: Members of a group in a formerly non-Christian culture who become Christian invariably lose much of their original cultural identity. Therefore, the fact that Native Americans became Christian under Spanish rule helped bring about the radical change in their culture.

pages
214–220

Native American Catholicism

SAINT ROSE OF LIMA

OUR LADY OF GUADALUPE

Spanish Catholicism Moves North

JUAN DE PADILLA

EUSEBIO FRANCISCO KINO

JUNIPERO SERRA AND THE CALIFORNIA MISSIONS

1. You might divide your class into eight groups and assign one of the above eight sub-sections to each group (exclude the paragraph on **Native American Catholicism**). Direct students to read over their section and to provide the rest of the class a summary of the information included there.
2. You might add to this assignment by instructing each group to find more information about their topic and to include in their presentation whatever additional information they found on the topic. (You could send your class to a computer-equipped room or to the library to prepare this assignment.)

page 214   **FYI**

Using the FYI

In many parts of the country, there are members of third orders (lay people and/or religious). Consider having one of these people attend a class in order to be interviewed by the students. Work with the students to prepare questions ahead of time.

page 215   ACTIVITY

Using the Activity

Have the students share their suggestions in small groups. Then ask the small groups to choose three suggestions to share with the class. Discuss as needed.

---

pages 216–217

Bartolome de Las Casas/The Reductions of Paraguay

Have the students read and summerize the boxed text on pages 216–217.

---

page 219   **FYI**

page 220   ACTIVITY

Using the Activity

Have the students share their lists and create a combined list of city names. Group them according to states.

Additional Activities

OUR LADY OF GUADALUPE

1. In Mexico and among Mexicans, devotion to Our Lady of Guadalupe is strong. Even many young Mexican men make their way on their knees to the cathedral that houses the image of Mary. You might divide the class into five groups and ask each group to write up a first-person account of the story of Mary's appearances and the response that they received. Assign a group to each of the following:
   - The Blessed Mother
   - Juan Diego
   - The bishop
   - The native Mexicans
   - The Spanish people living in Mexico
2. Allow the students ten to fifteen minutes to think about how their particular person or group might view the events. Instruct each group to prepare a statement from that perspective to be read to the class.

3. After the presentations, discuss with the students: Does the nature of the Blessed Mother's appearance to Juan Diego reflect the original spirit of Christianity? Why or why not?

(You might remind the students that something similarly unexpected happened in the early day of Christianity—the Holy Spirit came and gave hope to a desperate group. Also, Christianity opened its doors to people of all nations and cultural backgrounds. Finally, Jesus' message took root among people of his time who were poor and outcast. These early characteristics of Christianity are represented in the story of Our Lady of Guadalupe.)

HISPANIC AMERICANS—A CONTINUING PRESENCE

1. The Hispanic influence on the United States did not end when the United States defeated Mexico and annexed the area of the Southwest. By the 1980s the United States ranked fifth among Spanish-speaking populations, behind Mexico, Spain, Argentina, and Colombia. The U.S. Catholic Bishops wrote about the Hispanic presence in 1983. **Handout 9–B, The Hispanic Presence: Challenge and Commitment,** lists positive contributions that that presence makes to the U.S. Church. Distribute the handout and direct the students to respond to the questions.

2. In conjunction with this assignment, you might direct the students to gather information about the Hispanic presence in the United States today:
   - What percentage of the U.S. population is Hispanic?
   - What religions are represented in that population?
   - How many Hispanic Catholic bishops serve the Church in the United States?
   - What types of conflicts do various Hispanic groups in the United States face today?

CONCEPT REVIEW

If you haven't addressed the following questions already, discuss with the students:
- When Junipero Serra was declared "blessed" in 1988, some Native Americans protested the announcement, charging him with mistreating their ancestors. Should the work of any early missionaries to the Americas be viewed as saintly work, or was their work always a part of the cultural domination that brought ruin to native people?
- Can conquest of one group of people by another ever be accomplished without mistreatment of the conquered people?
- Are all members of a conquering group guilty of exploitation of those who are conquered, no matter how well-meaning and kind they are?

(Here again it is important for the students to remember that once Europeans began exploration of America, a clash of cultures had to result. Many missionaries tried to make interaction between Spanish and Native peoples less destructive and more creative.)

1. **What responsibility did the pope give the governments of Spain and Portugal in 1493?**

   In 1493 the pope of the time granted to Spain and Portugal the responsibility to oversee the spread of the Christian message to the New World.

2. **Who were the conquistadores?**

   Conquistadores were Spanish soldiers who came to the Americas, particularly in search of wealth.

3. **What three factors led to the decrease of the Native American populations who had contact with the Spanish?**

   Diseases introduced by the Spanish, destruction of the Native American social systems, and direct killing combined to decrease the native populations of the Americas.

4. **How did local Spanish leaders respond to Antonio Valdivieso's criticism of their treatment of Native American people?**

   In 1550 the Nicaraguan governor's son and several accomplices stabbed to death Valdivieso and two other Dominicans.

5. **What were the two most powerful Native American groups during the time of the Spanish conquest of the Americas?**

   During the time of the Spanish conquest, the Aztecs and the Incas were the two most powerful native groups in Latin America.

6. **Who were the voices speaking out for Native American groups during the time of the Spanish conquest?**

   The main voices speaking out for Native Americans were the missionaries.

7. **Who was the greatest defender of Native Americans among the Spanish?**

   Bartolome de Las Casas was the greatest defender of Native Americans among the Spanish.

8. **Who is the first American declared a saint?**

   Rose of Lima, Peru, is the first American declared a saint.

9. **How was Juan Diego's bishop convinced to build a chapel in honor of Mary?**

   Juan Diego opened his cloak and on it could be seen a picture of young woman believed to be the Virgin Mary.

10. **Where was the oldest parish in the present-day United States founded?**

    The oldest parish in the present-day United States is in St. Augustine, Florida.

11. **Who was the first martyr in what is today the United States?**

    Juan de Padilla was the first martyr in what is today the United States.

12. **Who was the German Jesuit who began missions in southern Arizona and California?**

    Eusebio Kino began missions in southern Arizona and California.

13. **What Franciscan founded a series of missions along the California coast?**

    Junipero Serra founded a series of missions along the California coast.

French America

French missionaries introduce northern Native Americans to Catholicism and create a Catholic presence in Canada.

pages 221–224

THE FRENCH PRESENCE

Jesuit Work among Northern Native Americans

SAINT ISAAC JOGUES

BLESSED KATERI TEKAKWITHA, LILY OF THE MOHAWKS

How Successful Were the Missionaries?

1. Ask the students to read these sections on French America on pages 221–224.

2. Then ask the students:

   • How was the French experience in the New World different from that of the Spanish?

   • How was the experience of French missionaries different from that of Spanish missionaries?

     (Generally speaking, French missionaries were much less successful in making converts among the Indians they encountered than the Spanish were. Also, in contrast to the Spanish experience, the story of French missionaries is filled with accounts of men who suffered greatly trying to bring the gospel message to native people.)

3. Take note of the map on page 223.

In-Text Activities

page 222 ACTIVITY

Using the Activity

1. Be sure to schedule class prayer time for these prayer services.

2. This topic may generate some debate among the students. Remind the students that such debate was probably true for the missionaries as well.

Pere Jacques Marquette

The text states that Fr. Marquette was asked by Louis Jolliet to be the chaplain of the expedition. Have students research Fr. Marquette's contribution to the expedition and report their findings to the class.

In-Text Activities

page 224   ## ACTIVITY

Using the Activity

Provide class time for the students to present their work.

Additional Activities

KATERI TEKAKWITHA—PATRON OF NATURE AND PEOPLE IN EXILE

1. Write the following words on the board:
   - ecologists, ecology, and the environment
   - exiles
   - people who have lost their parents
   - people ridiculed for their piety
2. Point out to the students that Blessed Kateri is a patron of these four groups.
   - Discuss why she is associated with each of these groups.
   - Then discuss what it must have been like for a young woman to adopt the beliefs of a religion different from that of most people in her community.

CoNCept RevieW

Ask the students: Compared to the Spanish experience, what image of Native Americans do you have based on the stories about the French experience with them?

(The students may have an image of Native Americans in Spanish-dominated areas as being more docile, while the Native Americans encountered by the French were more hostile. Much of that difference in image comes from the degree of domination achieved by the Spanish compared to the French. Remind the students that the Iroquois, who tortured Isaac Jogues and others, also had a highly developed League of Five Nations by which various tribes lived together peacefully. Benjamin Franklin proposed the Iroquois model when the Constitution of the United States was being written.)

page 224   ## Review Questions and Answers

1. **What two reasons led French explorers to go to Canada? What two sources of wealth did the French find there?**

   French explorers initially went to Canada seeking a Northwest Passage to Asia. The two sources of wealth that the French found in the area were fish off the coast and furs.

2. **Why did the Jesuits want the French colonization of North America?**

   The Jesuits believed that French colonies would provide opportunities for missionary work among the natives of North America.

3. **What obstacle did the Jesuits face in their attempts to convert the Native Americans they encountered?**

   An obstacle faced by Jesuits in attempts to convert Native Americans was that each tribe was constantly at war with other tribes.

4. **What was the cause of the death of Saint Isaac Jogues?**

   An Iroquois warrior killed Isaac Jogues because he thought he was responsible for an outbreak of illness and for crop failure experienced by his tribe.

5. **Why did the people around Montreal treat Kateri Tekakwitha with great reverence?**

   Many people around Montreal noticed that Kateri Tekakwitha seemed to possess mystical powers.

6. **Among what group of Native Americans did Father Marquette work?**

   Father Marquette worked especially with the Illinois.

7. **Why were the French missions less successful in bringing about conversions among the Native Americans than the Spanish missions were?**

   Conversions in French-controlled territory did not match that of the Spanish missions because the French presence was not nearly as strong as the Spanish presence was in Latin America, the disbanding of the Jesuits diminished the number of missionaries, and the Native Americans of the North held onto their traditional ways more forcefully than those of the South.

English America

Catholics in the English colonies attempt to express their Catholicism in a predominantly Protestant society.

1. Before they read this section, point out to the students that Catholics not only made up a very small percentage of the population in the English colonies, but also that Puritan-leaning Protestants viewed them with suspicion. Although Catholics governed in Maryland, the majority of its population was Protestant. William Penn offered freedom of religion in Pennsylvania, but even there Catholics were so few in number that they were not viewed as a threat.

2. Begin discussion of this section by posing the question: Catholic leaders in Europe were against "religious freedom." In the British colonies of North America, Catholic leaders advocated "religious freedom." Why?

   (Point out to the students that the Catholic Church officially endorsed much of the U.S. American position on religious freedom in the 1960s at Vatican Council II.)

pages
225–228

CATHOLICISM IN THE COLONIES

Maryland—A Safe Haven for Catholics

JOHN CARROLL OF MARYLAND, THE NATION'S FIRST BISHOP

Religious Freedom

Instruct the students to read the sections on pages 225–228. Then summarize in discussion each section of the text.

Chapter Nine

page 227   **FYI**

Using the FYI

Discuss reasons this procedure was followed in this case; see the text on page 227.

page 228   **FYI**

Using the FYI

The website **www.ushistory.org/tour** has virtual tours of both churches. See also **www.oldstjoseph.org**.

ACTIVITY

Using the Activity

Have students who are researching the same person gather and prepare a presentation for the class.

Additional Activities

MARYLAND'S ACT OF TOLERATION

Handout 9–C, Excerpts from The Maryland Toleration Act (1649), contains two paragraphs from that proclamation granting religious freedom to all Christians and making it unlawful to criticize members of other Christian religions. Since the language is difficult to understand, distribute the handout and read the passage aloud. Go over the meaning of the two passages and then ask the students to discuss the proclamation using the questions on the handout.

CoNCept ReviEw

Discuss the following statement with the students: The experience of living as a minority group in the Protestant-dominated English colonies proved to be beneficial for Catholics as they entered the modern world.

(The statement implies that the colonial American experience, with its endorsement of various freedoms—including freedom of religion, set the stage for universally accepted principles of the modern world as stated in the UN Declaration on Human Rights and the document on religious freedom by the Catholic bishops of Vatican Council II.)

page 228   ## Review Questions and Answers

1. **In what sense was the Catholic experience in the English colonies different from that in the Spanish and French colonies?**

   Unlike the situation in the Spanish and French colonies, Catholics were a distrusted minority in the English colonies where Protestantism prevailed.

2. **What advice did Lord Baltimore give to the Catholics traveling to Maryland?**

   Since so few Catholics were traveling to Maryland, Lord Baltimore advised them not to speak publicly of their religion.

3. **What was the Act of Toleration?**

   In 1649 the colonial government of Maryland passed the act granting religious freedom to Christians in the colony.

4. **Who is the Apostle of Maryland?**

   Father Andrew White, a Jesuit priest who arrived with the first colonists to Maryland, is known as the "Apostle of Maryland." He first said Mass in the colony, established a mission, and worked with the Algonquin Indians.

5. **Why did Catholics initially not want Rome to appoint a bishop for the United States?**

   United States Catholic leaders feared that Protestants would view a Catholic bishop as an extension of bad experiences they had had with Catholic Church leaders in Europe.

6. **Who was the first U.S. Catholic bishop? How was he chosen?**

   The first U.S. Catholic bishop was John Carroll, who was elected by the United States clergy in 1789.

7. **What religious group controlled colonial Pennsylvania? What policy did they espouse toward other religions?**

   The Society of Friends, or Quakers, controlled colonial Pennsylvania and espoused toleration toward other religions.

Catholicism in the Early United States

Catholicism grows from a small percentage of the population of the new nation to the largest single religious denomination by 1850. Predominantly immigrant Catholics face challenges in a new kind of political environment.

pages 229–231

THE AMERICAN SYSTEM

Democracy in America

1. After the students have read pages 229–231, ask them:
   - What is lay trusteeism?
   - What American document did Bishop England apply to governance of his diocese?

2. Point out that during the early days of the United States, it was viewed as expected and acceptable to blend the democratic American system with Catholicism. Thus both greater lay leadership in parish affairs and Bishop England's ideas of a constitution and constitutional conventions were incorporated into Catholicism in the United States. Discuss with the students how the American Catholic experience might have been different if these two practices had been implemented for the entire Catholic Church in the United States.

In-Text Activities

page 230   **DISCUSSION**

Using the Discussion

This would be a good time to invite a lay person who works in a parish to speak with the class about his or her work. With the class, brainstorm questions ahead of time.

DISCUSSION

Using the Discussion

For each question, ask the students to choose sides; gather the "agree" side in one part of the classroom and the "disagree" side on the other. Have the groups list their arguments; then call on each group to share their points, and discuss as needed. During the discussion, the students should feel free to move to the other side if they change their mind.

Additional Activities

AMERICAN CULTURAL VALUES, CATHOLIC VALUES

1. Divide the class into two groups. Ask one group of students to identify and list what they believe are fundamental American (U.S.) values. Ask the other group to identify and list what they believe are fundamental Catholic values. Each group should write its list on newsprint or some other medium so that when the task is completed all class members can see the values. Ask a representative from each group to explain its list.

2. Discuss values that are shared and values that may be in conflict. Ask the students whether or not they experience conflict between being Catholic and being U.S. Americans. Ask the students whether they believe there were times when the conflict between being Catholic and being U.S. Americans was greater and to explain why they think so.

CONCEPT REVIEW

Read aloud the passage from the 1837 Provincial Council on page 230. Discuss with the students:

- What fears of non-Catholic U.S. Americans is the passage addressing?
- Are such fears held by many non-Catholics in the U.S. today? If not, what has happened to allay those fears?

(Point out to the students that for over a century many people in the United States believed that Catholics gave "civil and political supremacy" to the pope and therefore were unfit to serve in an independent, democratic government. In 1960 John Kennedy needed to address this concern, which he did in a major address during his candidacy for president.)

Review Questions and Answers

1. Define lay trusteeism.

Lay trusteeism refers to the policy of having an elected body of laypeople controlling the funds and resources of a parish.

2. Who was John England?

John England was an Irishman who was appointed bishop of Charleston, South Carolina; he took an active role in U.S. Church leadership during the early 1800s.

3. What position on being Catholic and being American did the United States Catholic bishops state in 1837?

At a Provincial Council in 1837 the U.S. bishops relayed to the country that no one need fear the loyalty of Catholics to the nation. People could be Catholic and American without conflict.

THE IMMIGRANT CHURCH
Preserving the Catholic Faith of Immigrants
African American Catholics

AMERICAN CATHOLICS AND SLAVERY

1. Instruct the students to read the sections on pages 232–237.

2. Since the ancestors of most students were immigrants to the United States at some time, invite the students to find out when members of their families first came to this country and/or to this part of the country. Ask them to find out, if possible, what the experience was like for the first generation of their family in this country and to report to the class whatever information they can.

3. You might also ask the students to research what the experience of members of their particular nationality was like in U.S. history.

In-Text Activities

page 232 **YOUTH NEWS**

Using the Youth News

As much as possible, openly address prejudices and stereotypes held by the students. Particularly, spend time with prejudicial and derogatory language heard around the school. Make clear to the students that such language and behavior is contrary to the gospel.

DISCUSSION

Using the Discussion

In the discussion take note of events that result in a reevaluation of immigration policies, such as terrorist attacks. Note also the economic status of countries that U.S. immigration policies tend to restrict.

page 233

Bishop John Hughes of New York

More information about Saint Patrick's Cathedral can be found at: **http://www. fordham.edu/halsall/medny/stpat1.html**

Sisters of Our Lady of Mercy

Choose a small group of students to do further research on the Yellow Fever epidemic and the Sisters of Our Lady of Mercy and report their findings to the class.

page 234   **FYI**

Using the FYI

The students might find it interesting to research the numbers of parishes and priests when their diocese was formed and the numbers now.

ACTIVITY

Using the Activity

Be sure to explore the reasons *for* the existence of Catholic schools today.

Saint Elizabeth Ann Seton—Pioneer of Catholic Schools

Have a student read aloud the text about Saint Elizabeth Ann Seton. The text mentions that she was particularly drawn to the belief in the Real Presence of Christ in the Eucharist. Use this text to segue into a class discussion on the Real Presence of Christ in the Eucharist.

---

page 236   **WWW.**

Using the www.

Follow up by having the students research or estimate the ethnic makeup of the parishes in the vicinity.

ACTIVITY

Using the Activity

Possible resources: Internet (African American Catholic bishops, African popes), Catholic encyclopedias, Catholic almanacs.

Additional Activities

THREE PHASES OF AMERICAN CATHOLIC HISTORY

Historian David J. O'Brien identifies three phases in the history of Catholicism in the United States. **Handout 9–D, Three Phases of American Catholic History,** outlines those periods and provides activities to help the students think about the impact of each phase.

THE IMMIGRANT EXPERIENCE

1. If appropriate with your demographics, instruct the students to research stories about the experiences that people of their nationality had in coming to the United States. Tell them to look for information about the role that religion played in the immigrants' lives. You might divide the students up by nationality and have them create posters of the various nationalities and ethnic groups to have on display during discussion of the topic of Catholicism in the United States.

2. If you have students in your class who are immigrants, you might invite them to speak of their experience or that of their family as immigrants today. You might also invite other immigrants in your school or community to speak about their experiences. Follow their presentation with discussion of how the immigrant experience during different time periods in U.S. history would be similar to or different from the immigrant experience today.

CATHOLICISM AND SLAVERY

You might direct some of the students to research the topic of Catholic teaching on slavery and report their findings to the rest of the class. Remind the students that, although Church leaders did not fully condemn slavery until 1839, since then they have taught that slavery violates both gospel values and natural law principles.

Concept Review

Discuss with the students:

- What does U.S. American culture have to offer Catholicism?
- What does Catholicism have to offer U.S. American culture?
- Nativists were right: Catholicism and America are fundamentally incompatible.

page 236 ## Review Questions and Answers

1. What is Nativism, and why did it flourish?

Nativism was a movement to drastically reduce the number of immigrants entering the United States. It flourished because of a fear of foreigners, a fear that Catholics were taking over the country, a fear of returning to a medieval world, the threat of change to the social landscape of the country, and the belief that immigrants were taking jobs from native-born workers.

2. Why did the United States Catholic bishops call for the creation of Catholic schools?

The bishops recognized that public schools of the time promoted Protestant beliefs and practices and feared that Catholic immigrants might lose their faith if they attended public schools.

3. Who were James Augustine Healy and Augustine Tolton?

James Augustine Healy was the first person of mixed race to be appointed a Catholic bishop in the United States. Augustus Tolton was the first full-blooded African American priest. He was ordained in 1886.

4. What position did the average Catholic in general take toward the Civil War?

There were Catholics on each side during the war. Typically, average Catholics held the same opinions as their neighbors.

Chapter Review and Conclusion

REVIEW

1. Ask the students to summarize the main points in the chapter using their own words. Write notes on the board from their contributions. To reinforce their summary, you might want to review the major concepts in this chapter as found in the teaching manual. Then read the **Conclusion** on page 237.

2. Review the vocabulary in this chapter:

   conquistadores—Spanish word for "conquerors"; the Spanish soliders who first came to the Americas especially in search of wealth (page 211)

   Our Lady of Guadalupe—patron of the Americas (page 215)

   mestizo—a person of mixed European and Native American ancestry (page 215)

   Northwest Passage—a non-existent waterway through the northern part of the Americas that explorers hoped would lead from the Atlantic Ocean to the Pacific Ocean (page 221)

   Black Robes—northern Native American term given to the Jesuits because of their distinctive garb (page 221)

   Act of Toleration—decree by the government of Maryland granting freedom of religion for the colony (page 225)

   lay trusteeism—control of parish funds and resources by an elected body of laypeople (page 229)

   Nativism—anti-catholic and anti-immigrant movement (page 232)

   Know Nothing Party—anti-foreign, anti-Catholic political organization that flourished in the United States between 1852 and 1856 (page 232)

TEST

Give the students the Chapter 9 Test or an alternative assessment. The tests have been placed on the Harcourt Religion Publishers' Web page. This has been done to enable the teacher to customize this material for local needs. First contact Harcourt Religion Publishers' high school consultant at 800-922-7696, ext. 3781 for a user ID and password. Then connect with the Harcourt Religion Publishers' Web site at **www.harcourtreligion.com** to download the information. Collect the tests for grading.

Chapter 9 Test Answers

MATCHING (Spanish and French America) (1 point each)

1. C	4. G	7. E
2. D	5. H	8. B
3. F	6. A	9. I

MATCHING (English America) (1 point each)

1. C	3. H	5. D	7. F	9. I
2. G	4. A	6. B	8. E	10. J

MULTIPLE CHOICE (2 points each)

1. c	5. c	9. c	13. a	17. b
2. d	6. a	10. d	14. d	18. a
3. b	7. c	11. a	15. a	19. b
4. a	8. d	12. a	16. c	

IDENTIFICATION (2 points each)

1. Lily of the Mohawks—Blessed Kateri Tekakwitha
2. Pioneer of Catholic schools—Saint Elizabeth Ann Seton
3. Know Nothing Party—anti-foreign, anti-Catholic political organization that flourished in the United States between 1852 and 1856
4. Lay trusteeism—control of parish funds and resources by an elected body of laypeople
5. Act of Toleration—decree by the government of Maryland granting freedom of religion for the colony
6. Black Robes—northern Native American term given to the Jesuits because of their distinctive garb
7. Reductions—the Jesuit practice in Paraguay of bringing together diverse Native American groups into communities
8. Our Lady of Guadalupe—patron of the Americas
9. Conquistadores—Spanish word for "conquerors"; the Spanish soliders who first came to the Americas especially in search of wealth

ESSAYS (5 points each)

1. Answers may vary. For instance, the Jesuits created *reductions* in Brazil to blend Indian and European practices.
2. French missionaries were not as successful as Spanish missionaries in bringing Native Americans to Catholicism. One reason for the lack of success by French missionaries is that French people did not colonize French-controlled territory to the extent that Spanish settlers did. Another reason is that the Native American groups who lived in territory controlled by the Spanish had a history of different rulers coming to dominance in the area.
3. In imitation of the American system, the priests of the new nation elected the first United States bishop. Some dioceses also adopted constitutions for their governance. Finally, lay trusteeism, control of parishes by their lay members, was commonplace in Catholic parishes.
4. During the nineteenth century nativists feared the influx of foreigners into the United States, they viewed Catholicism itself as a religion that was adversarial to Protestantism—the majority religion in the country—and they associated immigrants with the social ills rampant in big cities where immigrants congregated. Catholic Church leaders instituted Catholic schools to counter the Protestant-leaning public schools, and they called for a catechism that would explain Catholic beliefs in a simple, easy-to-remember format.
5. Catholics and Church leaders generally responded to slavery the way their neighbors did. That is, southern Catholics supported slavery in equal numbers to other southerners, while northern Catholics generally opposed slavery.

Prayer

Music Suggestions

"All Things New" by Rory Cooney from *Give Your Gifts, the Basics* (GIA, Harcourt Religion Publishers).

"Bwana Awabariki, May the Lord Bless You Forever," African folk hymn, from *Lead Me, Guide Me* (GIA), *Gather (Comprehensive)* (GIA).

"For Everything There Is a Time" by Donald Reagan from *Glory & Praise (Comprehensive)* (OCP).

"Gather Your People" by Bob Hurd from *Today's Missal* (OCP).

"On Holy Ground" by Donna Peña from *Give Your Gifts, the Songs* (GIA, Harcourt Religion Publishers).

"Song of the Body of Christ"/ "Canción del Cuerpo de Cristo" by David Haas, Spanish Trans. by Donna Peña, from *Gather (Comprehensive)* (GIA), *Today's Missal* (OCP).

"We Are Many Parts" by Marty Haugen from *Gather (Comprehensive)* (GIA), *We Celebrate* (J.S. Paluch Co., Inc.), *Today's Missal* (OCP).

Scripture Suggestions

Isaiah 44:1–4, 6–8

Acts 22:17–21

Matthew 9:35–38

Prayer

God of power and mercy,
you blessed the Americas at Tepeyac
with the presence of the Virgin Mary of Guadalupe.
May her prayers help all men and women
to accept each other as brothers and sisters.
Through your justice present in our hearts
may your peace reign in the world.
We ask this through our Lord Jesus Christ, your Son,
who lives and reigns with you and the Holy Spirit,
one God, for ever and ever.
Amen.

Opening Prayer, Feast of Our Lady of Guadalupe.

CHAPTER 9 TEST

Name_____ Date_____ Class period_____

Test is made up of questions with suggested point values totaling 100 points.

Matching (Spanish and French America) (1 point each)

_____ 1. Bartolome de Las Casas   A. Founded missions along California's coastline

_____ 2. Rose of Lima   B. Indian convert to Catholicism

_____ 3. Juan Diego   C. Returned to Spain to defend Native Americans

_____ 4. Juan de Padilla   D. First American-born saint

_____ 5. Eusebio Kino   E. Missionary to Iroquois

_____ 6. Junipero Serra   F. Presented bishop with image of Mary on his cloak

_____ 7. Isaac Jogues   G. First martyr in what became the U.S.

_____ 8. Kateri Tekakwitha   H. Explored and mapped out the Southwest

_____ 9. Jacques Marquette   I. Traveled the Mississippi River; worked with the Illinois

Matching (English America) (1 point each)

_____ 1. John Carroll   A. Wrote about democracy in America

_____ 2. William Penn   B. Opened a school in Emmitsburg, MD

_____ 3. John England   C. First bishop of the U.S.

_____ 4. Alexis de Tocqueville   D. New York bishop who began Saint Patrick's Cathedral

_____ 5. John Hughes   E. First full-blooded African American priest

_____ 6. Elizabeth Ann Seton   F. Bishop, son of Irish immigrant and black slave

_____ 7. Augustine Healy   G. Granted religious freedom in his colony

_____ 8. Augustus Tolton   H. Irishman appointed bishop of Charleston

_____ 9. Andrew White   I. Sailed with English Catholics to Maryland

_____ 10. George Calvert   J. Received a charter to found colony of Maryland

Chapter Nine

Multiple Choice (2 points each)

_____ 1. Conquistadores came to America primarily to
   a. spread Christianity
   b. find a Northwest Passage
   c. gain wealth
   d. explore the New World

_____ 2. The dominant Native American group in Mexico at the time of European conquest were the
   a. Meztizos
   b. Incas
   c. Cherokee
   d. Aztecs

_____ 3. Our Lady of Guadalupe appeared as
   a. a European princess
   b. someone with mixed ancestry
   c. an Indian peasant
   d. a Carmelite nun

_____ 4. The Reductions of Paraguay attempted to
   a. blend European and Indian practices
   b. prepare Indians for slavery
   c. preserve Native American religion
   d. reduce Native American populations

_____ 5. The oldest parish in continual use in the U.S. is in
   a. Santa Fe, NM
   b. San Antonio, TX
   c. St. Augustine, FL
   d. San Diego, CA

_____ 6. The priest whose statue represents Arizona in the U.S. Capitol building is
   a. Eusebio Kino
   b. Junipero Serra
   c. Ponce de Leon
   d. Bartolome de Las Casas

_____ 7. The Franciscan who founded a series of missions in California built them
   a. where tribes had their villages
   b. alternately along the coast and inland
   c. a day's walk from each other
   d. according to the Book of Revelation

_____ 8. French explorers initially came to the New World in search of
    a. gold
    b. spreading Christianity
    c. furs
    d. a Northwest Passage

_____ 9. A major problem hindering missionary work among Native American tribes in North America was that
    a. missionaries could not speak the languages
    b. few missionaries joined the effort
    c. tribes were constantly at war among themselves
    d. dense forest hindered extensive travel

_____ 10. The Native American name for Jesuit missionaries was
    a. medicine men
    b. Yankee priests
    c. White Fathers
    d. Black Robes

_____ 11. Isaac Jogues was killed because
    a. a warrior thought he had caused disease and crop failure
    b. he represented the French to a tribe friendly with the English
    c. he attempted to baptize Native American children
    d. Protestants and Catholics were at war at the time

_____ 12. Immediately after Kateri Tekakwitha's death,
    a. her face cleared of blemishes
    b. a bright light surrounded her
    c. everyone in her tribe became Christian
    d. she was declared Blessed

_____ 13. The first U.S. Catholic bishop was
    a. elected by U.S. priests
    b. appointed by the pope
    c. sent over from Ireland
    d. recommended by President Washington

_____ 14. The first diocese of the United States was
    a. New York
    b. Philadelphia
    c. Charleston
    d. Baltimore

_____ 15. The first major wave of Catholic immigrants to America came from
    a. Ireland
    b. Germany
    c. France
    d. Italy

_____16. Nativism was a movement to
   a. help immigrants become American
   b. restore land to Native Americans
   c. limit immigrants to the U.S.
   d. promote religious toleration

_____17. One means the Church used to help preserve the faith of Catholic immigrants was
   a. an English translation of the Bible
   b. the founding of Catholic schools
   c. voter drives at local parishes
   d. electing Catholic governors

_____18. Generally speaking, during the Civil War, Catholics
   a. held the same views as their neighbors
   b. sided with the North against slavery
   c. upheld the Southern position on slavery
   d. remained neutral about the conflict

_____19. The first full-blooded African American ordained a priest
   a. attended seminary in New Orleans but served in Chicago
   b. studied in Rome since no U.S. seminary would accept him
   c. ended up serving as a priest in France and Spain
   d. became the first bishop of Quincy, Illinois

Identification (2 points each)

1. Lily of the Mohawks—

2. Pioneer of Catholic schools—

3. Know Nothing Party—

4. Lay trusteeism—

5. Act of Toleration—

6. Black Robes—

7. Reductions—

8. Our Lady of Guadalupe—

9. Conquistadores—

Essays (5 points each)

1. Describe one example of how missionaries attempted to assist Native Americans under Spanish rule.

2. Compared to the missionary experience in New Spain, how successful were French missionaries in converting Native Americans to Catholicism? Explain factors that would account for the difference.

3. Give two examples illustrating how the Catholic Church during the early years of the United States adopted the style of the new nation.

4. Name three causes underlying nativism in the U.S. during the nineteenth century. Describe two ways that Catholic leaders attempted to help Catholic immigrants to the United States.

5. How did Catholics and Church leaders generally respond to the slavery question in pre-Civil War America?

NATIVE AMERICAN IMAGES AND TEAM NAMES— EXPLOITATION CONTINUES?

Name_____ Date_____ Class period_____

On April 13, 2001, The United States Commission on Civil Rights issued the following "Statement on the Use of Native American Images and Nicknames as Sports Symbols."

- List the reasons the commission gives for condemning this practice.
- Write a response to the statement as if you were Native American.

The U.S. Commission on Civil Rights calls for an end to the use of Native American images and team names by non-Native schools. The Commission deeply respects the rights of all Americans to freedom of expression under the First Amendment and in no way would attempt to prescribe how people can express themselves. However, the Commission believes that the use of Native American images and nicknames in school is insensitive and should be avoided. In addition, some Native American and civil rights advocates maintain that these mascots may violate anti-discrimination laws. These references, whether mascots and their performances, logos, or names, are disrespectful and offensive to American Indians and others who are offended by such stereotyping. They are particularly inappropriate and insensitive in light of the long history of forced assimilation that American Indian people have endured in this country.

Since the civil rights movement of the 1960s many overtly derogatory symbols and images offensive to African-Americans have been eliminated. However, many secondary schools, post-secondary institutions, and a number of professional sports teams continue to use Native American nicknames and imagery. Since the 1970s, American Indian leaders and organizations have vigorously voiced their opposition to these mascots and team names because they mock and trivialize Native American religion and culture.

It is particularly disturbing that Native American references are still to be found in educational institutions, whether elementary, secondary or post-secondary. Schools are places where diverse groups of people come together to learn not only the "Three Rs," but also how to interact respectfully with people from different cultures. The use of stereotypical images of Native Americans by educational institutions has the potential to create a racially hostile educational environment that may be intimidating to Indian students. American Indians have the lowest high school graduation rates in the nation and even lower college attendance and graduation rates. The perpetuation of harmful stereotypes may exacerbate these problems.

Name_____ Date_____ Class period_____

The stereotyping of any racial, ethnic, religious or other groups when promoted by our public educational institutions, teaches all the students that stereotyping of minority groups is acceptable, a dangerous lesson in a diverse society. Schools have a responsibility to educate their students; they should not use their influence to perpetuate misrepresentations of any culture or people. Children at the elementary and secondary level usually have no choice about which school they attend. Further, the assumption that a college student may freely choose another educational institution if she feels uncomfortable around Indian-based imagery is a false one. Many factors, from educational programs to financial aid to proximity to home, limit a college student's choices. It is particularly onerous if the student must also consider whether or not the institution is maintaining a racially hostile environment for Indian students.

Schools that continue to use Indian imagery and references claim that their use stimulates interest in Native American culture and honors Native Americans. . . . [However] Even those that purport to be positive are romantic stereotypes that give a distorted view of the past. These false portrayals prevent non-Native Americans from understanding the true historical and cultural experiences of American Indians. Sadly, they also encourage biases and prejudices that have a negative effect on contemporary Indian people. These references may encourage interest in mythical "Indians" created by the dominant culture, but they block genuine understanding of contemporary Native people as fellow Americans.

. . . The elimination of Native American nicknames and images as sports mascots will benefit not only Native Americans, but all Americans. The elimination of stereotypes will make room for education about real Indian people, current Native American issues, and the rich variety of American Indian cultures in our country.

THE HISPANIC PRESENCE:
CHALLENGE AND COMMITMENT

Name_____ Date_____ Class period_____

In 1983 the U.S. Catholic Bishops wrote a pastoral letter titled, "The Hispanic Presence: Challenge and Commitment." In that letter the bishops identified five values that are central to Hispanic culture (number 3). Describe specific ways that each of these values could be incorporated into U.S. culture and the Catholic Church in the United States.

1. Profound respect for the dignity of each *person*, reflecting the example of Christ in the Gospels

2. Deep and reverential love for *family life*, where the entire extended family discovers its roots, its identity, and its strengths

3. A marvelous sense of *community* that celebrates life through "fiesta"

4. Loving appreciation for God's gift of *life*, and an understanding of time which allows one to savor that gift

5. Authentic and consistent devotion to Mary, the Mother of God

EXCERPTS FROM THE MARYLAND TOLERATION ACT (1649)

Name_____ Date_____ Class period_____

And be it also further enacted by the same authority advise and assent that whatsoever person or persons shall from henceforth upon any occasion of offence or otherwise in a reproachful manner or way declare, call, or denominate any person or persons whatsoever inhabiting, residing, trafficking, trading, or commercing within this Province or within any of the ports, harbors, creeks, or havens to the same belonging an heritic, scismatic, idolator, puritan, independent, Presbyterian, popish priest, Jesuit, Jesuit papist, Lutheran, Calvinist, Anabaptist, Brownist, Antinomian, Barrowist, Roundhead, Separatist, or any other name or term in a reproachful manner relating to matter of religion shall for every such offence forfeit and lose the sum of ten shillings sterling or the value thereof to be levied on the goods and chattels of every such offender and offenders, the one half thereof to be forfeited and paid unto the person and persons of whom such reproachful words are or shall be spoken or uttered, and the other half thereof to the Lord Proprietary and his heirs Lords and Proprietarys of this Province.

And whereas the enforcing of the conscience in matters of religion has frequently fallen out to be of dangerous consequence in those commonwealths where it has been practiced, and for the more quiet and peaceable government of this Province, and the better to preserve mutual love and amity among the inhabitants thereof,

Be it therefore also by the Lord Proprietary with the advise and consent of this Assembly ordained and enacted . . . that no person or persons whatsoever within this Province, or the islands, ports, harbors, creeks, or havens thereunto professing to believe in Jesus Christ, shall from henceforth be in any ways troubled, molested, or discountenanced for or in respect of his or her religion nor in the free exercise thereof within this Province or the islands thereunto belonging, nor any way compelled to the belief or exercise of any other religion against his or her consent, so as they be not unfaithful to the Lord Proprietary, or molest or conspire against the civil government established or to be established in this Province under him or his heirs.

(Changes made in spelling, capitalization, and punctuation from the original to facilitate readability.)

1. What attitude does the Proclamation have toward those who criticize others for their religious beliefs?

2. Why does the proclamation call for religious toleration?

3. What restrictions does the proclamation make regarding who can practice religion freely in Maryland?

4. How is the spirit of this proclamation different from the attitude toward religious freedom in Europe and in the other colonies of the time?

THREE PHASES OF U.S. AMERICAN CATHOLIC HISTORY

Name_____ Date_____ Class period_____

One Catholic historian identifies three phases in the relationship between Catholicism and the United States. For each of these phases, describe how the experiences and values associated with it have shaped U.S. American Catholicism today.

1. **The Republican Phase.** Following the lead of the nation at large, early U.S. American Catholic leaders endorsed separation of church and state, freedom of individuals to choose and practice the religion of their choice, a climate of religious pluralism, and some democracy in Church affairs.

2. **The Immigrant Phase.** Religious practices, family life, identification with one's ethnic group, and education were in general separate from the mainstream. Mainstream U.S. America appeared to be an affront to Catholicism and Catholic identity; therefore, a tension between the Catholic religion and the culture existed. Catholics saw themselves as a subculture within the dominant (Protestant) culture.

3. **The Evangelical Phase.** After the election of President John Kennedy and Vatican Council II, U.S. Catholics saw themselves as active participants in American culture. They felt comfortable criticizing aspects of U.S. American culture and saw themselves as called upon to live the Christian life and to promote gospel values (thus the term *evangelical*).

ACTIVITIES

1. Write a report on the concept of separation of church and state as it is practiced in the United States. What are its pros? Cons?

2. Find out in the history of the Catholic Church how many African Americans have served as bishops in the U.S. Catholic Church and how many men from the continent of Africa have served as popes.

3. Research John Kennedy's response to those who thought the pope would control the United States if Kennedy became president.

A SPIRITUAL AND MORAL PRESENCE

The Church in the Modern World

A Teacher's Prayer

Jesus, who calmed the storm on Galilee's sea, help my students see beyond the busy-ness of today's world and find peace and calm through you, with you, in you. Amen.

Overview

Two characteristics of the modern world, industrialization and pursuit of national self-interest, reach their culmination in the two devastating world wars of the twentieth century. The first section of this chapter examines the bold stance taken by Pope Leo XIII in addressing problems associated with industrialization. His 1891 encyclical initiates one of the strongest characteristics of the Catholic Church since then: to be a voice for justice and for oppressed people in the world. Church leaders also struggled with how to be a moral voice during an era when nations saw the Church as an outside entity and thus as a threat to their power. Meanwhile, heroic models of Catholic spirituality such as Saint Thérèse, one of the most popular saints of all time, continue to grace the world with a message of God's love.

Major Concepts Covered in This Chapter

① Introduction

② Modern Catholic Social Teaching

③ The Church and Politics in the Modern World

④ Modern Catholic Spirituality

⑤ The Church and the World Wars

⑥ Chapter Review and Conclusion

Introduction

Prayer

pages
238–240

■ **Music Suggestions**

"Amazing Grace," Traditional from *Gather (Comprehensive)* (GIA), *Glory & Praise (Comprehensive)* (OCP), *Today's Missal* (OCP), *We Celebrate* (J.S. Paluch Co., Inc.), *Lead Me, Guide Me* (GIA).

"Beatitudes" by Darryl Ducote from *Glory & Praise (Comprehensive)* (OCP), *Today's Missal* (OCP).

"City of God" by Dan Schutte from *Glory & Praise (Comprehensive)* (OCP), *Gather (Comprehensive)* (GIA), *Today's Missal* (OCP).

"God of the Hungry" by Scott Soper from *Today's Missal* (OCP).

"Send Down the Fire (Penitential Rite) by Gary Gaigle from *Give Your Gifts, the Basics* (GIA, Harcourt Religion Publishers).

"Servant Song" by Donna M. McGargill from *Today's Missal* (OCP).

"The Harvest of Justice" by David Haas from *Gather (Comprehensive)* (GIA).

■ **Scripture Suggestions**

Micah 7:1–4, 7

James 5:1–8

Matthew 12:15–21

■ **Prayer**

Isaiah 58:6–7, 10 (See textbook, page 238.)

pages
238–240

Overview

1. Have the students read the **Chapter Overview** and timeline on pages 238-239. Briefly discuss some of the points and events noted.

2. Read the paragraphs under **The Industrial Revolution** on page 240, and ask the students to share what they know about the event.

3. Have the students complete the **Before We Begin . . .** activity. (You might instead assign this activity as homework before beginning the chapter and ask the students to come to class prepared to discuss the questions.)

Modern Catholic Social Teaching

Pope Leo XIII begins modern Catholic social teaching, making the Church a leading voice for justice.

1. Begin this section by writing on the board or overhead the words *Industrial Revolution.* Ask the students:

   - What does the term *Industrial Revolution* mean?
   - In what sense was it a revolution?
   - How did the Industrial Revolution change life in industrialized areas?
   - What problems did it create?
   - What could the Church do in response to this revolution?

2. Then have the students read pages 241–247; discuss with them:

   - How did Pope Leo XIII respond to industrialization?
   - How did Catholics on local levels deal with problems associated with it?

     (Pope Leo's *Rerum Novarum* called for justice and humane treatment of workers, including support for the right of workers to participate in decision-making. In the U.S. in particular, industrial workers were predominantly Catholic. Therefore, the U.S. Catholic Church became a strong advocate for workers' rights.)

pages 241–247

THE INDUSTRIAL REVOLUTION

Responses to the Industrial Revolution

"On the Condition of the Working Classes"

THE LASTING IMPACT OF *RERUM NOVARUM*

United States Contributions to Catholic Social Teaching

Divide the class into five groups and assign one of the sections (excluding **The Industrial Revolution** on page 241) to each group. Ask the groups to summarize their reading for the class.

In-Text Activities

page 244 ### DISCUSSION

Using the Discussion

1. List on the board or overhead the changes suggested.

2. Discuss what the Church would probably say about each suggested change; use the Church's documents and the Catechism as needed to facilitate a decision.

ACTIVITY

Using the Activity

Have the students work in small groups to discuss this concept and to share their examples. Then have each group select three examples to share with the class. Discuss as needed.

In-Text Activities

page 247   ## ACTIVITY

Using the Activity

This activity could be done as small-group projects. Whether the activity is done individually or in small groups, the students should have the opportunity to share their responses with the class.

Additional Activities

AN OVERVIEW OF MODERN CATHOLIC SOCIAL TEACHING

If your students will not have a required course on justice, you might find a justice textbook and look for an overview of modern Catholic social teaching which is typically included in such texts.

1. Briefly discuss each issue covered in the textbook. Perhaps assign one topic to each of several small groups; the groups would be responsible for a report on the issue to the class.
2. Point out to the students that since 1891 popes have regularly written on justice issues. Along with other Church documents, these papal encyclicals emcompass a developing body of Catholic doctrine on matters of justice.

THE CHURCH AND SOCIETY

It's helpful for the students to understand what they think is the role of the Catholic Church in justice issues. **Handout 10–A, The Church and Society** presents several forced choices that will help the students clarify their understanding of the Church's role. Lively discussion may result from disagreements on the forced choices.

DOROTHY DAY AND THE CATHOLIC WORKER MOVEMENT

Dorothy Day is an interesting figure in the story of the modern Church and justice. In her youth she was a socialist, but she came to see in the Church and in the writings of the popes more hope for people who were poor than in the writings of Karl Marx. Along with Peter Maurin, she began the Catholic Worker Movement.

Have the students research Dorothy Day and the Catholic Worker Movement. **Handout 10–B, Dorothy Day on Catholic Faith and Poverty,** provides quotes from her and questions allowing the students to reflect on the way Day relates Catholicism and working with people who are poor. Questions can be answered individually and then shared in small groups or with the class.

CoNCepT RevIEw

Discuss with the students: The Church's social teaching seeks a middle course between the dangers of individualism and collectivism. Name problems of excessive individualism and of excessive collectivism. What types of laws or policies would you suggest in order to balance the two?

page 247   ## Review Questions and Answers

1. **What is the difference between *laissez-faire* capitalism and socialism?**

   Laissez-faire capitalism is an economic system that advocates that people with money, or capital, can use their money as they wish. Socialism advocates government control of the instruments of production, such as farms and factories.

2. **What position did Catholic Church leaders take toward capitalism and socialism?**

   Catholic leaders took a middle-of-the-road position, criticizing capitalist thinkers who proposed that private property was an absolute right and socialist thinkers for completely rejecting the right to private property.

3. **What contribution did Pope Leo XIII make to Catholic social teaching in 1891?**

   In 1891 Pope Leo XIII wrote the encyclical *Rerum Novarum,* which was most responsible for initiating a Catholic position on problems associated with industrialization.

4. **What four principles did Pope Leo XIII propose to help workers?**

   Pope Leo XIII proposed the following four principles as ways to help workers:

   - Wealthy industrialists should not abuse workers.
   - Governments should step in when problems arise.
   - Workers have a right to a living wage.
   - Workers have a right to form unions.

5. **How did publication of *Rerum Novarum* help make the Church a spiritual and moral presence in the modern world?**

   Rerum Novarum began a series of encyclicals on justice written by popes since 1891. They are a voice for people suffering from injustice throughout the world.

6. **What was the Knights of Labor? What position did Cardinal Gibbons take toward the Knights of Labor?**

   The Knights of Labor was one of the first labor unions in the United States and Canada. Cardinal Gibbons of Baltimore appealed to the pope not to condemn the Knights as a "secret society."

7. **What four proposals did the U.S. bishops make in 1919?**

   In 1919 the U.S. bishops proposed that:

   - There should be a minimum wage.
   - High rates of wages should be created and maintained.
   - Origination of a government-mandated social security insurance for all workers.
   - Workers should participate in the management of industry.

The Church and Politics in the Modern World

1. The Church addresses ongoing political conflicts associated with the modern world. Begin discussion of this concept in the following way: In this section we will discover that approximately a century ago popes condemned what they called "Americanism" and "modernism." (In doing so, they didn't condemn either North America or the modern world.) What qualities associated with either North America or with the modern spirit do you think the popes were disturbed about?

2. After discussing this question, direct the students to read the sections on pages 248–254 and to identify what the text says about the Americanist and Modernist controversies.

pages 248–254

POLITICAL CONTROVERSIES

The Church in Mexico

The Americanist Controversy

The Modernist Controversy

After the students have read pages 248–254, gather key ideas from each of these sections of reading.

In-Text Activities

page 248

ACTIVITY

Using the Activity

1. Suggestions: genuflecting, the Sign of the Cross, the saints, prayers to Mary and the saints, the rosary, adoration of the Blessed Sacrament, the Sacraments of Healing (Reconciliation and Anointing of the Sick), daily Mass, the crucifix, statues of saints, Catholic schools, the Rite of Christian Initiation of Adults, celibate priesthood, the pope, cardinals, Vatican City, the Sistine Chapel, Swiss Guards, the Nuptial Mass, funeral Mass, abstaining from meat on Ash Wednesday, Good Friday, and the Fridays of Lent.

2. Provide class time for the students to share their reports, and post those that can be.

page 250

FYI

Using the FYI

Suggest that the students ask their non-Catholic friends for their reaction to the term *separated brethren*. Then discuss in class.

page 251

FYI

Using the FYI

Follow-up activities:

1. Research the missionaries who first staffed the local parishes.

2. Check with diocesan offices to see if the diocese cooperates in any mission work outside of the country. If it does, share information on the venture with the class.

page 251 ACTIVITY

Using the Activity

1. If the students are going to interview any immigrants or children of immigrants, prep them on using questions that do not intimidate those being interviewed.

2. Guide the discussion along lines in keeping with Catholic principles on human dignity and the rights of immigrants.

page 252

James Cardinal Gibbons

Once the students have read the text on James Cardinal Gibbons, assign them to research his work with the Knights of Labor and report back to the class what they have found.

page 253 ACTIVITY

Using the Activity

Consider dividing the class into three groups and assigning one of the figures to each group for research and class presentation.

Additional Activities

WHAT IS "THE VATICAN"?

Handout 10–C, What Is the Vatican? provides information about the Vatican that can clarify for the students that the Vatican is an independent city-state. It also directs the students to a website where they can learn more about this political center of the Catholic Church.

CoNCept ReviEw

Discuss with the students: The end of the nineteenth century found Church leaders in conflict with certain ideologies popular at the time. What would you say are the major points of contention about which Church leaders were battling?

(Two positions criticized by Church leaders in the chapter are excessive nationalism and naturalism—placing science and the natural realm above the supernatural, which they associated with "modernism.")

page 254

Pope Pius X

For additional information on Pope Pius X, contact the following websites:
http://www.catholic-forum.com/saints/saintp06com.htm
http://www.ewtn.com/library/MARY/PIUSX.htm

1. **Why did Otto von Bismarck initiate his *Kulturkampf*?**

   Bismarck initiated his *Kulturkampf,* a "culture war" against the Church, as an attempt to strengthen the identity of the German people.

2. **How did many French intellectuals at the end of the 1800s view Catholicism?**

   Many French intellectuals still perceived Catholicism as being opposed to liberty.

3. **What action by Pope Leo XIII added to anti-Catholic feelings among Anglicans?**

   In 1896 Pope Leo XIII announced that Anglican orders were not valid, that is, he declared that Anglican priests and bishops were not validly ordained.

4. **Who was Miguel Pro?**

   Miguel Pro was a Mexican Jesuit priest who served the Catholic community during a time of government persecutions against Catholics. He died by firing squad at the age of thirty-six and became a hero of the underground Church in Mexico. He was beatified in 1988.

5. **What is assimilation? What two positions did U.S. Catholic leaders take toward assimilation?**

   Assimilation means members of a minority group adopting the values and characteristics of the dominant culture in which they live. Some U.S. Catholics believed that immigrant Catholics should keep to a minimum their adoption of values of dominant American culture; others believed that "Americanizing" Catholicism was a positive thing.

6. **What effect did Pope Leo XIII's condemnation of Americanism have on American theologians?**

   Pope Leo's condemnation of Americanism caused American theologians to be cautious when offering theological opinions for fear that they would slip into positions that would fall under the category of Americanism.

7. **In his 1902 response to the U.S. bishops, how did Pope Leo XIII view the U.S. Church?**

   In 1902 Pope Leo told the U.S. bishops that their "flourishing youthfulness, cheers Our heart and fills it with delight." In other words, he appreciated the great growth and vitality existing in U.S. Catholicism.

8. **Name two positions associated with modernism.**

   Two positions associated with modernism are that:

   • People cannot arrive at the existence of God through the use of reason.

   • The Church and Church practices developed over time in response to human need instead of their being divinely instituted by Christ.

9. **What effect did condemnation of modernism have on Catholic intellectual activity? What more traditional understanding of Catholic scholarship eventually replaced this viewpoint?**

   Condemnation of modernism stifled Catholic intellectual activity for some time. Eventually scholars reasserted a more traditional Catholic position, that Catholicism finds the use of reason and intellectual inquiry to be totally compatible with the life of faith.

Modern Catholic Spirituality

Catholics create a variety of ways to live the spiritual life in the modern world.

pages
255–258

CATHOLIC SPIRITUAL LIFE

Saint Damien—The Leper Priest

Saint Thérèse of Lisieux—"The Little Flower"

Frances Cabrini and Katharine Drexel

Missionaries and Monasteries in the U.S. Church

You might divide up the various models of spirituality described in this section and assign the students to do further research on them and report their findings to the class. There are also other models of spirituality from the time period worth examining, for instance, Saint Philippine Duchesne and Saint John Bosco.

In-Text Activities

page 258

FYI

Using the FYI

Maryknoll's website, **www.maryknoll.org**, has a wealth of information on the work and history of Maryknoll, including biographies of Father Thomas Price (**http://www.maryknoll.org/ABOUTUS/ARCHIV/arc_price.htm**) and Father James Walsh (**http://www.maryknoll.org/ABOUTUS/ARCHIV/arc_walsh.htm**). Some students may be familiar with *Maryknoll Magazine*; selections are available on the website.

ACTIVITY

Using the Activity

1. Again, consider dividing the class into three groups and assigning one of the figures to each group for research and class presentation.

2. Alert the students to these websites for information about the groups and their founders.
   - **www.taize.fr**
   - **www.larcheusa.com, www.larchecanada.org**
   - **www.madonnahouse.org**

Additional Activities

SAINT THÉRÈSE, THE LITTLE FLOWER

When the students have read about Saint Thérèse, point out to them that she has become one of the most popular saints of all time. Yet so much about her story runs counter to the modern spirit. In an age when "bigness" was celebrated, she advocated littleness. When action and the active life were in favor, she chose the contemplative life. She expressed great doubts about her faith, and yet she was passionately in love with Jesus. In her autobiography, Saint Thérèse described a spirituality of littleness. She equated herself to a child's toy that is overlooked in a corner of a playroom. She also spoke of doing little things out of love of God, thus giving inspiration to the "little people" of the past century.

Discuss with the students:

- What might a "spirituality of littleness" entail?
- What positive message does Thérèse hold for us today?

A GUEST SPEAKER ON MISSIONARY WORK

There may be a resource person in your area who has had experience doing missionary work, either locally or in another land. Perhaps there is a Catholic Worker house of hospitality, a Maryknoll residence: or you might draw upon some other representative of a group involved in ministry who could speak to your class. If you invite a guest speaker, have the class brainstorm questions ahead of time.

THOMAS MERTON ON PEACE

One of the most striking characteristics of the twentieth-century Trappist monk, Thomas Merton, was the way he led the life of a hermit and yet remained concerned about and actively involved in the great social and cultural issues of his day. **Handout 10–D, Thomas Merton on Peace,** contains portions of a prayer Merton wrote suggesting attitudes that people and national leaders should consider when deciding whether or not to enter into a war. The handout includes questions to lead the students in examining the message of the prayer.

CoNCept RevieW

Ask the students to review their text and their notes about the various saints discussed in the chapter. Give them a few moments to write about how one of these saints has something to say to them personally. Invite the students to share their observations.

page 258 **Review Questions and Answers**

1. **Give two examples of Catholic devotional practices.**

   Two Catholic devotional practices are recitation of the rosary and devotion to the Sacred Heart; students may mention other practices.

2. **How did Father Damien try to restore a sense of dignity to the people of Molokai?**

   One practice introduced by Father Damien aimed at restoring a sense of dignity was to provide proper burials and a decent cemetery for those who died of leprosy.

3. **Describe Saint Thérèse of Lisieux's approach to the spiritual life.**

   In her approach to the spiritual life, Saint Thérèse advocated doing little things well.

4. **Who was the first United States citizen to be declared a saint?**

   Frances Cabrini, an immigrant from Italy, was the first United States citizen to be declared a saint.

5. **With what groups did Katharine Drexel's sisters work?**

   Katharine Drexel's sisters worked with Native Americans and African Americans.

6. **What type of work do members of Maryknoll perform?**

   Members of Maryknoll perform missionary work throughout the world.

The Church and the World Wars

Church leaders seek ways to promote peace in an era of world wars.

pages
259–263

AN AGE OF WORLD WARS

Developments Between the Wars

From World War II to the Cold War

1. Like most people during the first half of the twentieth century, Church leaders were faced with how to respond to the great destruction of two world wars. Following these wars, popes came to assert their position as spiritual and moral leaders in a world desperately in need of inspiration and guidance. Ask the students to read pages 259–263.

2. Then ask them to name developments that occurred between the wars that led the way to changes in the Church that we take for granted today (for example, dialogue among religions, Church leaders representing most parts of the world, lay involvement in ministry).

3. Then consider using the **Additional Activity: The Popes and Nazism.** Use **Handout 10–E** to discuss how the popes during the period leading up to and during World War II acted and might have acted in response to the atrocities of Hitler, Nazism, and Fascism.

In-Text Activities

page 259 **FYI**

Using the Activity

The World Factbook, available on the CIA web site, presents interesting information regarding the relationship between Italy and the Holy See (Vatican City) (**www.odci.gov/cia/publications/factbook/geos/vt.html**).

page 262 **YOUTH NEWS**

Using the Youth News

1. Brainstorm the most urgent present-day situations of violence.

2. In small groups, formulate two solutions (partial, most likely) for each situation. If time is short, assign one area to each group and share solutions in the large group. Discuss as needed.

3. Set aside time for the students to write their representatives and senators on one or more issue of violence. Ask them to incorporate class suggestions.

page 263 **ACTIVITY**

Using the Activity

In addition to the Internet, the students might use Catholic encyclopedias. (The early twentieth-century encyclopedia, which is available on the web, obviously will not have information on these World War II personages.) Maximilian Kolbe and Edith Stein (Teresa Benedicta) are canonized saints.

THE POPES AND NAZISM

Much has been written lately about whether or not Pope Pius XII chose the right path by not speaking out more forcefully and specifically against Hitler and Nazi practices, especially in their policy of genocide against Jews. Some writers claim that the pope's silence on the issue indicates indifference to Jewish suffering or even an anti-Semitic position on his part.

Distribute **Handout 10–E, The Popes and Nazism,** and ask the students to read the handout. Discuss what the information contained there suggests about the position of the popes toward Nazism. Since much information is available about this issue, you might assign the students to research and report on what material from the Vatican library and other sources tell us about decisions made by Popes Pius XI and Pius XII. (For instance, the Red Cross and other organizations recommended to Pius XII that he not speak directly on the genocide since the result would likely make matters worse. Vatican library sources indicate that the pope followed their advice but anguished over this decision.)

CoNCept ReviEw

Discuss with the students:

- In light of the wars of the twentieth century, how important is it to have a strong Catholic Church that can challenge people and nations to seek peace and avoid resorting to violence in conflicts?

- Does the Catholic Church function as a moral voice in the world today? If so, how?

  (As we will see, recognition of the need to play a major role in the moral life of the modern world is one reason why Church leaders pursued the option of calling a council, which finally took place under Pope John XXIII in the 1960s.)

page 263 **Review Questions and Answers**

1. **What political position did Pope Benedict XV take during World War I?**

   During World War I Pope Benedict XV maintained a neutral position.

2. **What effect did World War I and postwar activities have on Catholic-Protestant relations?**

   During the war, Catholics and Protestants fought together on both sides. After the war, Catholic and Protestant organizations worked together to aid the victims of war.

3. **What steps did Pope Pius XI take to strengthen the Church in former mission countries?**

   Pope Pius XI ordained a number of native clergy as bishops in former mission countries. For instance, he appointed an Indian Jesuit as a bishop in India and ordained six native Chinese bishops.

4. **What is Catholic Action? Give two examples of organizations that promoted Catholic Action.**

   Catholic Action refers to the active involvement of laypeople in various forms of ministry. For instance, the Extension Society dedicated itself to building churches, rectories, and schools in isolated areas of the United States. The Grail movement in Holland promoted Christian values among women employed in social work, in medical fields, and in religious formation.

5. **What problem did Virgil Michel see in the way liturgy was typically experienced during his time?**

Virgil Michel pointed out that if Catholics are passive during the liturgy, they will be less likely to actively live the Christian life in the world.

6. **What position did Communism take toward religion?**

Communism was stridently anti-religious.

7. **Why did Pope Pius XII hesitate to confront Nazism too strongly?**

Pope Pius XII feared that continued confrontation with Hitler would actually lead to loss of more innocent lives.

8. **Give an example of how Pope Pius XII assisted Jews during World War II.**

In 1943 Nazis ordered Roman Jews to pay a large ransom or be shipped to a concentration camp. The pope ordered that sacred vessels should be melted down to help pay the ransom.

9. **What was Pope Pius XII's major political concern following World War II?**

Pope Pius XII's major political concern following World War II was restricting the spread and influence of communism.

Chapter Review and Conclusion

1. Ask the students to summarize the main points in the chapter using their own words. Write notes on the board from their contributions. To reinforce their summary, you might want to review in the teaching manual the major concepts in this chapter. Then read the **Conclusion** on page 263.

2. Review the vocabulary in this chapter:

laissez-faire **capitalism**—economic system that advocates that people with money (capital) can use their money as they wish without restrictions from governments or other sources (page 241)

socialism—economic system that advocates government control of all instruments of production, such as farms and factories (page 241)

assimilation—members of minority groups adopting the values and characteristics of the dominant culture in which they live (page 250)

ecumenism—actions aimed at dialogue and the restoration of unity among Christians (page 250)

devotional Catholicism—practices of religious piety among Catholics (page 255)

cloistered—literally, "behind walls," women and men religious who choose to live within monasteries (page 258)

Catholic Action—the movement calling for active involvement of laypeople in the Church (page 261)

TEST

Give the students the Chapter 10 Test or an alternative assessment. The tests have been placed on the Harcourt Religion Publishers' Web page. This has been done to enable the teacher to customize this material for local needs. First contact Harcourt Religion Publishers' high school consultant at 800-922-7696, ext. 3781 for a user ID and password. Then connect with the Harcourt Religion Publishers' Web site at **www.harcourtreligion.com** to download the information. Collect the tests for grading.

Chapter 10 Test Answers

MULTIPLE CHOICE (3 points each)

1. c	5. d	9. c	13. d
2. b	6. b	10. c	14. b
3. d	7. d	11. b	15. a
4. a	8. a	12. a	16. a

MATCHING (2 points each)

Set 1

1. E	5. I	9. D	
2. H	6. C	10. K	
3. F	7. G	11. J	
4. A	8. B		

Set 2

1. C	4. A
2. D	5. B
3. E	

ESSAYS (5 points each)

1. Prior to the industrial revolution, people who made things worked their way up to being skilled masters of their trade. With the industrial revolution, workers for the most part performed unskilled work and were interchangeable with other unskilled workers.

2. Archbishop Ketteler of Germany called for:

   a. prohibition of child labor
   b. limiting working hours
   c. separation of sexes in workshops
   d. sanitary working conditions
   e. Sunday rest
   f. care for disabled workers
   g. state-appointed factory inspector

3. Between the two world wars Catholicism saw increased positive relations between Catholics and Protestants, more native clergy, greater lay involvement in the Church, liturgical renewal, and the condemnation of communism.

4. In 1939 Pope Pius XII issued a condemnation of the Hitler regime but, acting upon the advice of a number of international advisors, he didn't further confront Hitler directly for Nazi treatment of Jews. Instead, he and other Church leaders worked behind the scenes to assist Jews who were in danger of death at the hands of Nazi Germany.

Prayer

MUSIC SUGGESTIONS

"Anthem" by Tom Conry from *Glory & Praise (Comprehensive)* (OCP), *Today's Missal* (OCP), *Gather (Comprehensive)* (GIA).

"Blest Are They" by David Haas from *Gather (Comprehensive)* (GIA), *Glory & Praise (Comprehensive)* (OCP), *Today's Missal* (OCP), *Walking by Faith* (Harcourt Religion Publishers, GIA).

"Give Your Gifts" by Michael Mahler from *Give Your Gifts, the New Songs* (GIA, Harcourt Religion Publishers).

"Prayer of Saint Francis" by Sebastian Temple from *Today's Missal* (OCP), *We Celebrate* (J.S. Paluch Co., Inc.), *Glory & Praise Comprehensive* (OCP).

"Servant Song" by Ziggy Stardust and Bobby Fisher from *Gather (Comprehensive)* (GIA).

"Service" by The Dameans from *Glory & Praise (Comprehensive)* (OCP).

SCRIPTURE SUGGESTIONS

Jeremiah 20:12–13

2 Corinthians 4:5–16a

Luke 19:1–10

PRAYER

O God, the Lord of all,
your Son commanded us to love our enemies
and to pray for them.
Lead us from prejudice to truth;
deliver us from hatred, cruelty, and revenge;
and enable us to stand before you,
reconciled through your Son, Jesus Christ our Lord.
Amen.

"Blessing in Time of Suffering and Need," *Catholic Household Blessings & Prayers* (Washington, DC: USCC, 1988), 314.

CHAPTER 10 TEST

Name_____ Date_____ Class period_____

Test is made up of questions with suggested values totaling 100 points.

Multiple Choice (3 points each)

_____ 1. *Laissez-faire* capitalism advocates
   a. workers' right to unionize
   b. state control of industry
   c. no restrictions on production and use of wealth
   d. concern for the common good

_____ 2. Karl Marx was a leading advocate of
   a. capitalism
   b. socialism
   c. Church reform
   d. the guild system

_____ 3. Pope Leo XIII's encyclical *Rerum Novarum* addressed
   a. the coming threat of world war
   b. Protestant–Catholic relations
   c. the Americanist controversy
   d. the conditions of working people

_____ 4. The Knights of Labor was
   a. an early labor union in the U.S.
   b. a secret society antagonistic to the Church
   c. a forerunner of the Ku Klux Klan
   d. a society of wealthy industrialists

_____ 5. A 1919 statement by the U.S. Catholic bishops advocated
   a. a minimum wage
   b. social security for workers
   c. worker participation in management
   d. all of the above

_____ 6. Mother Jones was a famous
   a. religion teacher
   b. labor leader
   c. founder of a religious order
   d. novelist

_____ 7. With his *Kulturkampf,* Prime Minister Bismarck was demonstrating his
   a. support for the Church in Germany
   b. position on German industrialization
   c. concern for improving education
   d. intent to limit the Church's power

_____ 8. In the late 1800s, many French intellectuals believed that
   a. Catholicism opposed liberty
   b. the pope supported their views
   c. Napoleon's son should be emperor
   d. the French monarchy should be restored

_____ 9. In 1896 Pope Leo XIII upset Anglicans because he
   a. sided with France in a border dispute
   b. refused to recognize Queen Victoria
   c. declared Anglican orders invalid
   d. condemned the Oxford Movement

_____ 10. Assimilation refers to
   a. members of different religions working together
   b. losing jobs because of industrialization
   c. minority groups becoming like the dominant culture
   d. two or more countries becoming one nation

_____ 11. After the pope's condemnation of Americanism, North American theologians tended to
   a. find work in state universities
   b. be cautious in their opinions
   c. study European theologians
   d. join the Episcopalian Church

_____ 12. The Third Plenary Council of Baltimore in 1884 called for
   a. parish schools
   b. liturgy in English
   c. election of bishops
   d. more American cardinals

_____ 13. To counter modernism, Pope Pius X required all priests to
   a. wear clerical clothing
   b. take courses in Latin
   c. live in rectories
   d. take an oath

_____ 14. Pope Pius X encouraged
   a. regular Bible reading
   b. daily Communion
   c. Confirmation of infants
   d. scientific study of Scripture

_____ 15. In the 1929 Lateran Treaty, Pope Pius XI
  a. gave up claims to the former Papal States
  b. supported Fascism and Nazism
  c. condemned German takeover of Poland
  d. encouraged modern Scripture study

_____ 16. The position Pope Pius XII took toward communism after World War II was to
  a. condemn communism
  b. work with communist leaders
  c. favor many communist principles
  d. call for dialogue among groups

Matching (2 points each)

SET 1

_____ 1. Miguel Pro
_____ 2. Isaac Hecker
_____ 3. Cardinal Gibbons
_____ 4. Saint Damien
_____ 5. Saint Thérèse of Lisieux
_____ 6. Saint Frances Cabrini
_____ 7. Saint Katharine Drexel
_____ 8. Thomas Merton
_____ 9. James Walsh and Thomas Price
_____ 10. Virgil Michel
_____ 11. Pope Pius XII

A. Worked with lepers in Hawaii
B. Famous U.S. monk
C. First U.S. citizen saint
D. Founded Maryknoll Missionaries
E. Martyred in Mexico
F. Baltimore's advocate for American workers
G. Worked with Native and African Americans
H. Wanted to "Americanize" Catholicism
I. Proposed doing little things well
J. Church leader during World War II
K. Called for active participation in liturgy

SET 2

_____ 1. Ecumenism
_____ 2. Americanism
_____ 3. Modernism
_____ 4. Assimilation
_____ 5. Devotional Catholicism

A. Becoming like the dominant culture
B. Pious religious practices
C. Dialogue among religions
D. Associated with Isaac Hecker
E. Resulted in priests taking an oath against it

Essays (5 points each)

1. How did the industrial revolution change the relationship between workers and their work?

2. Name three proposals made by Archbishop Ketteler in 1869 that eventually became standard practice in industrialized countries.

3. Name three developments that took place in the Church between the two world wars.

4. What position did the pope of the time take toward Hitler's treatment of Jews during World War II? Why did he take this position?

THE CHURCH AND SOCIETY

Name_____ Date_____ Class period_____

Some people question whether Church leaders should be involved in addressing social issues to the degree and in the manner in which they have done since Pope Leo XIII's *Rerum Novarum.*
    Read over the following contrasting opinions and explain why you would support one view or the other.

Church leaders should speak out about matters affecting workers, such as minimum wage and social security.	Church leaders should address only matters proper to religion, such as care of souls and how to get to heaven.
Catholics who hold public office should follow Church teachings when deciding political matters.	Catholics who hold public office should disregard Church teachings and make judgments strictly as politicians.
Church leaders should meet with heads of state whenever they can to discuss social and political matters	Church leaders should not be directly involved with political leaders in any manner.

DOROTHY DAY ON CATHOLIC FAITH AND POVERTY

Name_____ Date_____ Class period_____

Dorothy Day, former socialist who converted to Catholicism, took to heart the social teachings of the Church and co-founded the Catholic Worker Movement. Here are some of her observations from years of living and working with people in New York who were poor. (Quotes are from her *Meditations* [New York: Paulist Press, 1970].)

I'd like to have everyone see the poor worn feet, clad in shoes that are falling apart, which find their way to The Catholic Worker *office. A man came in this rainy morning and when he took off one dilapidated rag of footwear, his sock had huge holes in the heel and was soaking wet at that. We made him put on a dry sock before trying on the pair of shoes we found for him, and he changed diffidently, there under the eye of the Blessed Virgin on the bookcase, looking down from her shrine of Christmas greens.* (pages 29–30)

When I talk about poverty I do not mean destitution *which is something quite different. Nor do I want to "talk poor mouth" as my mother used to say. I talk about the poverty of young people newly married, the girl without a dowry, the young man without anything, either a team or horses, or a sum of money, or a truck, to make a start in life.* (pages 41–42)

Let us canvas blocks, factories, schools, form groups to study, not Marxism, but the encyclicals of the Popes—the writings of the Church on social questions as well as on the liturgy. The two should go together. There should be daily Mass, a community act, as well as the individual work which we must each do. (page 28)

We must minister to people's bodies in order to reach their souls. We hear of the faith through our ears, we speak of it with our mouths. The Catholic Worker movement, working for a new social order, has come to be known as a community which breaks bread with brothers of whatever race, color or creed. "This is my body," Christ said at the Last Supper, as He held out bread to His apostles. When we receive the Bread of life each day, the grace we receive remains a dead weight in the soul unless we cooperate with that grace. When we cooperate with Christ, we "work with" Christ, in ministering to our brothers. (page 75)

1. Dorothy Day recognized poverty in a man's feet red from exposure to cold and wet. She provided some relief with dry socks and new shoes. What image do you associate with poverty? What actions could help alleviate poverty?

2. Do you believe that there are still people who lack what it takes to "make a start in life"? If so, what are they lacking? What could help them?

3. Is faith something you hear or something you do? Explain.

4. Dorothy Day sees a vital connection between the Mass and helping people in need. How can she make this connection? What connection do you see between these two aspects of the Christian life?

5. What would the "new social order" envisioned by Dorothy Day look like? Would you like to see such an order? Why?

WHAT IS THE VATICAN?

Name_____ Date_____ Class period_____

In our study of Church history we learned that the Papal States existed as a separate country under the leadership of the pope from around the time of Charlemagne until 1870. What remained of the pope's domain after that time is known as the Vatican.

Since its creation, the Vatican has enjoyed the status of a country. With the exception of a great open space facing Saint Peter's Square, it is a completely walled-in city comprising 108.7 acres. It is smaller than the grounds of the Capitol building in Washington, DC, and only one-eighth the size of New York's Central Park. You can walk around it in less than an hour.

Nearly 4,000 people work in the Vatican, but only about 300 actually live within its borders—the pope, 89 Swiss Guards, and 50 cardinals who head congregations of the Vatican. About a dozen buildings outside of the city walls are also under the sovereignty of the Vatican, including the pope's summer residence at Castel Gandolfo and the three major basilicas Saint John Lateran, Mary Major, and Saint Paul Outside-the-Walls.

The primary purpose of the Vatican State today is to assure the political independence of the pope as head of the Catholic Church. As the sovereign of a city-state, the pope is not subject to any government or political power. The United Nations has declared the Vatican a World Heritage site for its cultural importance, thus entitling it to special protection. No other country has been so designated.

Over 120 countries have diplomatic relations with the Vatican. The United States maintained consular relations with the Papal States and diplomatic relations with the pope as head of the Papal States from 1787 to 1870. The U.S. did not have diplomatic relations with the Vatican again until 1984.

You can take a visual tour of the Vatican by visiting web site **www.vatican.va.** Find out:

• How did the Swiss Guards come to be the protectors of the pope?

• The president of the United States had a personal representative at the Vatican from 1939 until 1950. Who was it?

• What was the status of the relationship between the two countries between 1950 and 1984?

• Who is the current U.S. ambassador to the Vatican?

• Who is the Vatican's ambassador to the United States?

THOMAS MERTON ON PEACE

Name_____ Date_____ Class period_____

Here are portions of a "prayer for peace" that the twentieth-century monk Thomas Merton wrote. In the prayer Merton captures some of the attitudes that can lead to war and suggests alternative attitudes that can result in peace. For each passage, explain in your own words:

- What does Merton say can lead to war?
- What alternative viewpoint would foster peace?

1. Armed with a titanic weapon, and convinced of our own right
   We face a powerful adversary, armed with the same weapon, equally convinced that he is right.

2. Save us then from our obsessions! Open our eyes, dissipate our confusions, teach us to understand ourselves and our adversary!

3. Help us to be masters of the weapons that threaten to master us.
   Help us to use our science for peace and plenty, not for war and destruction.
   Show us how to use atomic power to bless our children's children, not to blight them.

4. Save us from the compulsion to follow our adversaries in all that we most hate
   Confirming them in their hatred and suspicion of us.

5. Grant us prudence in proportion to our power,
   Wisdom in proportion to our science,
   Humaneness in proportion to our wealth and might,
   And bless our earnest will to help all races and peoples to travel, in friendship with us,
   Along the road to justice, liberty, and lasting peace.

A Thomas Merton Reader, edited by Thomas P. McDonnell
(New York: Doubleday, Image Books, 1974), 282–284.

THE POPES AND NAZISM

Name_____ Date_____ Class period_____

A 1963 fictional play, "The Deputy" by Rolf Hochhuth, portrayed Pope Pius XII as remaining silent and indifferent while Jews and others suffered and died under Hitler. Was there any truth to this portrayal? In March, 1937, Pope Pius XII's predecessor published an encyclical to the German bishops condemning the racism and excessive nationalism that underlay Nazism. Eugenio Pacelli (later Pope Pius XII), the Vatican Secretary of State and fluent in German, wrote the encyclical for Pius XI. Here is a passage from the encyclical.

Whoever exalts race, or the people, or the State, or a particular form of State, or the deposition of power, or any other fundamental value of the human community—however necessary and honorable be their function in worldly things—whoever raises these notions above their standard value and divinizes them to an idolatrous level, distorts and perverts an order of the world planned and created by God: he is far from the true faith in God and from the concept of life which that faith upholds. . . .

Our God is the Personal God. . . . This God, this Sovereign Master, has issued commandments whose value is independent of time and space, of country and race. As God's sun shines on every human face, so His law knows neither privilege nor exception. Rulers and subjects, crowned and uncrowned, rich and poor, are equally subject to His word. From the fullness of the Creator's right there naturally arises the fullness of His right to be obeyed by individuals and communities, whoever they are. This obedience permeates all branches of activity in which moral values claim harmony with the law of God, and pervades all integration of the ever-changing laws of man into the immutable laws of God.

None but superficial minds could stumble into concepts of a national God, of a national religion; or attempt to lock within the frontiers of a single people, within the narrow limits of a single race, God, the Creator of the universe, King and Legislator of all nations, before whose immensity they are "as a drop of a bucket". . . .

Quoted in Anne Fremantle, *The Papal Encyclicals in Their Historical Context*
(New York: The New American Library, 1956), 251–253.

Time magazine for December 23, 1940, quotes the great German-Jewish scientist Albert Einstein as saying:

Being a lover of freedom, when the revolution came in Germany, I looked to the universities to defend it, knowing that they had always boasted of their devotion to the cause of truth; but, no, the universities immediately were silenced. Then I looked to the great editors of the newspapers whose flaming editorials in days gone by had proclaimed their love of freedom; but they, like the universities, were silenced in a few short weeks. . . . Only the Church stood squarely across the path of Hitler's campaign for suppressing the truth. I never had any special interest in the Church before, but now I feel a great affection and admiration because the Church alone has had the courage and persistence to stand for intellectual truth and moral freedom. I am forced thus to confess that what I once despised I now praise unreservedly.

Name_____ Date_____ Class period_____

In 1945, Rabbi Herzog of Jerusalem sent a "special blessing" to Pope Pius XII "for his life-saving efforts on behalf of the Jews during the Nazi occupation of Italy." When Pius XII died, Israel's Foreign Minister gave a moving eulogy at the United Nations.

In an interview reported in the Vatican newspaper *L'Osservatore Romano* for September 5, 2001, historian Rabbi David Dalin said:

> *I call today's critics [of Pope Pius XII] revisionists because they reverse the judgement of history, namely the recognition given to Pius XII by his contemporaries, among whom is Nobel Prize [winner] Albert Einstein, chief Rabbi Isaac Herzog of Israel, Prime Ministers Golda Meir and Moshe Sharett, and in Italy, people like Raffaele Contoni, who was at the time president of the Italian Union of Jewish Communities.*
>
> *During the German occupation of Rome, Pius secretly instructed the Catholic Clergy to use all means to save as many human lives as possible. While 80% of European Jews died during the war, 80% of Italian Jews were saved. In Rome, alone, 155 convents and monasteries gave refuge to some 5,000 Jews. For nine months, 60 Jews lived with the Jesuits at the Pontifical Gregorian University, and many others were hidden in the basement of the Biblical Institute.*
>
> *An explicit and severe denunciation of the Nazis by the Pope would have been an invitation to reprisals. We have evidence that, when the bishop of Munster [Germany] wished to pronounce himself against the persecution of the Jews in Germany, the leaders of the Jewish communities of his diocese begged him not to do so, as it would have caused a harsher repression against them.*
>
> *Pius XII was not Hitler's Pope, but the greatest defender that we Jews have ever had, and precisely at the time when we needed it.*

1. Should the pope have gone against civil authorities and hidden Jews as he did? Why?

2. In hindsight, should the pope have denounced Nazi treatment of Jews directly?

3. Should the pope have condemned the Nazi regime and called upon all Catholics to resist Nazism in whatever way they could?

4. Should the pope have called for the use of violence to overthrow Hitler and the Nazi regime?

Chapter Ten

CHAPTER ELEVEN

THE CHURCH OF VATICAN COUNCIL II

A Teacher's Prayer

God, grant me the serenity to accept the things I cannot change, courage to change the things I can, and the wisdom to know the difference. Amen.

Overview

1. Have the students read the Chapter Overview and timeline on pages 264–265. Briefly discuss some of the points and events noted.

2. Read the paragraphs under **The Church Is Transformed** on 267, and ask the students to share what they know about the Second Vatican Council.

3. Have the students complete the **Before We Begin . . .** activity. (You might instead assign this activity as homework before beginning the chapter and ask the students to come to class prepared to discuss their work.)

Major Concepts Covered in This Chapter

① Introduction

② Pope John XXIII and the Council

③ Pope Paul VI and Implementing the Council

④ Chapter Review and Conclusion

LESSON STRATEGIES

Introduction

Prayer

- **Music Suggestions**

  "All Things New" by Rory Cooney from *Give Your Gifts, the Basics* (GIA, Harcourt Religion Publishers).

  "City of God" by Dan Schutte from *Glory & Praise (Comprehensive)* (OCP), *Gather (Comprehensive)* (GIA), *Today's Missal* (OCP).

  "Follow the Light" by Richard Putori and Christopher Dutkiewicz from *Give Your Gifts, the New Songs* (GIA, Harcourt Religion Publishers).

  "Live in the Light" by Michael Mahler from *Give Your Gifts, the New Songs* (GIA, Harcourt Religion Publishers).

  "On That Day" by Kate Cuddy from *Give Your Gifts, the New Songs* (GIA, Harcourt Religion Publishers).

  "Service" by The Dameans from *Glory & Praise (Comprehensive)* (OCP).

  "Sign Me Up" by Kevin Yancy and Jerome Metcalfe from *Lead Me, Guide Me* (GIA).

- **Scripture Suggestions**

  Deuteronomy 30:15–19

  Hebrews 13:1–6

  John 15:1–12

- **Prayer**

  See page 264 of the textbook.

Pope John XXIII and the Council

This chapter looks at the Second Vatican Council as a response to historical circumstances in place at the time. World War II had created physical destruction as well as a spiritual and moral vacuum. The Cold War and nuclear weapons had the world on the edge of self-destruction. And an increasingly interdependent global community meant that problems in one corner of the world had ramifications throughout the world. Pope John XXIII saw a council as the best way to renew and update the Catholic Church and as the best way for the Church to bring the light of Christ to bear on a world desperately in need of a renewed vision.

THE CHURCH IS TRANSFORMED

A Spiritual and Moral World Crisis

The Post-War World and the Pre-Vatican II Church

Pope John XXIII

A POPE *FROM* AND *OF* THE PEOPLE

Direct the students to read pages 267–271. Then ask the students:

- What were some of the political and economic conditions in the world that led up to the election of Pope John XXIII?

- What are some expressions of the "spiritual and moral crisis" that existed in the world during the post-war era?

- What had been the dominant attitude of Church leaders toward developments in the modern world during the century before this era?

(The text mentions crises relating to nuclear weapons, communism, the global community, and liberation movements. The dominant attitude of Church leaders toward the "modern world" had been to condemn most of what was associated with it and to remain in isolation from the changes taking place in the world. Pope John changed this attitude with his program of *aggiornamento*.)

In-Text Activities

page 267 | **DISCUSSION**

Using the Discussion

The students may find it easier to relate to this concept if they consider more recent acts of war and terrorism.

page 269 | **FYI**

Using the FYI

Have the students explain the meaning of each of the italicized terms as it relates to the world today and to defend their definitions.

ACTIVITY

Using the Activity

Depending on the culture of a particular class in any given year, you might create two lists during the follow-up discussion: *positive effects* and *negative effects*. Try to avoid stereotyping and prejudicial comments. Ask the students to support their suggestions of positive or negative effects with solid information and reasoned conclusions.

Additional Activities

READING THE SIGNS OF THE TIMES

1. Mention to the students that Pope John XXIII spoke often about the need for "reading the signs of the times." He used the phrase to mean "identifying and analyzing major trends," both problems and hopeful developments, taking place in the world. He wanted the Church to be responsive to these signs. In the early 1960s Pope John identified three of these signs as: women asserting their rights, an end to colonialism, and working conditions of laborers.

2. Ask the students to take a few minutes to write down what they would see as "signs of the times" for today. Instruct them to think about both problems as well as hopeful signs, and to think both locally as well as globally.

3. When the students have identified some signs, place them in small groups to select three of the major signs of the times for today. Instruct each group to describe ways that the universal Church and individual Church members could respond to these signs.

One commentator identified the following qualities with Pope John XXIII. Write them on the board and invite the students to spend a few minutes writing down their thoughts about how they could incorporate these qualities into their own lives.

- He overlooked much and criticized little.
- He complimented others when he could.
- His company was peaceful.
- He gave few orders.
- He was quick to abandon a path that proved fruitless.

Alberic Stacpoole OSB, in *Vatican II Revisited* (Minneapolis, MN: Winston Press, 1986), 5.

page 271

Review Questions and Answers

1. **What event associated with World War II led Church leaders to realize that the world faced a moral and spiritual vacuum?**

   The Holocaust and circumstances surrounding it indicated that the world faced a serious spiritual and moral crisis.

2. **What change in perspective did the Church need to make if it was to address the problems facing the world following World War II?**

   If the Church was to use the gifts of her founder and provide direction and hope to a despairing world, it would have to enter into serious dialogue with people from the world's many nations and religions. It would also need to address expressions of contemporary culture.

3. **What four developments in the post-war world led the Church to examine its role in the world?**

   Four developments in particular led the Church to examine its role in the world after World War II: nuclear weapons, communism, the expanding sense of a global community of nations, and liberation movements.

4. **Name two assignments served by Pope John XXIII that helped prepare him for the papacy during a time of change. Explain.**

   During World War I, Pope John XXIII served as a chaplain in the army medical corps. Later he served in Eastern Europe where he encountered members of the Eastern Churches, other religions, and minority groups. He also represented the pope in France during the tense post-World War II period.

5. **What does it mean to say that Pope John XXIII was initially thought to be a *papa de passagio*?**

   Most people thought that John XXIII would be a transitional pope, someone who did little until a younger, longer reigning pope would be elected.

Vatican II—Christ's Presence
Pope John Sets the Tone for the Council
Bishop Peter Cule of Mostar

The Death of Pope John XXIII

Have the students read and summarize each of the readings on pages 272–275. Then in a large-group discussion, gather summary ideas for each section.

In-Text Activities

page 274 **FYI**

www.

Using the www.

See the Internet site below. Note especially the Crypt Church: The Papal Exhibit, the tiara of Pope Paul VI.

page 275 **Discussion**

Using the Discussion

1. Give the students time to reflect on this topic and to write a paragraph on each characteristic.

2. Divide the class into small groups to share one of their paragraphs.

3. Call on each group to present to the class one characteristic and their reasons. Discuss as needed.

Additional Activities

Vatican Council II at a Glance

The Second Vatican Council was not simply a ground-breaking event in the story of the Church in the modern world, it was also a monumental event for the entire history of the Church. Theologian Karl Rahner described it as the moment when Catholicism became truly a world Church. **Handout 11–A, Vatican II at a Glance,** lists some unique characteristics of the council. Distribute the handout and then ask the students: Think back on key moments in the history of the Church as you have studied it this semester. What are some of the ways that Vatican Council II was a ground-breaking event for the Church?

(If they have difficulty making contrasts, suggest that the students think about the spirit of the Church leading up to the East–West Schism, during the Reformation, during the age of Metternich and Vatican Council I. Following Vatican II, the mutual excommunications of the pope and patriarch of Constantinople were rescinded, Protestants were invited to be observers at the council, and the bishops had a more open attitude toward "the modern world" than the attitude that prevailed during the age of Metternich and Vatican I.)

CONCEPT REVIEW

Discuss with the students:

- If your school has a decision-making body that includes administration, teachers, and students, how does it function? What are the strengths and weaknesses of having such a multi-level body?

- If your school does not have a decision-making body that includes administration, teachers, and students, what effect do you think it would have on the school? What would be the strengths and weaknesses of having such a multi-level body?

- How did the first session of Vatican Council II end? How did some observers view this ending? How did Pope John view it?

  (Expanding decision-making typically slows down governance of an organization. This happened at Vatican II, when the first session ended with no decrees passed. Pope John did not view this as a failure, however. He felt the time spent by bishops examining issues and getting to know one another was fruitful.)

page 275   **Review Questions and Answers**

1. **What is the meaning of *aggiornamento?***

   Aggiornamento means to make things ready for today—today's needs, today's times, today's people.

2. **What type of direct involvement did Pope John XXIII make in the deliberations of Vatican Council II? What effect did this have on council deliberations?**

   Pope John XXIII did not become directly involved in council deliberations. As a result, he assured the bishops that the process would be one in which they were free to discuss and make decisions for the Church.

3. **How did Pope John XXIII respond to the work of the first session?**

   When the first session of the council ended, some people called it a failure since no decrees were approved. However, Pope John expressed his pleasure at the work accomplished, pointing out that starting slowly gave bishops an opportunity to get to know one another.

pages
276–279

THE IMPACT OF VATICAN II

The Council Was More Than Its Documents

The Documents

THE DOCUMENTS OF VATICAN COUNCIL II—MAJOR THEMES AND IMPLICATIONS

1. Direct the students to read these sections of the text.

2. You might assign a student or a group of students to each of the documents listed in the chart on 278–279; ask them to prepare a brief report on the principal themes and implications of their particular document. The series of books, *Vatican II in Plain English,* by Bill Huebsch (published by RCL), is a good resource; it includes Book 1 *(The Council),* Book 2 *(The Constitutions),* and Book 3 *(The Decrees & Declarations).*

3. Set aside class time for the reports and for discussion of the themes of the documents.

278

Chapter Eleven

Additional Activities

U.S. CHURCH NUMBERS

Use **Handout 11–B, The U.S. Church Before and After the Council,** to help the students grasp some of the changes in the Catholic Church in the United States following the council. After they have done the research and shared the results, discuss with the students the possible positive and negative effects of the council on the Church in the U.S. (Note that even a negative change in number can at times result in positive results.)

CONCEPT REVIEW

Discuss with the students: What does it mean to say that "the council was more than its documents"?

(As an example, you might point out that the Declaration of Independence symbolized a spirit that has made an impact on the world ever since it was written. Its meaning was more than its words. In similar fashion, the council signaled a spirit in the Church that cannot be reduced simply to its written decrees.)

page 277 **Review Questions and Answers**

1. **In what sense was Vatican Council II greater than the documents it produced?**

    In addition to the sixteen documents that the council produced, it also carried with it a spirit of inquiry and self-reflection, an attitude of dialogue, and an openness to change.

2. **What changes continued to occur in the Church for years following the council?**

    The council established a number of commissions to study various Church practices, such as the sacraments. These commissions instituted changes over the next decade after the council.

3. **How did younger Catholics view the Sacrament of Reconciliation compared to the way older Catholics were accustomed to viewing it?**

    Younger Catholics learned about "celebrating the Sacrament of Reconciliation" while older Catholics talked about "going to confession."

Pope Paul VI and Implementing the Council

Pope Paul VI continues the council and implements changes following Vatican II.

pages 280–282

POPE PAUL VI

An Advocate of Ecumenism

The Pope of Social Justice

The Pope of Liturgical Reform

After the students have read these sections, use the **In-Text Activity** and/or the **Handouts** accompanying the additional activities to help the students reflect on the information provided in the text.

page 281

DISCUSSION

Using the Discussion

1. OBSERVE—What is happening? Why is it happening? What is our responsibility? JUDGE—What would be a Christian response? ACT—What will we do? How will we do it? When? How did we do?

2. Possible issues: priest shortage in some countries, roles for women in the Church, difficulties with community in large parishes, inadequate people resources in small parishes, insufficient giving, supporting and promoting Catholic schools, the need to evangelize.

3. If there is time, expand the discussion to "world issues," such as unequal distribution of wealth, the wasting of natural resources, terrorism, conflicts between people of different religions or denominations.

YOUTH NEWS

Using the Youth News

1. List the seven themes horizontally on the board or overhead. Under each, with the help of the students, list specific areas of concern or issues.

2. Then ask the students to write an essay on one of the topics, including their understanding of the topic and the Church's teaching on it.

ACTIVITY

Using the Activity

See these websites for the documents:
www.vatican.va/holy_father/paul_vi/index.htm
www.catholic.net/RCC/Indices/subs/by-subject.html
www.vatican.va/holy_father/paul_vi/index.htm

page 282

FYI

Using the FYI

Discuss the policy of the students' diocese(s).

ACTIVITY

Using the Activity

1. Depending on the person's actual involvement in the Church at the time, he or she will be able to give the students some sense of the changes that followed the council. If available, older priests and men and women religious can probably provide a great deal of insight.

2. Consider inviting one of the more knowledgeable persons interviewed to speak with the class.

An Ecumenical Church

Your students likely are not aware of the unfriendly attitude that existed between Catholics and people of other religions that was dominant in the pre-Vatican II world. And they may not be aware of the variety of ecumenical activities that are currently going on in the world. Following the council the Catholic Church went from being largely a non-participant in such activities to being a leader in ecumenism. **Handout 11–C, An Ecumenical Church,** describes types of ecumenical activity outlined by a head of a Vatican commission on such activities.

Distribute the handout to the students. First ask volunteers to explain what each statement on the handout means, and then give the students a few minutes to write down possible examples of the various activities. Share and discuss these in large or small-group discussion.

A Post-Vatican II Vision of Justice

After the council, the Church increased its emphasis on being an advocate for justice. For instance, the U.S. Catholic Church had always had Catholic Charities organizations, but those organizations became more justice-oriented after the council. Monsignor Robert Fox helped guide the Church in that direction during the 1970s. **Handout 11–D, Catholic Charities in the Spirit of Vatican II,** offers passages from Monsignor Fox's address to representatives of Catholic Charities in Chicago in 1971. Distribute the handout to the students. Ask them to read it; then discuss with them the spirit of justice and the vision of charity that the statement offers.

Liturgical Change

Invite the school chaplain or another guest speaker to describe the way Mass and the sacraments were celebrated prior to the changes instituted by Vatican Council II. If possible, hold the lecture in the school chapel so that the guest speaker can demonstrate the way Mass was celebrated. Invite the students to discuss what it must have been like to experience Mass and the sacraments in that way. You might also distribute **Handout 11–E, Mass in the Pre-Vatican II Church,** and invite the students to discuss how characteristics of the Mass prior to the conciliar changes fostered a different atmosphere from that found in the Mass as it is currently celebrated.

Concept Review

Discuss with the students the following question: After the council, some Catholics disliked the changes that were taking place in the Church. Why do you think this was the case?

(Some Catholics felt that Mass in Latin and attendance in passive silence added a sense of mystery that became lost when the words were spoken in English and congregations actively participated. Some Catholics felt that because of the increased participation of laypeople in the Church, the aura of sacredness surrounding priests was dissipated. Some Catholics felt that the Church was becoming too concerned about world affairs rather than about spiritual affairs narrowly understood.)

Review Questions and Answers

1. **What four aims for the council did Pope Paul VI identify?**

   In his opening address Pope Paul VI laid out his understanding of the council's four principal aims: the Church must impart to herself and to the world a new awareness of her inner nature, there must be a renewal and reform of the Church, the Church should work to bring about Christian unity, and the Church should be in dialogue with today's world.

2. **What was Pope Paul VI's stance toward the Orthodox Patriarch of Constantinople and the communist governments of Eastern Europe?**

   In 1964, when Pope Paul VI met with the Patriarch of Constantinople, the two leaders removed the mutual excommunications that had been in place since 1054. To improve relations between the Church and communist governments, Pope Paul VI took a more open stance toward those governments—called *ostpolitik*.

3. **What three conclusions did the Latin American bishops arrive at that reshaped Catholic social teaching?**

   The Latin American bishops realized that the gospel message could not be separated from the work of justice. Second, people who are poor need to develop a sense of their own dignity and needed to grow in power. Third, poverty in Latin America was tied to a broad system that created wealth for some but kept large numbers of people poor.

4. **Name three changes in the liturgy that occurred during the papacy of Pope Paul VI.**

   During the time of Pope Paul VI, Mass and the sacraments went from being celebrated in Latin to being celebrated in the language of the people. The altar came to look like and serve the function of a table, around which the community gathered, rather than exclusively a place of sacrifice. People became more active participants in the liturgy, and Scripture became a more important focus than it had been.

Chapter Review and Conclusion

1. Ask the students to summarize the main points in the chapter using their own words. Write notes on the board from their contributions. To reinforce their summary, you might want to review the major concepts in this chapter in the teaching manual. Then read the **Conclusion** on page 283.

2. Review the vocabulary in this chapter:

   colonialism—the rule of one country by another (page 269)

   aggiornamento—the spirit of updating the Church that Pope John XXIII wanted to underlie Vatican Council II (page 273)

   permanent deacons—men ordained to assist the bishop and priests in various pastoral duties and ministries of hospitality and charity (page 282)

TEST

Give the students the Chapter 11 Test or an alternative assessment. The tests have been placed on the Harcourt Religion Publishers' Web page. This has been done to enable the teacher to customize this material for local needs. First contact Harcourt Religion Publishers' high school consultant at 800-922-7696, ext. 3781 for a user ID and password. Then connect with the Harcourt Religion Publishers' Web site at **www.harcourtreligion.com** to download the information. Collect the tests for grading.

Chapter 11 Test Answers

MULTIPLE CHOICE (5 points each)

1. b	4. d	7. a	10. a	13. c
2. a	5. d	8. a	11. c	14. a
3. c	6. a	9. c	12. b	

SHORT ANSWERS

1. Describe (15 points total)
   - the end of World War II—Europe was in a state of turmoil. The Church saw itself as in a position to assist the world during this time of crisis and rebuilding.
   - Nuclear weapons—The Church saw the threat of mass destruction as requiring a moral voice for guidance, which it could provide.
   - Communisim—The Church wanted to counteract the spread of communism, which stridently rejected God and all religion.
   - The end of colonialism—The Church represented an international organization whose concern was universal human welfare, not national self-interest.
   - Liberation movements—The Church called for justice as various groups seeking liberation were also calling for justice and equality—such as women and poor people in underdeveloped countries.

2. Name (5 points total)

   Answers may vary. Pope John XXIII served in the East where he met members of other religions. He also served in France after World War II where a voice of diplomacy was needed.

3. Define (10 points total)
   - *aggiornamento*—the spirit of updating the Church that Pope John XXIII wanted to underlie Vatican Council II
   - ecumenism—the movement toward Christian unity
   - *ostpolitik*—the dialogue between the Church and Eastern European communist governments at the time of Pope Paul VI
   - permanent deacons—men ordained to assist the bishop and priests in various pastoral duties and ministries of hospitality and charity

Prayer

MUSIC SUGGESTIONS

"Canticle of the Turning" (Irish Traditional) from *Give Your Gifts, the Basics* (GIA, Harcourt Religion Publishers).

"Church of God" by Margaret Daly from *Gather (Comprehensive)* (GIA), *Glory & Praise (Comprehensive)* (OCP), *Today's Missal* (OCP).

"For Everything There Is a Time" by Donald Reagan from *Glory & Praise (Comprehensive)* (OCP).

"Hope at the Crossroads" by Michael Mahler from *Give Your Gifts, the New Songs* (GIA, Harcourt Religion Publishers).

"Open Our Ears" by Darryl Ducote from *Give Your Gifts, the Basics* (GIA, Harcourt Religion Publishers).

"Send Down the Fire" by Marty Haugen from *Give Your Gifts, the Basics* (GIA, Harcourt Religion Publishers).

"We Will Serve the Lord" by David Haas or Rory Cooney from *Gather (Comprehensive)* (GIA).

SCRIPTURE SUGGESTIONS

Proverbs 1:1–8

Acts 20:17–24

John 21:4–6

PRAYER

Psalm 150

CHAPTER 11 TEST

Name_____ Date_____ Class period_____

Test is made up of questions with suggested values totaling 100 points.

Multiple Choice (5 points each)

_____ 1. There have been ____ Church councils since the Council of Trent (1545-1563).
   a. one
   b. two
   c. three
   d. four

_____ 2. When Pope John XXIII called for a council, many people in the Vatican opposed the idea because they believed that
   a. the pope and his staff could settle any issues
   b. few bishops would choose to attend
   c. too many councils had recently been held
   d. the pope had no authority to call a council

_____ 3. Vatican Council II took place during the
   a. 1940s
   b. 1950s
   c. 1960s
   d. 1970s

_____ 4. Pope John XXIII called for a spirit of *aggiornamento,* meaning
   a. fidelity to the Church
   b. open discussion of ideas
   c. reaching consensus
   d. updating with the times

_____ 5. In the first session of Vatican Council II, the vast majority of bishops
   a. were not present at the sessions
   b. asked the pope to decide matters
   c. ratified prepared documents
   d. voted against prepared documents

_____ 6. During council sessions, Pope John XXIII
   a. watched proceedings on close-circuit television
   b. participated actively in discussions
   c. oversaw the daily workings of commissions
   d. wrote documents to be discussed

_____ 7. One innovation at Vatican Council II was that fifteen women were
     a. official listeners and later worked on committees
     b. chosen to participate fully in council sessions
     c. elected from their countries to speak before the council
     d. translators of documents into various languages

_____ 8. Bishop Peter Cule of Mostar wanted
     a. Saint Joseph's name included in the canon of the Mass
     b. to speak about Our Lady of Fatima
     c. communists to be invited to the council
     d. council sessions held in Vienna

_____ 9. At the end of the first session of the council, Pope John said it was
     a. a failure for not passing any decrees
     b. a success because it passed three decrees
     c. a success despite not passing any decrees
     d. time to end the council and resume work

_____10. Since the council could not address all issues, the bishops
     a. set up commissions to deal with various aspects of Church life
     b. called for another council to be held in ten years
     c. left the council upset over unresolved conflicts
     d. elected twenty-five of their number to advise the pope

_____11. When elected, Pope Paul VI
     a. discontinued the council
     b. continued the council reluctantly
     c. continued the council and its direction
     d. refused to recognize council documents

_____12. Pope Paul VI shocked many bishops when he told observers from other Christian communities that
     a. their ancestors were responsible for the split in Christianity
     b. the Church asked their forgiveness if they felt they had been injured by the Church
     c. they would be invited to speak at official council sessions
     d. they should ask their leaders to return to the Catholic Church

_____13. Bishops who led the Church in applying gospel teachings to poverty were from
     a. communist countries
     b. Asian countries
     c. Latin America
     d. North America

_____14. After Vatican Council II, Scripture readings at Mass
     a. received greater emphasis
     b. were shortened in length
     c. were left unchanged
     d. were said in Latin

Short Answers

1. Describe how each of the following helped create a climate increasing the need for the Catholic Church to examine its role in modern society. (15 points total)

    • the end of World War II—

    • nuclear weapons—

    • communism—

    • the end of colonialism—

    • liberation movements—

2. Name one position held by Pope John XXIII that helped prepare him for the papacy during a time of change. (5 points total)

3. Define the following terms: (10 points total)

    • *aggiornamento*—

    • ecumenism—

    • *ostpolitik*—

    • permanent deacons—

© Harcourt Religion Publishers

The Church of Vatican Council II

287

VATICAN COUNCIL II AT A GLANCE

Name_____ Date_____ Class period_____

Vatican Council II was truly a ground-breaking event in the history of the Church. 2,540 bishops of a possible 2,908 from all over the world attended the council. United States delegates numbered 241, the second largest number of attendees after Italy. The Asian and African churches were well represented, giving the council a distinctly global spirit. (By contrast, 800 bishops attended Vatican Council I (1869–1970), 400 of whom were from European dioceses. At that time bishops from mission lands were also of European descent. 100 American bishops attended.) Only a few bishops from countries under communist control were able to attend Vatican Council II. The council issued sixteen documents dealing with a variety of matters associated with Church teaching and life.

- Vatican Council II was the largest gathering of bishops in the Church's history.
- Participants represented the great cultural diversity that exists in the universal Church.
- Representatives of local Churches in union with Rome participated actively and demonstrated the diversity that has always existed in the Church.
- The council instituted many changes without their actions resulting in a schism within the Church, as often happened with past councils. However, a retired French archbishop, Marcel Lefebvre, led a movement called "Catholic Traditionalists" who rejected the council's changes. He was excommunicated in 1988.
- Bishops, who were the official participants in the council's deliberations, had noted that theologians from around the world helped them formulate decrees. Bishops even attended sessions held by theologians to learn for themselves what some of the changes meant.
- In conjunction with formal council sessions, lively exchanges took place among bishops, women and laymen, non-Catholic observers, clergy and religious, and many other interested parties.
- Instead of taking place in secret, council deliberations were made known to the world as they were happening; all interested parties could reflect on and discuss changes.

What were some shifts in perspective represented by the council? A complete list of such changes would be lengthy. One commentator suggests four primary shifts in emphasis:

1. From a juridical Church to a mystery/sacrament Church (that is, less concern with following specific, detailed rules and greater concern with being a sign of Christ's presence in the world)

2. From obedient faithful to co-responsible faithful (That is, increased involvement of laypeople in the Church)

3. From contempt for the world to sanctification of matter (that is, Catholics were not to ignore "this world" in their journey to the "next world." Heaven and earth are intricately linked, and the Church is "in the world," not outside of it.)

4. From fidelity to laws and moral excellence to involvement with Christ in creating the world according to God's plan (That is, Catholics were urged not just to avoid wrongdoing but to participate actively in world affairs.)

THE U.S. CHURCH BEFORE AND AFTER THE COUNCIL

Name_____ Date_____ Class period_____

Statistics don't reveal the spirit of an organization. Nonetheless, it is helpful to look at statistical information to get a sense of the direction that an organization is taking. Here are numbers from *The Official Catholic Directory* for 1961 (reported in Clyde F. Crews, *American and Catholic* [Cincinnati, OH: St. Anthony Messenger Press, 1994], 144). Look in a recent *Catholic Almanac* or other source, such as the *Official Catholic Directory* (OCD), or use the Internet, to find out the most recent data for the categories listed here. Also, list other statistical information that provides a sense of how the Catholic Church in the United States has changed in recent decades.

	1961	Today
Catholic population	4, 204, 900	
Priests	54, 682	
Permanent deacons	0	
Seminarians	41,871	
Religious sisters	170,438	
Religious brothers	10,928	
Catholic hospitals	814	
Elementary schools	10,593	
Elementary students	4,389,779	
Secondary schools	2,433	
Secondary students	886,295	

AN ECUMENICAL CHURCH

Name_____ Date_____ Class period_____

In 1987 Cardinal Francis Arinze of Nigeria, President of the Pontifical Council for Interreligious Dialogue, described five types of interreligious activity. For each one, describe one way that someone could participate in that activity.

1. **Dialogue of life.** Everyone who lives in a religiously pluralistic environment can live and work in harmony while bearing witness to his or her own faith.

2. **Dialogue of Social Action.** People of different religions can work together for the good of humanity, for justice and peace, for those who suffer and for education and development.

3. **Dialogue of Prayer.** People of different religions can come together to pray for a common purpose. Some prayer is in common, and each religious family also prays separately according to its own tradition.

4. **Dialogue of sharing religious experience.** For those who have achieved a level of trust and openness, members of different religions who know each other well can speak honestly about what is deepest in their lives.

5. **Dialogue of Experts or Theologians.** Scholars from different religions can study areas where their beliefs and practices come together and also where they diverge.

See *Church in Dialogue* (San Francisco, CA: Ignatius Press, 1990), 215–216.

CATHOLIC CHARITIES IN THE SPIRIT OF VATICAN II

Name_____ Date_____ Class period_____

Charitable works have always been part of the Church's mission. Vatican Council II inspired the Catholic Charities organizations of the United States to reevaluate the work they were doing. In 1971 Monsignor Robert Fox addressed representatives from Catholic Charities from around the country in preparation for adopting a restatement of their mission. Read the following excerpts from his speech and then describe in your own words Monsignor Fox's understanding of the Church's mission.

The first and fundamental premise is the fact that Charities is an integral part of the Church, responsible not only for delivering services or doing the job for the Church or taking care of the poor, but also I would say primarily responsible for contributing to and shaping the thinking and life and life-style of the Church. . . . Once that is stated, it should also be stated that both scripture and tradition seem to indicate that the most graphic revelation of God is lodged in the poor and in the oppressed.

The whole Gospel is replete with examples of Christ's good news coming from his encounter with people who were subject to oppression. An encounter that did not simply, in a superficial way, help the people adjust to whatever the problem was, but challenged them to confront that problem to the point where they got some sense of the cause of it.

We as Catholic Charities, and similarly we as a Church, are responsible not so much for praying for the oppressed and the poor that we serve, but rather praying with the people that we serve in an effort to get them to reflect themselves into a deeper confrontation with themselves and their problems. We have to recognize that it is the oppressed who have the greatest possibility of coming to this indepth vision of God revealed in and through their oppression, and not those who serve the oppressed.

If we're to be ministers . . . we're charged with the responsibility of stimulating and encouraging people to face their own deaths . . . [a] death perhaps to some of the staid ways of experiencing ourselves and seeing ourselves as the Church, or a Charities movement, some of the time-honored ways we have of doing things; maybe some of the securities that we find in the present ways of fumbling and living out our existence.

The other challenge that this process asks of us . . . is the need for us to be ministers of penance. Not simply the one-to-one relation in the confessional but a recognition that if we are to embark on this deep confrontation with the problems and needs that face people, that we are going to involve ourselves in a lot of failure, that we are going to then identify with people in life-thrusts that are necessarily going to involve mistakes and wrong directions. And it asks of us a willingness to get away from the defensiveness that we sometimes bring up when certain aspects of the life of the Church or the life of a social movement or the life of the Charities movement are challenged because of their deficiencies . . . being a minister of penance is being a person who [is] . . . willing and able to denounce that which we discover as dead in us at the same time that we announce and stand for tentative, new, fresh, unsophisticated forms of life that are coming about.

Robert Fox, *Fox-Sight* (Huntington, IN: Our Sunday Visitor, 1989), 107–112.

MASS IN THE PRE-VATICAN II CHURCH

Name_____ Date_____ Class period_____

Here are some characteristics of Mass as it was celebrated before the changes mandated after Vatican Council II. After reading through the list, write down what you think would be the atmosphere and sense of spirituality created by Mass celebrated in this fashion. How is Mass as it is currently celebrated similar to and different from pre-Vatican II Mass?

- Mass was in Latin except for gospel readings on Sundays.

- The priest celebrated Mass facing the altar, which was against the front wall, and as a result the celebrant did not face the congregation.

- An altar rail separated the sanctuary from the rest of the church.

- Only the priest and altar boys were in the sanctuary. The congregation remained silent during most of the Mass.

- People did not greet or acknowledge one another's presence within church.

- Some people recited rosaries silently, lit candles before a statue, or went to confession during Mass.

- Typically a small percentage of the congregation received Communion, which was the sacred host received only on the tongue and handled only by the priest. People knelt at an altar rail to receive Communion.

- There were "high Masses," which included a choir singing parts of the Mass in Latin, and "low Masses," which included no singing and could be completed very quickly—in about twenty minutes if there was no sermon. Typically, only Sunday Mass included a brief sermon by the priest.

THE GOSPEL OF LIFE
The Church in the Global Community

A Teacher's Prayer

> *Jesus, Lord of life, during this course we have struggled to know your presence in our world. Help my students find you in their lives and in their own stories, in their communities and in the world. Amen.*

Overview

1. Have the students read the Chapter Overview and timeline on pages 284–285. Briefly discuss some of the points and events noted.

2. Read the paragraphs under **Transformation of the Church** on page 287.

3. Have the students complete the **Before We Begin . . .** activity. (You might instead assign this activity as homework before beginning the chapter and ask the students to come to class prepared to discuss their work.)

Major Concepts Covered in This Chapter

① Introduction

② Recent Developments in the U.S. Church

③ Pope John Paul II

④ Today's Global Church

⑤ Chapter Review and Conclusion

Introduction

Prayer

pages
284–286

■ **Music Suggestions**

"All the Ends of the Earth" by Bob Dufford from *Gather (Comprehensive)* (GIA), *Lead Me, Guide Me* (GIA), *Today's Missal* (OCP), *Glory & Praise Comprehensive* (OCP).

"Bring Forth the Kingdom" by Marty Haugen from *Gather (Comprehensive)* (GIA).

"Gather Your People" by Bob Hurd from *Today's Missal* (OCP).

"I Want to Walk as a Child of the Light" by Kathleen Thomerson from *Gather (Comprehensive)* (GIA).

"On That Day" by Kate Cuddy from *Give Your Gifts, the New Songs* (GIA, Harcourt Religion Publishers).

"Send Down the Fire" by Marty Haugen from *Give Your Gifts, the Basics* (GIA, Harcourt Religion Publishers).

■ **Scripture Suggestions**

Exodus 16:1–5, 17:5–6

Colossians 2:6–7

Matthew 4:18–22

■ **Prayer**

See page 284 of the textbook.

Recent Developments in the U.S. Church

The Catholic Church in the United States seeks to define its role.

pages
287–288

TRANSFORMATION OF THE CHURCH

Controversial Pastoral Letters

Direct the students to read the section on recent developments in the U.S. Church on pages 287–288. Ask them: What is the "transformation" in the U.S. Church that the text is talking about?

(If need be, point out to the students that prior to the 1960s, leaders of the Catholic Church in the U.S. generally were concerned about being accepted in mainstream society. By the 60s, when Catholics felt part of the mainstream, Church leaders saw the need to be critical of certain aspects of U.S. culture, as reflected in a number of pastoral letters.)

In-Text Activities

page 288 ACTIVITY

Using the Activity

When you assign these research activities, remind the students to look for signs that the people and organizations involved reflect Catholic values.

USCC STATEMENTS

The text points out that since the 1960s the United States Catholic bishops have issued a number of statements that challenge policies of the U.S. government and values that are dominant in North American culture. You might direct the students to find and read through pastoral letters of the U.S. bishops from the past thirty years to look for statements that are challenging and forceful.

CoNCept ReViEw

Read aloud the following statement and then discuss with the students the accompanying question: In their 1986 pastoral letter on the economy the U.S. bishops wrote that: *"As Americans . . .* [w]e believe that we honor our history best by working for the day when all our sisters and brothers share adequately in the American dream" (number 9). What challenges and criticisms do you think leaders of the Catholic Church would give to leaders of economic life in the United States?

Pope John Paul II

Pope John Paul II guides the Church into the twenty-first century.

pages
289–291

Pope John Paul I—The "Smiling Pope"

Pope John Paul II: A New Pope for a New Time

Pope John Paul II and the Fall of Communism

After the students have read the text on pages 289–291, ask them to work together to summarize each section. Discuss as needed.

In-Text Activities

page 291 ACTIVITY

Using the Activity

1. Many videos on Pope John Paul II are available; check the diocesan media center, and make the videos available to interested students. The Internet is another rich source of information and visuals on the pope.

2. Set aside class time for these presentations; ask probing questions to move the students beyond the superficial in their presentations.

THE CANONIZATION PROCESS

As the text indicates, Pope John Paul II has greatly increased the number of officially canonized saints in the Church. **Handout 12–A, The Canonization of Saints,** describes the canonization process and its history. Distribute the handout and place the students in small groups to complete the accompanying assignment.

Concept Review

Discuss with the students the following question: When Pope John Paul II became pope in 1978, a central theme of his message to the world was, "Be not afraid!" Why do you think he felt that this was the message that people of the time needed to hear? What do you think he saw as the basis for overcoming fear?

page 291

Review Questions and Answers

1. **How did the place of Catholics in U.S. society change from the late 1940s to the '60s?**

   Up until World War II, Catholics in the U.S. belonged to the immigrant Church. After that time Catholics became part of mainstream U.S. culture.

2. **Give three examples of how Catholic leaders, beginning in the late 1960s, became critical of U.S. society.**

   During the Vietnam War era, the U.S. Catholic bishops supported the morality of selective conscientious objection, a position not permissible in U.S. law. During the 1980s the bishops wrote challenging and controversial pastoral letters on peace and the U.S. economy.

3. **Name two protest movements in which individual Catholics participated beginning in the '60s.**

   Individual Catholics participated both in the civil rights and in anti-war movements.

4. **Name three characteristics that made Pope John Paul II unique among modern popes.**

   Pope John Paul II was relatively young when elected, he was a non-Italian, and he was from a communist country.

5. **List four ways that Pope John Paul II contributed to the modern world.**

   Pope John Paul II traveled extensively, becoming the first pope to visit many parts of the world. He wrote many encyclicals. Under him the Church adopted a new code of Canon Law and a new catechism. He named many new saints. He contributed to the fall of communism in Eastern Europe and the former Soviet Union.

Today's Global Church

In this section the students receive an overview of the contemporary Church as it carries forth Christ's mission throughout the world. While the overview is not all-inclusive, it is important for the students to realize that the Catholic Church is a world Church and as such is very much involved in world affairs. The section describes models of spirituality.

pages 292–300

A VOICE FOR LIFE

The Church in El Salvador

WOMEN MARTYRS IN EL SALVADOR

The Church in India

The Church in Canada

The Church in Africa

The Church in Europe

The Church in the United States

In-Text Activities

page 293 **ACTIVITY**

Using the Activity

Have available copies of the bishops' pastoral on peace *(The Challenge of Peace)* and economics *(Economic Justice for All)*. One side of each debate topic should be able to support its stand with quotations from one or the other of these documents.

page 294 **ACTIVITY**

Using the Activity

1. Resources
   • Video: Roses in December, Choices of the Heart
   • Internet sites: **www.rtfcam.org/martyrs/women; www.maryknoll.org/MARY-KNOLL/SISTERS/ms_martyrs.htm**
2. Set aside class time for these presentations.

page 295 **YOUTH NEWS**

Using the Youth News

The website for Food for the Hungry is **www.fh.org** or **www.food-for-the-hungry.com.**

ACTIVITY

Using the Activity

Obtain a book that contains the writings of Mother Teresa. Describe and explain how three of Mother Teresa's messages can be applied to your own life.
Suggested books:

• *Mother Teresa: In My Own Words: 1910–1997* by Mother Teresa and Cervantes Saavedra (Random House, 1997).

The Gospel of Life

- *Mother Teresa: A Simple Path* by Mother Teresa, Lucinda Vardey (Compiler) (Ballantine Books, 1995).
- *Everything Starts from Prayer: Mother Teresa's Meditations on Spiritual Life for People of All Faiths* by Mother Teresa of Calcutta, Anthony Stern (Editor) (White Cloud Press, 2000).
- *The Joy in Loving: A Guide to Daily Living* by Mother Teresa of Calcutta (Viking Penguin, 2000).
- *Meditations from A Simple Path* by Mother Teresa of Calcutta, Lucinda Vardey (Compiler) (Random House, 1996).
- *Thirsting for God: A Yearbook of Prayers and Meditations* by Mother Teresa of Calcutta, Angelo D. Scolozzi (Compiler) (Servant Publications, 2000).
- *In the Heart of the World: Thoughts, Prayers, and Stories* by Mother Teresa of Calcutta (New World Library, 1997).
- *My Life for the Poor: Mother Teresa of Calcutta* by Mother Teresa of Calcutta, Jane Playfoot (Editor) (Ballantine Books, 1987).
- *Words to Love By . . .* by Mother Teresa (Ave Maria Press, 1982).
- *Heart of Joy* by Mother Teresa (Servant Publications, 1990).
- *Total Surrender* by Mother Teresa, Angelo Devananda (Editor) (Servant Publications, 1990).

page 296   **FYI**

Using the FYI

These websites were suggested in chapter 10 and may be useful for further research at this time: **www.larcheusa.com, www.larchecanada.org**.

DISCUSSION

Using the Discussion

1. With the last question, help the students make the connection between their need for community and the community dimension of the Church.

2. Use this discussion item to review some of the main events in the history of the Church. The students might begin with Pentecost and the early Church community as depicted in Acts and move through each chapter of the textbook to find other examples.

page 297   **ACTIVITY**

Using the Activity

1. A general search on the Internet can supply many leads for this research. Magazines of missionary groups can also be helpful; see, for example, Maryknoll magazine.

2. Provide time for the students' presentations. Post any artwork.

Sister Thea Bowman—A Dancing Prophet

For further information on Sister Thea Bowman, contact the following websites:

> **http://www.bc.edu/bc_org/svp/ahana/thea.html**
> **http://www.fspa.org/whoweare/fspanews/theabook.htm**
> **http://www.fspa.org/whoweare/fspanews/theafest.htm**

In-Text Activities

ACTIVITY

Using the Activity

This document is available on **www.elca.org/ea/jddj/declaration.html**. The Vatican's website has the Catholic/Lutheran responses:
**www.vatican.va/roman_curia/pontifical_councils/chrstuni/documents/rc_pc_chrstuni
_doc_31101999_cath-luth-official-statement_en.html**.

CoNCept RevIEw

On the day before you complete discussion of this chapter, ask the students to find a photograph or draw a picture that they believe communicates something about the Catholic Church today. Encourage them to think symbolically. That is, the picture need not include people or words. Ask the students to bring in their pictures and place them around the room for everyone to view. Give the students time to look at the pictures and then to write what they believe one or two of the pictures says about the Church today. After ten minutes, invite the students to read a portion of their comments.

In-Text Activities

WWW.

Using the www.

You might take this opportunity to have each of the students research a different group and report back to the class.

ACTIVITY

Using the Activity

This would make an excellent small-group project, with follow-up reports and discussion in the large group.

Review Questions and Answers

1. **How did Archbishop Oscar Romero's stance on political involvement change after the death of Father Rutilio Grande?**

   After the death of his friend, Father Rutilio Grande, Archbishop Romero began to speak out forcefully for those in his country who were poor and oppressed.

2. **In what ways did Jean Donovan serve the people of San Salvador?**

   Jean Donovan worked mainly with refugees in El Salvador. In particular she cared for children who were wounded or who had lost their families in the conflict that was taking place at the time.

3. **For what type of work is Mother Teresa noted?**

   Mother Teresa dedicated herself to working with "the poorest of the poor."

4. **What is the name of the religious order founded by Mother Teresa?**

   Mother Teresa founded the Missionaries of Charity.

5. **Name four reasons why African Catholics welcomed the changes encouraged by Vatican Council II.**

   African Catholics welcomed the changes of Vatican Council II because (1) they didn't want "being Catholic" to mean "being European." (2) They welcomed the opportunity to continue adding elements of African culture into the liturgy. They applauded (3) Vatican II's stand for social justice and (4) against colonialism.

6. **Name two signs of hope for the European Church.**

   Europe has seen Christian martyrs in the twentieth century. Many Christians exhibit holiness. (See the chart on page 299.)

7. **Give three examples of signs of life in the U.S. Catholic Church.**
   - Teens and adults assist at parish liturgies and volunteer their time to run sports programs and tutor children.
   - U.S. parishes often coordinate clothing drives and food preparation for homeless shelters.
   - Men and women participate in spirituality groups or Bible study or attend daily Mass.

Additional Activities

CONTEMPORARY SPIRITUALITIES

In order for the students to appreciate that Catholic spirituality has remained strong and active in the Church over recent decades, direct them—either as individuals or in groups—to choose one of the persons listed on **Handout 12–B, Models of Modern Spirituality.** Instruct the students to prepare a presentation for the class on the person they select. (You might add more recent or locally recognized models of spirituality to this list.)

Chapter Review and Conclusion

1. Ask the students to summarize the main points in the chapter using their own words. Write notes on the board from their contributions. To reinforce their summary, you might want to review the major concepts in this chapter as found in the teaching manual. Then read the **Conclusion** on page 301.

2. Review the vocabulary in this chapter:

   conscientious objector—one who refuses in conscience to participate in all wars (page 287)

   selective conscientious objector—refusing in conscience to participate in one particular war that a person believes to be immoral (page 287)

TEST

Give the students the Chapter 12 Test or an alternative assessment. The tests have been placed on the Harcourt Religion Publisher's Web page. This has been done to enable the teacher to customize this material for local needs. First contact Harcourt Religion Publishers' high school consultant at 800-922-7696, ext. 3781 for a user ID and password. Then connect with the Harcourt Religion Publishers' Web site at **www.harcourtreligion.com** to download the information. Collect the tests for grading.

Chapter 12 Test Answers

MULTIPLE CHOICE (3 points each)

1. c	4. c	7. a	10. a	13. a
2. c	5. c	8. b	11. a	14. b
3. d	6. d	9. a	12. c	

MATCHING (3 points each)

1. E	3. B	5. A
2. D	4. C	6. F

ESSAYS (5 points each)

1. By the time of the 1960s Catholics had gained both an acceptance within American society and also a high degree of economic and political success. Catholic leaders, therefore, felt that they needed to criticize aspects of U.S. values and culture that contradicted Catholic values. The pastoral letters on peace and the economy in the 1980s are the most famous examples of such a critique.

2. Answers may vary. Pope John Paul II traveled a great deal, meeting first-hand people from all areas of the world. He named a great number of saints. He is credited with helping to bring to an end communist rule over Eastern Europe and the former Soviet Union. He wrote many encyclicals and oversaw publication of a new official catechism that clarifies Catholic teaching.

3. Before being named archbishop of San Salvador, Oscar Romero spoke against Church leaders being involved in the social and political issues facing his country. After he became archbishop, a priest-friend who was involved in helping poor people was killed. Romero then became an outspoken critic of violence and policies harmful to the poor people of El Salvador.

4. Mother Teresa's order is dedicated to helping "the poorest of the poor" throughout the world.

5. Jean Vanier formed communities where people with mental and physical disabilities live in community with people who did not possess disabilities.

6. The African Church welcomed the vision of a "world Church" called for by the council, the endorsement of diversity within the Church made by the council, and its call for justice.

7. During the 1990s the Church in Europe addressed problems resulting from the fall of communism and from the great increase in prosperity that many experienced at the time.

8. Answers may vary. Catholics in the United States provide services for families and children, help with homeless shelters and poverty programs, and participate in a variety of spiritual activities through their parishes.

Prayer

MUSIC SUGGESTIONS

"Anthem" by Tom Conry from *Glory & Praise (Comprehensive)* (OCP), *Today's Missal* (OCP), *Gather (Comprehensive)* (GIA).

"Come, All You People" by Alexander Gondo from *Give Your Gifts, the Basics* (GIA, Harcourt Religion Publishers).

"Follow the Light" by Richard Putori and Christopher Dutkiewicz from *Give Your Gifts, the New Songs* (GIA, Harcourt Religion Publishers).

"God of All Creation" by David Haas from *Gather (Comprehensive)* (GIA).

"New Life" by Carey Landry from *Glory & Praise* (OCP).

"Song of the Body of Christ"/ "Canción del Cuerpo de Cristo" by David Haas, Spanish Trans. by Donna Peña, from *Gather (Comprehensive)* (GIA), *Today's Missal* (OCP).

"You Will Show Me the Path of Life" by Marty Haugen from *Gather* (GIA).

SCRIPTURE SUGGESTIONS

Isaiah 27:2–5

Acts 5:12–16

Mark 6:30–44

PRAYER

All that God has created and sustains, all the events he guides, and all human works that are good and have a good purpose, prompt those who believe to praise and bless the Lord with hearts and voices. God is the source and origin of every blessing . . . we proclaim our belief that all things work together for the good of those who fear and love God. We are sure that in all things, we must seek the help of God, so that in complete reliance on his will we may, in Christ, do everything for his glory.

Catholic Household Blessings & Prayers, pages 321–322.

CHAPTER 12 TEST

Name_____ Date_____ Class period_____

Test is made up of questions with suggested values totaling 100 points.

Multiple Choice (3 points each)

_____ 1. Beginning in the 1960s U.S. Catholic bishops began to
   a. elect their replacements
   b. be native-born American citizens
   c. become more critical of some U.S. policies
   d. consider ordaining women priests

_____ 2. During the Vietnam War, U.S. Catholic bishops
   a. condemned anti-war protestors for lack of patriotism
   b. supported U.S. military action wholeheartedly
   c. recognized anti-war principles as being consistent with Catholicism
   d. refused to address issues related to war and peace

_____ 3. During the 1980s the U.S. bishops wrote controversial pastoral letters on
   a. the nature of the Holy Trinity
   b. the Immaculate Conception and the Virgin Birth
   c. discrimination against Catholics in the U.S.
   d. peace and the U.S. economy

_____ 4. One distinguishing characteristic of Pope John Paul II was that he was
   a. elected when very old
   b. from the continent of Asia
   c. non-Italian
   d. a convert to Catholicism

_____ 5. One important contribution of Pope John Paul II was that he
   a. restored the Papal States
   b. supported communism
   c. canonized many saints
   d. began Vatican Council II

_____ 6. Oscar Romero was an archbishop in
   a. Peru
   b. Mexico
   c. Chile
   d. El Salvador

_____ 7. Archbishop Romero died while
      a. celebrating Mass in a chapel
      b. flying in a plane to the U.S.
      c. helping wounded peasants
      d. speaking to government officials

_____ 8. Jean Donovan was in El Salvador as a
      a. Maryknoll nun
      b. laywoman
      c. visitor
      d. citizen

_____ 9. In El Salvador Jean Donovan worked
      a. with refugees and children
      b. as a government employee
      c. with U.S. soldiers stationed there
      d. as a newspaper reporter

_____10. The three women who died with Jean Donovan were
      a. U.S. nuns
      b. reporters
      c. Salvadorans
      d. soldiers

_____11. Mother Teresa was originally from
      a. Albania
      b. Lebanon
      c. India
      d. England

_____12. Mother Teresa felt called to work with
      a. children in grade schools
      b. elderly shut-ins
      c. the poorest of the poor
      d. young men in seminaries

_____13. Jean Vanier worked with
      a. mentally disabled adults
      b. children in grade schools
      c. refugees in France
      d. orphans in the Middle East

_____14. Generally speaking, African Catholics
      a. disapproved of Vatican II
      b. welcomed Vatican II changes
      c. left the Church after Vatican II
      d. imitated European ways

Matching (3 points each)

_____ 1. RCIA

_____ 2. L'Arche

_____ 3. Missionaries of Charity

_____ 4. *Illustrissimi*

_____ 5. Karol Wojtyla

_____ 6. Institute of Black Catholic Studies

A. Pope John Paul II

B. Mother Teresa

C. Pope John Paul I

D. Jean Vanier

E. adult Baptism process

F. Sister Thea Bowman

Essays (5 points each)

1. Explain why Catholic leaders felt that by the 1960s they were in a position to criticize some U.S. values and culture. Give an example of such a critique.

2. Name three contributions that Pope John Paul II made to the Church.

3. What transformation did Oscar Romero undertake when he became archbishop of San Salvador? What led him to such a transformation?

4. To what kind of work is Mother Teresa's order of sisters dedicated?

5. What characterized the communities founded by Jean Vanier?

6. Give three reasons why the African Church welcomed the changes of Vatican Council II.

7. Name two problems that the Church in Europe addressed during the 1990s.

8. Name three examples of current life in the U.S. Church.

THE CANONIZATION OF SAINTS

Name_____ Date_____ Class period_____

During this course you have met many people of faith. You might have noticed that only some of them bear the title *saint*. Why is that?

Over the centuries the Church has developed a long and careful procedure for declaring sainthood. It was not always so. In the early days of the Church, many people were simply acclaimed as saints by their local communities. Early on, Church leaders declared that if you died a martyr, you went straight to heaven. Martyrs were so special that the day of their death was considered their "birthday into eternal life," and the Christian community would come together to celebrate Eucharist that day. (Daily Mass was not a regular practice until the late Middle Ages. Therefore, celebrating Mass on a martyr's feast day indicated how important the Church viewed those who died for the faith.)

At times, a cult grew up around local saints. For instance, Saint Uplio died a martyr's death. He is still honored in the Italian town of Trevigo, which holds a festival every year on his feast day, August 12. However, Saint Uplio was never declared a saint for universal veneration. In 1969 a Church commission attempted to document historical evidence for saints because many legends existed that tended to confuse the facts. Some "saints" were found to be mere legends, for instance, Saint Ursula, while others, such as the popular Saint Christopher, were removed from the universal calendar but could be celebrated by local churches.

The process for declaring a person a saint is called *canonization*. Representatives of the local church study the life and writings of likely candidates, and the bishop forwards the results to the Congregation of Saints at the Vatican. After its own study, the congregation can declare this "servant of God" to be Venerable, meaning that people can offer prayers to the person, asking the person to intercede with God. The next step in the canonization process is to be declared Blessed. Such a declaration is made only after further investigation into the person's life and also after a miracle—verified by medical personnel in the case of healings—has occurred that is linked to this person. If an additional miracle can be attributed to the intercession of this person, the congregation then petitions the pope to canonize him or her, that is, declare the person to be a saint—in heaven and worthy to be a model of the Christian faith. When saints are determined to be deserving of worldwide devotion, their feast day may be included in the universal calendar. If their appeal would be to a particular area or community, their feasts might be celebrated locally even though not part of the universal calendar.

Catholics, of course, do not worship saints. Catholics honor saints and pray for their intercession before God. Only God is worshiped.

Name_____ Date_____ Class period_____

- Find out the names of two saints who were citizens of the United States.

- Name one person from the United States who is currently being considered for canonization. Write a brief account of that person's life.

- Write the story of a saint who has a parish dedicated to him or her in your area.

- Name a saint from:

    —Latin America

    —Africa

    —Asia

- Saints have been designated patrons of various occupations, needs, and concerns—such as airplane pilots, television, and travel. Write the story of one such patron saint.

MODELS OF MODERN SPIRITUALITY

Name_____ Date_____ Class period_____

The Church believes that Christ, who died and was raised up for all, can through his Spirit offer man the light and the strength to measure up to his supreme destiny.

The Documents of Vatican II, "The Church in the Modern World," number 10.

Over the last decades, the Church has been blessed with many examples of holiness. A number of people have also written about spirituality, attempting to suggest how people today can live the Christian life. Choose one of the following people who, through their life or their writings, have witnessed to the Christian life. Describe that person's understanding of spirituality.

Pope John XXIII

Pope John Paul I

Mother Teresa

Archbishop Oscar Romero

Pope John Paul II

Henri Nouwen

Bishop Robert Morneau

Jesuit Martyrs and companions
    of El Salvador

Four Women Martyrs of El Salvador

Sister Thea Bowman

Jean Vanier

Anthony de Mello

Brother Roger of Taizé

Cardinal Joseph Bernadin

MAKING YOUR MARK
The Now and Future Church

A Teacher's Prayer

Lord Jesus, as we approach the end of our course, I pray that your message of loving kindness for your people and your world, manifest throughout history, will remain with my students. May they continue to discover you within them and among them. Amen.

Major Concepts Covered in This Chapter

① **Introduction**

② **Saints and Sinners**

③ **Blessed in God's Kingdom**

④ **Review and Prayer**

Introduction

Prayer

pages
302–304

■ **Music suggestions**

"Beatitudes" by Darryl Ducote from *Glory & Praise (Comprehensive)* (OCP), *Today's Missal* (OCP).

"Send Down the Fire (Penitential Rite) by Gary Gaigle from *Give Your Gifts, the Basics* (GIA, Harcourt Religion Publishers).

"We Are Called" by David Haas from *Gather (Comprehensive)* (GIA), *Give Your Gifts, the Songs* (Harcourt Religion Publishers, GIA).

■ **Scripture suggestions**

Wisdom 12:15–19

Hebrews 12:12–14, 28–29

Matthew 5:1–12

■ **Prayer**

Prayer of Saint Francis; see page 302.

Overview

1. Have the students read the Chapter Overview on page 303. Briefly discuss the points noted.

2. Read the paragraphs under **Present and Future** on page 305.

3. Have the students complete the **Before We Begin . . .** activity. (You might instead assign this activity as homework before beginning the chapter and ask the students to come to class prepared to discuss their work.) Take time now to discuss the students' choices or provide time for sharing the examples regarding each Beatitude is discussed in the Epilogue.

Saints and Sinners

The Church continues as a communion of saints, a communion of sinners. This epilogue encourages the students to recognize themselves as the Church of today and the future. The students may view themselves as not up to the task that lies ahead of them. The first section of the epilogue, therefore, reminds the students that the Church of the past was made up of people who were both sinners and saints.

pages
305–306

PRESENT AND FUTURE

The Communion of Saints; Communion of Sinners

Instruct the students to read the section on pages 305–306. (You might read aloud the quote from Cardinal Newman found at the beginning of the section.) Then ask them:

• Why do you think that the text describes the Church as a communion of saints as well as a communion of sinners?

• What does the text mean by the following statement: "we must not overlook the goodness that surrounds us simply because it is manifest in flesh and blood people rather than in characters described in a book"?

• Give examples to illustrate this statement.

page 306   ACTIVITY

Using the Activity

1. If this activity will be shared, let the students know that before they begin working on it.

2. Use small groups for the sharing of these projects.

ConCept Review

Read the following statement from the text: "All Christians *believe* in God, but saints have a *love relationship* with God." Then ask the students to journal on these questions (not to be shared):

- Do you have such a relationship?

- Would you like to have such a relationship?

- What might a person do to develop such a relationship?

Blessed in God's Kingdom

Matthew's Gospel offers the Beatitudes as descriptions of the followers of Jesus. The Beatitudes provide guidance for living the Christian life and contributing to the life of the Church.

pages
307–322

THE BEATITUDES

1. This section lists the Beatitudes, offers meditations on their meaning, and for each one provides at least two activities—one looking back to the historical information the students learned and one inviting the students to apply its message to their own lives. Assign the activities ahead of time so that they can be discussed as the Beatitude is addressed. Read through the suggestions for using each Activity before making the assignment, as the suggestions may determine the actual assignment you choose to give.

2. Before sharing the activities, ask the class to summarize the text for that Beatitude. Discuss as needed.

pages
307–309

Poor in Spirit, Open to God

THE POOR IN SPIRIT CLOSER TO HOME

Blessed are the poor in spirit, for theirs is the kingdom of heaven.

In-Text Activities

page 309   ACTIVITY

Using the Activity

1. It may work best to let the students choose a small group for this sharing. Circulate and comment as needed.

2. Begin this activity by having the students write their event on the board or overhead. Then vote on five to ten events to discuss in more detail. The person who wrote down the event might lead the discussion on it and first share his or her explanation.

pages
310–311

Those Who Mourn—Sharing the Gift of Tears

Blessed are those who mourn, for they will be comforted.

In-Text Activities

page 311   **ACTIVITY**

Using the Activity

1. Use small groups for this sharing. Then ask the groups to choose one collage and explanation to share with the class.

2. Have the students work in the same small groups to share their choices. Again, ask the groups to choose one example to share with the class.

pages
312–313

The Meek—Finding God in our Littleness

Blessed are the meek, for they will inherit the earth.

In-Text Activities

page 313   **ACTIVITY**

Using the Activity

1. Encourage the students to think of situations "close to home." The role-plays may be done in small groups, or small groups might present their role-plays for the class. Discuss as needed.

2. Ask the students to pair off and to share three of their problems and their reflections on them.

3. Set aside sufficient time for these presentations.

pages
314–315

Hunger and Thirst for Righteousness—Working for Justice

Blessed are those who hunger and thirst for righteousness, for they will be filled.

In-Text Activities

page 315   **ACTIVITY**

Using the Activity

1. Make available copies of encyclicals and pastoral letters on justice issues. Alternative: Direct the students to websites such as:

   • www.usccb.org/socialjustice.htm

   • http://catholicism.about.com/cs/socialjustice

2. As each example is discussed, ask the students to speculate on how the situation would be handled in the Church today.

pages
316–317

The Merciful—Finding God in Others

Blessed are the merciful, for they will receive mercy.

In-Text Activities

page 317   **ACTIVITY**

Using the Activity

1. Depending on the group you have, this may work best as a journal activity that would not be shared.

2. Across the board or on a strip of mural paper, draw a timeline from the time of Jesus to the present. Ask the students to write their example in the correct place on the timeline. Then discuss examples from each major period of the Church's history.

page 318   ## Pure in Heart—Looking More Deeply

Blessed are the poor in heart, for they will see God.

In-Text Activities

page 318   **ACTIVITY**

Using the Activity

1. After the students have shared their suggestions, choose three themes and create a class plan for a program. Submit the plan to area youth ministers and follow up with a discussion with them, perhaps in class. Encourage the students to participate in any program based on their suggestions.

2. Use small groups (four students at the most) to discuss these conflicts in depth. It may be that the students can provide a much better solution than was originally sought, due to the advantage of hindsight. Ask the groups to share their best solution, along with the problem, with the class.

pages
319–320

Peacemakers—Clinging to the Dream

Blessed are the peacemakers, for they will be called children of God.

In-Text Activities

page 320   **ACTIVITY**

Using the Activity

1. Some students may be familiar with such a program; if so, give them an opportunity to share their information and/or experience with the class. Other students may be members of families who have hosted exchange students; their experiences can be valuable for the class.

2. Have the students write these down first and then have them share them in small groups. Ask the small groups to choose five to share with the class. As a class, prioritize the list. Encourage the students to practice these suggestions. Perhaps you might create posters on each suggestion to post around the school.

3. Assign each of the groups to a small group. Then have the small groups present their findings to the class.

pages 321–322

Persecuted—Taking on the Challenge

Blessed are those who are persecuted for righteousness' sake, for theirs is the kingdom of heaven.

In-Text Activities

page 322

DISCUSSION

Using the Discussion

1. If the school is doing its job as a Catholic institution, the class should be able to readily and sensitively discuss the first point. If discussion is hesitant, this is a problem that needs to be addressed by the class and by the student body and school staff.

2. As each statement is discussed, designate one side of the room for *agree* and the other for *disagree*. Ask the students to move to their choice of sides and work together to present a short persuasive argument.

3. In the end, be sure the students can state a Christian response to the item.

page 322

ACTIVITY

Using the Activity

1. Compile a list of people and organizations suggested by the students. After reviewing them, make copies of those you approve and give the copies to the students for reference and future action.

2. Have the students work in small groups to choose an example and prepare a presentation for the class.

page 323

THE BEATITUDE FOR YOU!

Unlike most texts, this book does not include a typical Conclusion. The final activity invites the students to write their own conclusion to the course. Use this activity to provide the students with an opportunity to write about what they themselves felt were the key concepts that they learned through their study of Church history.

In-Text Activities

page 323

ACTIVITY

Using the Activity

• Determine ahead of time if or how much of the first two questions will be shared, and inform the students regarding this.

• Invite the students to share their hopes and conclusions with the rest of the class.

Review and Prayer

Give the students the Final Test or use number 4 in the Activity on page 323 as an alternative assessment. The tests have been placed on the Harcourt Religion Publishers' Web page. This has been done to enable the teacher to customize this material for local needs. First contact Harcourt Religion Publishers' high school consultant at 800-922-7696, ext. 3781 for a user ID and password. Then connect with the Harcourt Religion Publishers' Web site at **www.harcourtreligion.com** to download the information. Collect the tests for grading.

Prayer

MUSIC SUGGESTIONS

"Blest Are They" by David Haas from *Gather (Comprehensive)* (GIA), *Glory & Praise (Comprehensive)* (OCP), *Today's Missal* (OCP).

"The People of God" by Francis Patrick O'Brien from *Gather (Comprehensive)* (GIA).

"We Are the Light of the World" by Jean Anthony Greif from *Glory & Praise 2* (OCP), *Today's Missal* (OCP).

SCRIPTURE SUGGESTIONS

Wisdom 5:15–16

1 Corinthians 13:1–13

Luke 6:20–31

PRAYER

Father in heaven,
from the days of Abraham and Moses
until this gathering of your Church in prayer,
you have formed a people in the image of your Son.
Bless this people with the gift of your kingdom.
May we serve you with our every desire
and show love for one another
even as you have loved us.
Grant this through Christ our Lord.
Amen.

Alternative Opening Prayer, Fourth Sunday in Ordinary Time.

FINAL TEST

Final Test Answers

MULTIPLE CHOICE (1 point each)

1. b	9. d	17. c	25. a	33. c
2. a	10. c	18. b	26. c	34. a
3. a	11. a	19. c	27. a	35. c
4. c	12. a	20. b	28. d	36. a
5. b	13. b	21. a	29. d	37. c
6. c	14. c	22. a	30. c	38. d
7. c	15. b	23. c	31. a	39. b
8. c	16. a	24. b	32. a	40. c

MATCHING 1 (2 points each)

1. F	6. A
2. G	7. C
3. D	8. J
4. B	9. H
5. I	10. E

MATCHING 2 (2 points each)

1. F	6. A
2. G	7. C
3. J	8. D
4. I	9. E
5. H	10. B

MATCHING 3 (2 points each)

1. E	6. C
2. G	7. J
3. H	8. B
4. I	9. A
5. F	10. D

IDENTIFICATION (4 points each)

Pontifex Maximus—the term means "the greatest bridge-builder"; title for emperors and, eventually, the pope

ecumenical council—a meeting to which all bishops of the world are invited in the exercise of their collegial authority for the purpose of addressing common concerns facing the worldwide Church

Summa Theologica—Saint Thomas Aquinas's comprehensive systematic examination of Christian theology

The Book of Kells—a finely illustrated manuscript of the Four Gospels in Latin which was produced in the early Middle Ages

Avignon Papacy—period of seventy years during which the popes resided in the town of Avignon in the kingdom of Naples, France

Conversos— Jews and Muslims who converted to Christianity, either willingly or unwillingly, following the Christian takeover of Spain

Theocracy—form of government in which religious leaders are the effectively secular leaders as well

Lily of the Mohawks—Blessed Kateri Tekakwitha

Black Robes—northern Native American term given to the Jesuits because of their distinctive garb

Reductions—the Jesuits practice in Paraguay of bringing together diverse Native American groups into communities

ESSAYS (6 points each)
1. Pentecost is called the "birthday of the Church" because it marked the first time that the followers of Jesus actively carried on his work, as the Church is called to do.
2. Three women who had an impact on the Church during the fourth and fifth centuries were Saints Macrina and Scholastica, who helped establish monasticism, and Saint Clotilde, who helped convert her husband, King Clovis of the Franks, to Christianity.
3. The East–West Schism was preceded by a controversy over the phrase "and the Son" which was added to the Nicene Creed by the pope and the iconoclast controversy, when the pope sided with the patriarch of Constantinople against the emperor.
4. Mendicants lived as vowed religious among the rest of society. Previous to this time, vowed religious lived apart from the rest of society in monasteries.
5. The Spanish Inquisition began as Christian rulers were reclaiming control of Spain from Muslims. The Inquisition refers to trials, overseen by Church authorities, determining whether or not converts to Christianity from Judaism or Islam were sincere in their beliefs. The Inquisition created an atmosphere of fear and suspicion among people. It also led to numerous abuses, since people could accuse others of attacking Christianity either from within or from outside the Church.
6. (a) Protestantism emphasizes Scripture alone as the source of teachings; Catholicism combines Scripture with Tradition. (b) Protestantism emphasizes faith alone leading to justification before God; Catholicism emphasizes faith and good works.
   (c) Protestantism emphasizes the priesthood of all believers; Catholicism recognizes a separate priesthood serving a unique function in the Church.
7. Pope Pius IX can be considered the first modern pope because he was the first pope since the time of Charlemagne who was primarily a moral and spiritual leader and not also the head of a large country.

8. Catholics and Church leaders generally responded to slavery the way their neighbors did. That is, southern Catholics supported slavery in equal numbers to other southerners, while northern Catholics generally opposed slavery.

9. During World War I, Pope John XXIII served as a chaplain in the army medical corps. Later he served in Eastern Europe where he encountered members of the Eastern Churches, other religions, and minority groups. He also represented the pope in France during the tense post-World War II period.

10. Answers may vary. Catholics in the United States provide services for families and children, help with homeless shelters and poverty programs, and participate in a variety of spiritual activities through their parishes.

Final Test

Name_____ Date_____ Class period_____

Multiple Choice (1 point each)

_____ 1. The ascension refers to
     a. Mary's physical entrance into heaven
     b. Jesus' physical entrance into heaven
     c. the coming of the Holy Spirit
     d. Jesus rising from the dead

_____ 2. A person of non-Jewish origin was known as a
     a. Gentile
     b. Hebrew
     c. Christian
     d. Pharisee

_____ 3. The word *catholic* literally means
     a. universal
     b. Christ-like
     c. truthful
     d. holy

_____ 4. Attila the Hun is famous for
     a. speaking Latin and Greek
     b. killing the pope in battle
     c. sparing Rome from destruction
     d. accepting Baptism as a Christian

_____ 5. Charlemagne is called the "second Constantine" because he
     a. united the Eastern and Western empires
     b. formed all of Western Europe into one family of faith
     c. designed his own capital city and palace
     d. took control of the empire from his brothers

_____ 6. A conclave refers to
     a. a collection of manuscripts
     b. the pope and emperor sharing power
     c. cardinals meeting to elect a pope
     d. the ceiling of a cathedral

_____ 7. Besides bringing about the conversion of the Slavic people, Saints Cyril and Methodius
     a. ruled the Slavic nation
     b. converted the Vikings
     c. created a Slavic alphabet
     d. destroyed all pre-Christian temples

_____ 8. The *filioque* controversy had to do with
   a. who was leader of the Church
   b. priests marrying in the Eastern Church
   c. wording of the Nicene Creed
   d. Cardinal Humbert's view of the Eastern Church

_____ 9. Eastern Rite Catholics
   a. follow Western styles of worship
   b. are considered heretics by Rome
   c. are members of the Orthodox Church
   d. are in union with Rome

_____ 10. Mendicants are known for
   a. living in monasteries
   b. developing farm techniques
   c. relying on charity from others
   d. being the oldest form of religious life

_____ 11. Avignon was a city in
   a. the kingdom of Naples in modern-day France
   b. English territory in modern-day France
   c. the Papal States in modern-day Italy
   d. the Holy Roman Empire in modern-day Germany

_____ 12. Someone who helped bring about the return of the pope to Rome was
   a. Catherine of Siena
   b. Roger of Geneva
   c. King Philip IV
   d. Pope Celestine V

_____ 13. The bubonic plague began by way of
   a. knights returning from the crusades
   b. rats aboard ships
   c. untreated drinking water
   d. medieval medical practices

_____ 14. Mysticism refers to knowing God through
   a. reading Scriptures
   b. reciting prayers
   c. direct experience
   d. devotion to saints

_____ 15. In his letter to Archbishop Albrecht, Martin Luther addressed in particular Church practices related to
   a. the Mass
   b. indulgences
   c. naming saints
   d. priesthood

_____ 16. At the Diet of Worms, Luther said that he

     a. could not in conscience deny his beliefs

     b. would meet with the pope in Rome

     c. merely intended to spark scholarly debate

     d. would publicize his ideas using the printing press

_____ 17. Saint Charles Borromeo is known for

     a. traveling to the New World

     b. becoming pope at a young age

     c. applying the Council of Trent

     d. criticizing the pope of the time

_____ 18. Saint Ignatius Loyola spent his early life as a

     a. monk

     b. soldier

     c. missionary

     d. merchant

_____ 19. A geocentric view of the universe proposes that

     a. the earth began with volcanic eruptions

     b. the universe began with a "big bang"

     c. the sun and stars revolve around the earth

     d. God created the world in seven days

_____ 20. Deists believe that

     a. there is no God

     b. God is not actively involved in the world

     c. praying to God brings personal insights

     d. science has corrupted religion

_____ 21. A concordat was

     a. an agreement between Napoleon and the pope

     b. Napoleon's decree granting freedom of religion

     c. the pope's condemnation of Napoleon

     d. a treaty between Napoleon and Russia

_____ 22. The Christians of Saint Thomas were

     a. Indian Christians who trace their origins back to the first century

     b. Laypeople who engaged in missionary work in Asia

     c. Japanese Catholics who were crucified for accepting foreign beliefs

     d. Catholics who lived on islands in Southeast Asia

_____ 23. Conquistadores came to America primarily to

     a. spread Christianity

     b. find a Northwest Passage

     c. gain wealth

     d. explore the New World

_____ 24. Our Lady of Guadalupe appeared as
      a. a European princess
      b. someone with mixed ancestry
      c. an Indian peasant
      d. a Carmelite nun

_____ 25. The Reductions of Paraguay attempted to
      a. blend European and Indian cultures
      b. prepare Indians for slavery
      c. preserve Native American religion
      d. reduce Native American populations

_____ 26. The oldest parish in continual use in the U.S. is in
      a. Santa Fe, NM
      b. San Antonio, TX
      c. St. Augustine, FL
      d. San Diego, CA

_____ 27. Immediately after Kateri Tekakwitha's death,
      a. her face cleared of blemishes
      b. a bright light surrounded her
      c. everyone in her tribe became Christian
      d. she was declared Blessed

_____ 28. Pope Leo XIII's encyclical _Rerum Novarum_ addressed
      a. the coming threat of world war
      b. Protestant-Catholic relations
      c. the Americanist controversy
      d. the conditions of working people

_____ 29. A 1919 statement by the U.S. Catholic bishops advocated
      a. a minimum wage
      b. social security for workers
      c. worker participation in management
      d. all of the above

_____ 30. Assimilation refers to
      a. members of different religions working together
      b. losing jobs because of industrialization
      c. minority groups becoming like the dominant culture
      d. two or more countries becoming one nation

_____ 31. The position Pope Pius XII took toward communism after World War II was to
      a. condemn communism
      b. work with communist leaders
      c. favor many communist principles
      d. call for dialogue among groups

Final Test

_____ 32. When Pope John XXIII called for a council, many people in the Vatican opposed the idea because they believed that
   a. the pope and his staff could settle any issues
   b. few bishops would choose to attend
   c. too many councils had recently been held
   d. the pope had no authority to call a council

_____ 33. Vatican Council II took place during the
   a. 1940s
   b. 1950s
   c. 1960s
   d. 1970s

_____ 34. One innovation at Vatican Council II was that fifteen women were
   a. official listeners and later worked on committees
   b. chosen to participate fully in council sessions
   c. elected from their countries to speak before the council
   d. translators of documents into various languages

_____ 35. When elected, Pope Paul VI
   a. discontinued the council
   b. continued the council reluctantly
   c. continued the council and its direction
   d. refused to recognize council documents

_____ 36. Before Vatican Council II, the congregation at Mass
   a. was primarily silent
   b. stood throughout
   c. greeted one another
   d. sang hymns

_____ 37. One distinguishing characteristic of Pope John Paul II was that he was
   a. elected when very old
   b. from the continent of Asia
   c. non-Italian
   d. a convert to Catholicism

_____ 38. Oscar Romero was an archbishop in
   a. Peru
   b. Mexico
   c. Chile
   d. El Salvador

_____ 39. Jean Donovan was in El Salvador as a
     a. Maryknoll nun
     b. laywoman
     c. visitor
     d. citizen

_____ 40. Mother Teresa felt called to work with
     a. children in grade schools
     b. elderly shut-ins
     c. the poorest of the poor
     d. young men in seminaries

Matching 1 (1 point each)

_____ 1. Perpetua

_____ 2. Heretic

_____ 3. Martyr

_____ 4. Apologist

_____ 5. Monica

_____ 6. Augustine

_____ 7. Anthony of Egypt

_____ 8. Patrick

_____ 9. Marks of the Church

_____ 10. Charlemagne

A. wrote first true autobiography

B. someone who explains and defends the faith

C. First known Christian monk

D. Means "witness"

E. First Holy Roman Emperor

F. Early Christian who kept a diary in prison and died for the faith

G. Someone espousing a position contrary to officially defined teaching

H. one, holy, catholic, apostolic

I. Augustine's mother

J. returned to the land where he was enslaved

Matching 2 (1 point each)

_____ 1. Francis of Assisi

_____ 2. Pope Leo III

_____ 3. Torquemada

_____ 4. Clare

_____ 5. Interdict

_____ 6. Ninety-Five Theses

_____ 7. *sola scriptura*

_____ 8. Ignatius of Loyola

_____ 9. Diet of Worms

_____ 10. Angela Merici

A. Luther's list of complaints

B. Educated poor girls

C. The Bible is the only guide to truth

D. Founder of the Jesuits

E. meeting condemning Luther

F. Began the Friars Minor

G. Crowned Charlemagne Holy Roman Emperor

H. refusal to administer Sacraments

I. First member of the Order of Poor Ladies

J. Oversaw the Spanish Inquisition

Matching 3 (1 point each)

_____ 1. Teresa of Ávila

_____ 2. John Calvin

_____ 3. Louise de Marillac

_____ 4. Vincent de Paul

_____ 5. Juan Diego

_____ 6. Kateri Tekakwitha

_____ 7. Devotional Catholicism

_____ 8. Ecumenism

_____ 9. RCIA

_____ 10. Sr. Thea Bowman

A. adult Baptism process

B. dialogue among religions

C. Indian convert to Catholicism

D. Institute of Black Catholic studies

E. Reformed Carmelites

F. presented bishop with image of Mary on his cloak

G. Frenchman who emphasized predestination

H. organized women to work with the poor, founded Daughters of Charity

I. Realized priesthood should be service to the poor

J. pious religious practices

Identification (4 points each)

Pontifex Maximus—

Summa Theologica—

The Book of Kells—

Avignon Papacy—

Conversos—

Theocracy—

Lily of the Mohawks—

Black Robes—

Reductions—

Essays (6 points each)

1. Why is Pentecost called the "birthday of the Church"?

2. Name three women who had an impact on the Church during the fourth and fifth centuries.

3. What events led up to the East–West Schism?

4. Why were the mendicant orders a radical innovation for their time?

5. What was the Spanish Inquisition? What events created the atmosphere leading up to the Inquisition?

6. Explain three major differences between Catholic and Protestant theology.

7. Why is Pope Pius IX considered the first modern pope?

8. How did Catholics and Church leaders generally respond to the slavery question in pre-Civil War America?

9. Name one position held by Pope John XXIII that helped prepare him for the papacy during a time of change.

10. Name three examples of current life in the U.S. Church.

FAITH LIFE/BASIC BELIEFS
Catholics Believe
Rev. Michael Savelesky

SCRIPTURE
Journey Through the New Testament
Teresa LeCompte

Journey Through the Old Testament
Harcourt Religion Publishers

CHURCH HISTORY
The Church Through History
Rev. Maurice O'Connell & Joseph Stoutzenberger, Ph.D.

SACRAMENTS
Sacraments: Celebrations of God's Life
Joseph Martos, Ph.D.

MORALITY
Morality: An Invitation to Christian Living
Joseph Stoutzenberger, Ph.D.

Deciding
Michele McCarty

SOCIAL JUSTICE
Justice & Peace
Joseph Stoutzenberger, Ph.D.

LIFESTYLES & MARRIAGE
Christian Vocations
Michele McCarty

DEATH AND DYING
The Mystery of Suffering and Death
Janie Gustafson, Ph.D.

COMPARATIVE RELIGIONS
Religions in North America
Rev. Dwayne Thoman & Robert Santos

SERVICE/MINISTRY
Called By Name: An Invitation to Serve
Jerry Welte

Harcourt Religion Publishers

Harcourt Religion Publishers
1665 Embassy West Drive Suite 200
Dubuque, IA 52002
800-922-7696

On line assessment available
at www.harcourtreligion.com

EVALUATION FORM

Please Let Us Know What You Think!

Thank you for your interest in religion materials from Harcourt Religion Publishers. We are interested in your comments. Please take a few minutes to complete the questionnaire below.

Title _____

Does this book satisfy the needs of your religion program?   ❏ Yes   ❏ No

What are its strongest features/benefits? _____

_____

_____

How could the book be improved? _____

_____

_____

Name _____   Date Reviewed _____

School_____

Phone _____   Fax _____   E-mail _____

Office Hours _____

Grade Level _____   Enrollment _____

May we use your comments in future promotions?   ❏ Yes   ❏ No

Fax the survey to **563-557-3720** or **mail** to:

Harcourt Religion Publishers

1665 Embassy West Drive, Suite 200
Dubuque, Iowa 52002-2259
800-922-7696
www.harcourtreligion.com